AF251129

IDOLIZING MARY

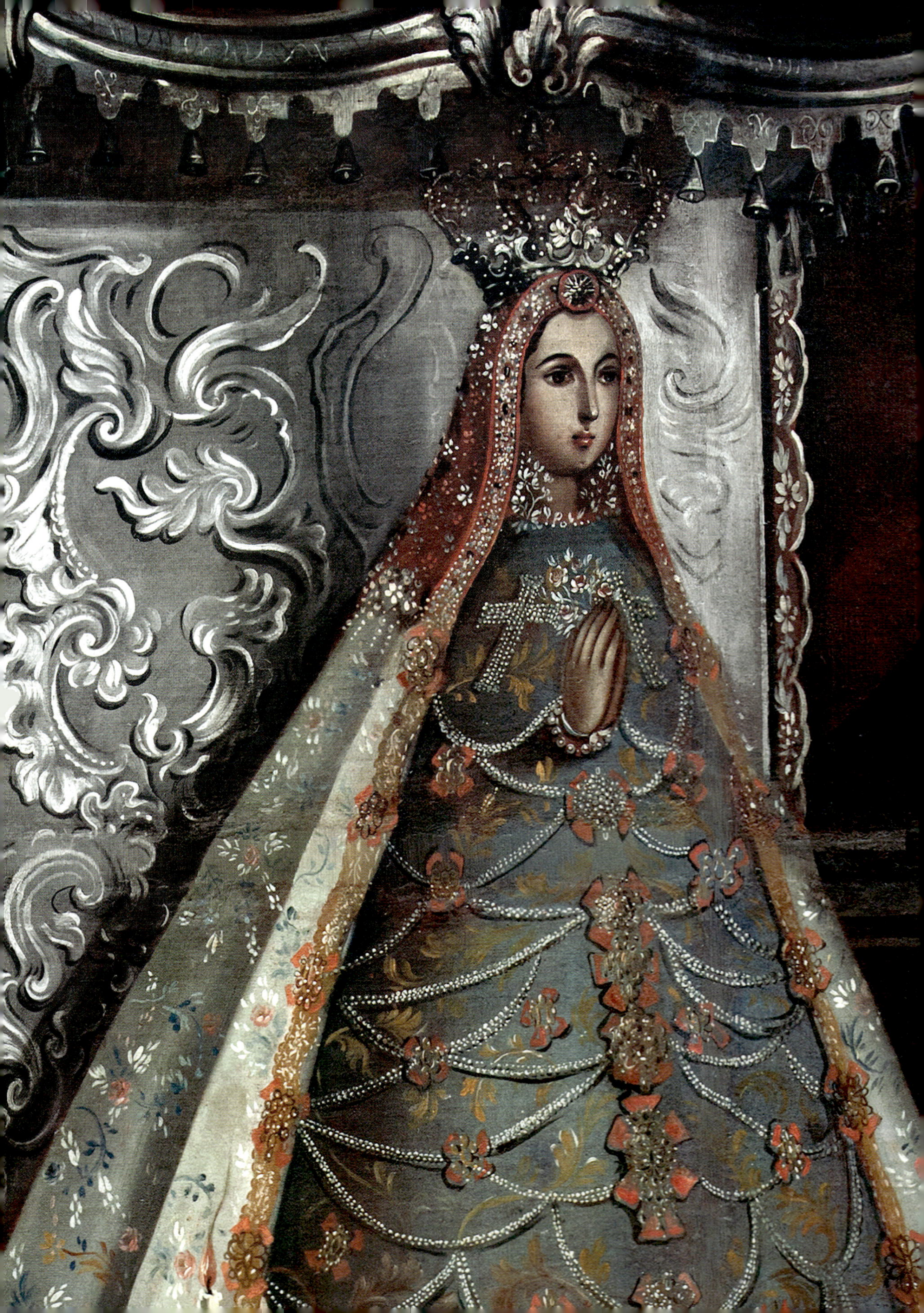

IDOLIZING MARY

Maya-Catholic Icons in Yucatán, Mexico

AMARA SOLARI

The Pennsylvania State University Press
University Park, Pennsylvania

FRONTISPIECE: *Canon Agustín Francisco Echano with the Virgin of Itzmal*, 1769, detail (fig. 3). Photo: Miguel Angel Martínez de la Fuente. Courtesy of Miguel A. Bretos.

Library of Congress Cataloging-in-Publication Data

Names: Solari, Amara, 1978– author.
Title: Idolizing Mary : Maya-Catholic icons in Yucatán, Mexico / Amara Solari.
Description: University Park, Pennsylvania : The Pennsylvania State University Press, [2019] | Includes bibliographical references and index.
Summary: "Investigates the origins of Maya veneration of the Virgin Mary and the processes of religious transformation during the first two hundred years of Spanish colonization in Yucatán"—Provided by publisher.
Identifiers: LCCN 2019007014 | ISBN 9780271083322 (cloth : alk. paper)
Subjects: LCSH: Mayas—Religion. | Mayas—Material culture. | Icons—Cult—Mexico—Yucatán (State)—History—16th century. | Icons—Cult—Mexico—Yucatán (State)—History—17th century. | Catholic Church—Mexico—Yucatán (State)—History—16th century. | Catholic Church—Mexico—Yucatán (State)—History—17th century. | Mary, Blessed Virgin, Saint—Art. | Mary, Blessed Virgin, Saint—Devotion to—Mexico—Yucatán (State) | Izamal, Our Lady of.
Classification: LCC F1435.3.R3 S65 2019 | DDC 972/.65—dc23
LC record available at https://lccn.loc.gov/2019007014

The Pennsylvania State University Press is a member of the Association of University Presses.

It is the policy of The Pennsylvania State University Press to use acid-free paper. Publications on uncoated stock satisfy the minimum requirements of American National Standard for Information Sciences—Permanence of Paper for Printed Library Material, ANSI Z39.48-1992.

For my mother and sister

Contents

Illustrations

MAPS

Preface and Acknowledgments

In the summer of 2003, on a fellowship, I visited Itzmal for the first time. Had I known that I would spend the next fifteen years of my life completing two monographs that prominently featured this Maya town, I might have headed for the hills (if Yucatán actually had any). Instead, I stayed and witnessed the singular event that has driven and sustained my fascination with this early modern artistic and architectural wonder for over a decade, the annual procession of the Virgin of Itzmal.

That first day, I slowly made my way up the sloping ramp to the atrium and entered Itzmal's immense forecourt. I crossed the open expanse, noticing the seventeenth-century polychrome murals that still decorate the facade of the monastic complex. The most vibrant image features a standardized depiction of a Santa Barbara icon; a Maya artist rendered her standing on a marble pedestal inscribed with her appellation. The saint's diagnostic edifice rests in the palm of her upturned hand, while she directly gazes at her spectators. As I drew closer, I noticed an elderly Maya woman, replete in a vibrantly embroidered *huipil*, engaged in what can only be described as a choreographed dance with this image. She twirled close to the picture plane, occasionally reaching out to touch Santa Barbara's sandaled foot, which visually edges out into the viewer's space, interrupting the usually strict divide between image and audience. This was not the Catholicism I had expected at the place that had hosted Pope John Paul II eleven years earlier. Something much more interesting was afoot.

I have spent the early part of my academic career attempting to figure out what that is. I suppose producing a second monograph is a bit like the common adage of producing a second baby; thankfully, we tend to block out the physical and emotional pain of the first experience to fully and naively engage with the second. In truth, the writing of this book has been joyful, as I've been able to devote large expanses of the past few years to the task all scholars love: complete immersion into the time, place, and human context of our chosen historical fields.

As with all such projects, I am eternally grateful for the time, insights, and humor bestowed on me by a trusted circle of colleagues whom I count among my closest friends. Tatiana Seijas, Martin Nesvig, Zeb Tortorici, and Miguel Martínez carefully read early drafts of a handful of chapters. Their positive feedback inspired me to continue on with the project. In the months that followed, Traci Ardren assisted me with much-needed advice from a real archaeologist of Yucatán, ensuring that my journey into the precontact world wouldn't be the disaster I anticipated. My dear friend and true partner in crime, Linda K. Williams, generously and graciously read the manuscript in its entirety, a chore for which I cannot effectively express my appreciation. Ongoing conversations with fellow scholars of Yucatán John Chuchiak, Mark Christensen, and Mark Lentz and fellow colonial art historians Dana Leibsohn, Barbara Mundy, and Jeanette Peterson have similarly shaped and then reshaped my thinking. Thanks are also owed to Karen-edis Barzman for organizing a CAA panel in 2015, which forced me to reconceptualize the contents of chapter 1. Similarly, the former editors of the *Hispanic American Historical Review*, Pete Sigal, Jocelyn Olcott, and John French, took a chance on a very early version of chapter 4, helping me to complicate this entire project.

I have also benefited from the privilege of much-needed release from teaching and service responsibilities at the Pennsylvania State University. Primary among these grants was a yearlong National Endowment for the Humanities Fellowship at the John Carter Brown Library during the academic year 2013–14. There I was able to access the library's remarkable collection of early modern texts, allowing me to more fully contextualize the historical theater that is the topic of this book. Among an impressive cohort of fellow fellows, especially Elvira Vilches and Miguel Martínez, I was able to more fully articulate the goals of this project, assisted by their smart insights and expert knowledge of early modern Spanish. My time at the JCB benefited from its remarkable staff, most especially, the director, Neil Safier; the former curator of Latin American books, Ken Ward; and the European books curator, Kimberly Nusco, as well as Susan Newbury, Adelina Axelrod, and Allison Rich. In the fall of 2015 I was awarded a residential fellowship at Penn State's Institute for the Arts and Humanities, during which I finalized the book's concluding two chapters. The Penn State Department of Art History's Krumrine endowment provided funds to secure image permissions. The Krumrine family's generosity also supported my colleague Larry Gorenflo, who expertly drew the maps for this text.

At Penn State I am privileged to be part of a large-scale academic community that includes, and extends beyond the confines of, my own department. In particular, Tatiana Seijas, Sarah Rich, Martha Few, Ronnie Hsia, Sophie de Schaepdrijver, Anthony Cutler, Elizabeth Smith, Bill Dewey, Brad Bouley, Dan Zolli, Laurent Cases, and Kathy Salzar have repeatedly made my professional life more pleasurable than I would have ever thought possible. Additionally, my graduate students, past and present, Catherine Popovici, Janet Purdy, Laura Almeida, Rebekah Martin, Scott Cave, Megan McDonie, Scott Doebler, Samantha Billing, Chris Valesey, and Samantha Davis have similarly reminded me of the joys of this profession and have similarly challenged and influenced my thinking. I have been given the privilege of watching them mature into academic peers.

I cannot say enough about the debt I owe to my editor at Penn State University Press, Ellie Goodman. Ellie has championed this book from our initial conversations.

Her editorial insights and inquisitive intellectualism permeate every page of this text. She is a most excellent art historian.

In our little community nestled within the Happy Valley, my close circle of James and Gretl Collins, Siela Maximova, Mark Guiltinan, Mark Koschny, Lara and Shawn Carter, and Anna and Matt Barone continually provide a much-needed reprieve from academic woes.

My family also deserves accolades in terms of their unwavering support. My father, Clifford; brother, Neil; sister-in-law, Nicole; and brother-in-law, Ian, have formed an ideal dream team of diversion.

I would be remiss if I did not properly acknowledge the wisdom and support of my husband, Matthew Restall. I cannot overstate the benefits of sharing one's life with a fellow academic. Beyond being the best scholar I know, Matthew fills our life with love and humor, the two ingredients that ensure a blissful home. I apologize to our four daughters, Sophie, Isabel, Lucy, and, most recently, baby Catalina Emilia, for having to endure countless hours of dinnertime debates about early modern Mexico. During the course of their childhoods and adolescences they have surely earned their own honorary doctorates in this field.

Finally, I dedicate this book to the two most influential women in my life, my mother, Kathy, and younger sister, Emily. Like the Virgin Mary in Maya communities, their love and faith sustain us all.

Introduction

[The Taínos] left the house of prayer, and they threw the [Christian] images on the ground; they covered them with soil and pissed on them, saying, "Now your fruits will be good and large."

—RAMÓN PANÉ, CA. 1498

There isn't a [Maya] house that doesn't have images of Christ our redeemer and of Our Lady and of others [saints], many crosses at the doors, and little ones on the rosaries around their necks. … The multitude of [Mayas] come together for Nuestra Señora de Itzmal from all the frontiers of this land and beyond…. [They] come to keep vigil with such spirit and faith that they would remain from the door of the church to the high altar, where the image is, asking her for health.

—GERÓNIMO DE PORRAS Y MONTALVO AND BERNARDO DE LIZANA, 1624

In the spring of 1494, the "poor hermit" Ramón Pané received a lofty challenge, a wholly new kind of theological commission: to provide the great admiral of the Ocean Sea, Christopher Columbus, with a treatise detailing the religious beliefs of the Taínos of Hispaniola.[1] The friar's ethnographic account, which today is extant only in the 1571 Italian edition of the *Life of the Admiral*, written by Columbus's son Fernando Colón, survives as the earliest description of an Amerindian cosmological system and its associated material culture.[2] Buried among Pané's lengthy description of Taíno sacred effigies, which he terms *cemini*, the friar provides short anecdotes of early encounter episodes, such as the moment quoted in the first epigraph. In this aside readers are told of a seemingly violent act committed against Catholic images.

As recorded in Colón's text, another friar, Giovan Borgognone, accompanied Pané, and together they established a "house of prayer" in the village of the great cacique (local ruler) Guarionex. After it became clear that Guarionex was not interested in the Christian faith, the two friars abandoned their mission for a neighboring village controlled by the cacique Mauiatué, who seemed more responsive to evangelism. Pané

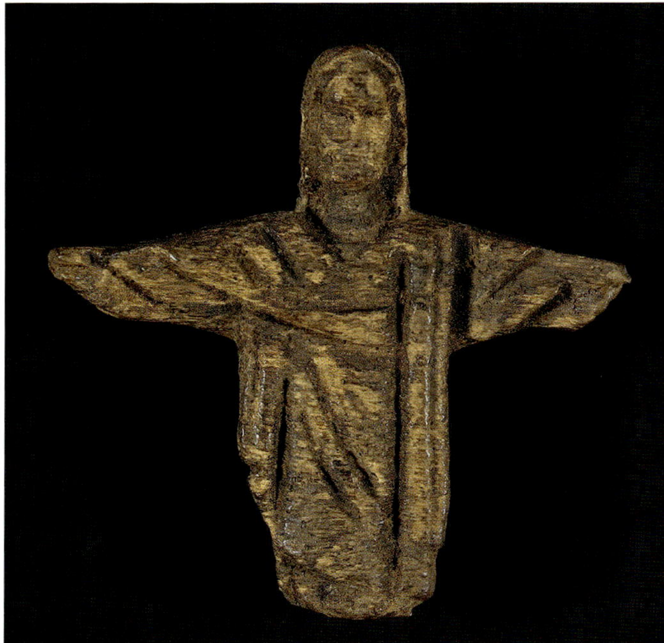

intentionally left behind a few Christian images in Guarionex's church for a handful of villagers committed to the faith; these objects likely resembled the humbly crafted Taíno crucifix found hidden in a cave in today's Dominican Republic (fig. 1). To his neophytes Pané also entrusted the care of the agricultural fields he had prudently tended for the past two years. Two days after the friars' departure, six allies of Guarionex bullied past some native children guarding the church and kidnapped the Catholic statuary. These men then absconded to the friars' agricultural fields, buried the statues, and urinated on their "graves" in an apparent mockery of Catholic rites.[3]

Today this tale reads like a parody of colonial interactions the world over. What Pané seems not to have fully understood, or at least was unwilling to acknowledge, was the active role the Catholic images played in the complex cultural landscape of the "encounter." In this scene, which prefigured the now infamous public outcry against Andres Serrano's photograph *Piss Christ* in 1989, one can only imagine the friars' revulsion when their loyal indigenous neophytes relayed this event.[4] Pané well understood how sculpted objects functioned in Taíno religiosity (nearly two-thirds of his report details these traditions), so it is remarkable that he didn't recognize that the iconoclastic act was an indigenous acknowledgment of the religious icons' inherent power. The Taínos conceived of the Christian images in terms that paralleled their traditional cemini, known to similarly manifest the totemic forces of unwelcome visitors. Through

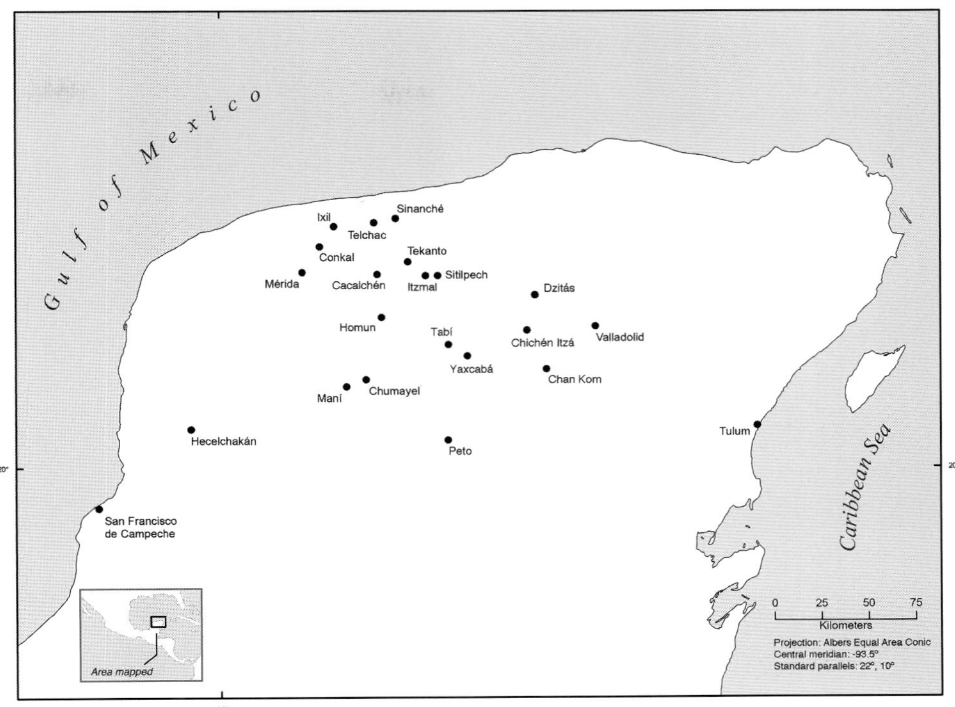

MAP 1 Northern Yucatán Peninsula. Map by L. J. Gorenflo.

the ritualized burial and "irrigation," Gaurionex's men had remade the Catholic icons into malicious power objects.[5]

Yet, 130 years later, two Franciscan friars, Gerónimo de Porras y Montalvo and Bernardo de Lizana, described a nearly antithetical scene. Writing to the king from the similarly remote native town of Itzmal, Yucatán (map 1), to petition for funds to build yet another mission church, the mendicants detailed the success of the order's evangelical efforts.[6] For Porras and Lizana, evidence that the province's sizable Maya population now adhered to the "true faith" resided in their outpouring of affection directed toward Catholic material culture, their veneration of crucifixes, saint images, and, most significant, Marian icons. This indigenous piety was clearly visible in a variety of contexts, from the most private space of humble *chozas* (traditional Maya thatched houses) to public and elaborately orchestrated feast days, hosted by Maya confraternities, which occurred in the town's impressive missionary complex dedicated to San Antonio de Padua (fig. 2).

From Porras and Lizana's perspective, the most convincing aspect of indigenous devotion was the veneration expressed for the local sculpture of the Virgin Mary, Our

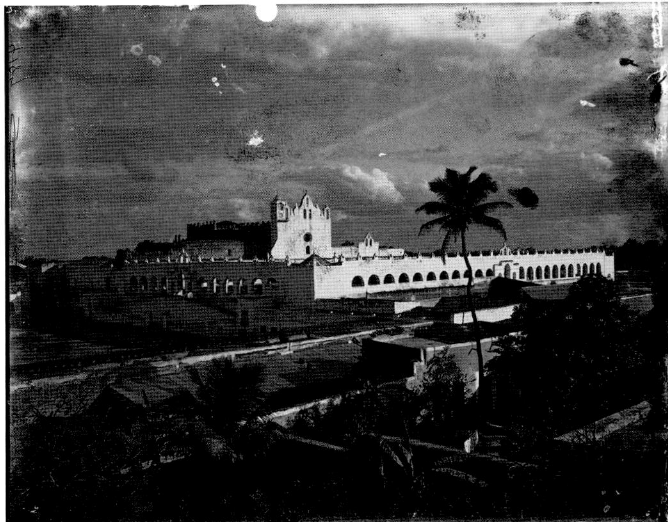

Lady of Itzmal, rendered here in two dimensions in a much-later eighteenth-century painting (fig. 3). Introduced in 1558, the icon had quickly gained popular and primarily indigenous appeal, owing in part to the miracles she performed in response to personal petitions for health. Given the devastating effect of infectious disease and related famines on the Maya population in these first decades of Spanish colonization, it is not difficult to comprehend why such a large public devotion toward a healing and apotropaic Catholic icon would have amassed. Moreover, for centuries Itzmal had functioned in the precontact era as a pilgrimage destination for Itzamnaaj, the Maya deity of healing. The local landscape was already understood to be particularly numinous.[7]

What is more difficult to understand is the apparent contradictory stance of the Franciscan order as a whole. From the earliest moments of the evangelical effort, these men of the cloth were extremely cautious, interpreting indigenous piety as potentially veiled forms of idolatry.[8] Inevitably, centuries of experience of converting Iberian Jews and Muslims to Catholicism flavored these mendicants' interactions with the Amerindian neophytes. Porras and Lizana thus display a surprising trust in the veracity of Yucatec devotion; there is not a single hint of suspicion in their words. While we must read their account within its political context as a monetary petition to the Catholic monarch (and thus excuse the propagandistic hyperbole), it is clear that the friars deemed outward expressions of devotion as perfected signs of their neophytes' interiorized religious beliefs. Like their predecessor Pané, these Franciscans seem incapable of contending with the possibility that the Amerindian relationship to Christian sculpture operated within a cultural system that predated the introduction of Catholicism. While the indigenous response to Catholic images had obviously undergone a

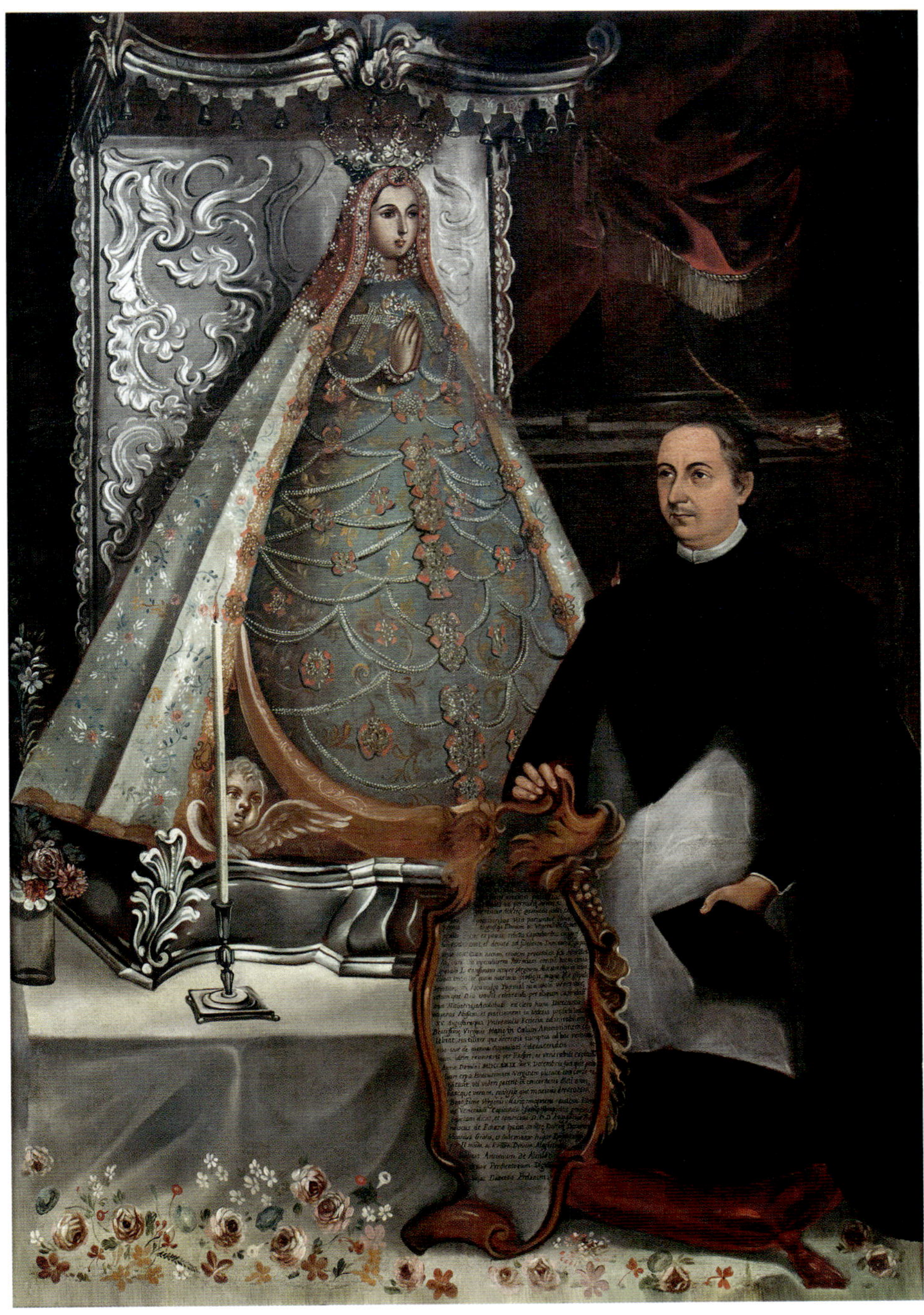

FIG. 3 Artist unknown, *Canon Agustín Francisco Echano with the Virgin of Itzmal*, 1769, Catedral de San Ildefonso, Mérida, Yucatán. Oil on canvas. Photo: Miguel Angel Martínez de la Fuente. Courtesy of Miguel A. Bretos.

substantial shift between the 1490s and the 1620s, the later mendicants were unable to explain the mechanics of this transformation. They happily attributed it to the singularly redemptive power of the Spanish Dios.

This book is an attempt to do what Porras and Lizana were not inclined or culturally capable of doing. In the chapters that follow I critically explain the popular devotion the Maya exhibited toward Catholic images in the Yucatán Peninsula. The oppositional nature of the epigraphs forces us to investigate what had transpired in the intervening decades between Spanish contact and the conquest of Yucatán. If we take Porras and Lizana at their word, and there is supplementary evidence that suggests that we should, how exactly was such a feat accomplished? How was an entire continent of Amerindians convinced that Catholic statuary had within its numinous capabilities the power to advocate for their needs to a new and strangely omnipotent God? What were the motivating factors that allowed such transference to be possible within the extremely fragmented social structure and cultural arena of the early colonial period? And, with the passage of even more time, how do we account for the multicultural nature of Yucatecan Catholicism? How and why were specifically "Maya" Catholic icons deemed useful to Spanish colonists and presumably Afro-Yucatecans? What kinds of mediating factors made possible the moments of *communitas* (communal experience of ritual liminality) witnessed during various moments of the peninsula's racially and ethnically divisive history?

A Method Materialized

The answers to all these questions involve an academic inquiry into comparative materiality, that is, an analysis of the ways in which the various contributing cultural groups (Mayas, Spaniards, and Afro-Yucatecans) conceived of matter, of the physical world. If we take the anecdotes as decontextualized bookends, they present a story of conversion as unproblematic and theoretically unnuanced as the one suggested by Robert Ricard in his seminal 1933 *La "conquête spirituelle" du Mexique*.[9] It would appear that where once the indigenous populations venerated precontact *ídolos*, after the arrival of Spanish clergy, native neophytes simply transferred their veneration toward Catholic statuary with little ado. This replacement model—or the somewhat more sophisticated model of "idols behind altars," whereby indigenous veneration of Catholic icons registers pagan practices lurking behind a veil of Christianity—has tended to dominate discourses of colonial religious conversion, as it is a simplified explanation for the outpouring of religious piety enacted by Amerindians.[10]

For example, writing in the 1970s about a later genre of these material icons, nineteenth-century Mexican *santos*, art historian Gloria Fraser Giffords begins her text by succinctly summarizing this model: "The worship of a household god or image representing supernatural powers is as old as man himself. Logically, then, the replacement of the New World's native gods with Christian religious personages was an obvious step in the conversion of the Indians. Catholicism supplanted an already deeply ingrained image-worshipping tradition with a new set of holy persons, often strikingly similar to the old gods. The desire to possess an image to ensure health, fertility, and abundance of crops often led to a simple transfer of beliefs from a pagan image to one of the Catholic hierarchy of saints."[11] Giffords's use of words such as "replacement," "supplanted," and "simple transfer of beliefs" glosses over the complexities of this religious transformation, in a single step confirming absolute Spanish religious authority and eliding even a whisper of indigenous agency. Beyond this, her assessment of Amerindian populations as "image-worshipping" reveals her (perhaps unintentional) collusion with early modern European notions of the "barbarous natives," defined as "idolaters." While one could expect this scholarly take when the book was first published in 1974, by the date of the text's second run, 1992, a more enlightened appraisal of indigenous Catholicism would have been timely. That particular year marked the quincentennial of Columbus's first landing on what would become "Hispaniola." Moreover, a revolution of indigenous language studies had occurred in the intervening two decades, revealing indigenous communities to be active participants in the creation of colonial society and its religious institutions.[12]

What is even more disheartening is the perseverance of this replacement model in much of the scholarship that dates from this millennium (the fact that scholars continue to use the term *idol* to refer to precontact statuary reveals the model's presence in contemporary academic discussion). While scholars have been keen to admit to its oversimplification, very little attention has been placed on the "replacement" of the model itself. Instead, native interest in newly introduced Catholic icons has been generally attributed to one of two primary motivators. The first is the serendipitous iconographical congruence between the Christian image and a precontact deity complex. For example, scholars have argued that certain native groups who venerated lunar goddesses, such as the Maya Ix Chel, were particularly responsive to the Virgin of the Immaculate Conception, as she is traditionally imaged with a crescent moon at her feet.[13] A second analytical method connects positive indigenous responses to the successful usurpation of traditional numinous landscapes. The central Mexican Virgin of Guadalupe's wide native appeal has often been attributed the virgin's appearance to a native man, Juan Diego, on a hill that in the precontact era had been used as a shrine for the Mexica goddess Tonatzin.[14] In fact, I myself have previously relied on this model to explain Maya interest in the Virgin of Itzmal and will expand on it in the following chapters.[15]

What is lacking in the scholarship, then, is an assessment of indigenous acceptance of Catholic icons that questions how these populations would have understood the sacred icon on its own terms, that is, outside the religious history that defined the precontact period but within traditional conceptualizations of the material world.[16] To the two modes of analysis discussed here, iconography and spatial usurpation, I wish to add a third motivating factor to help explain how indigenous communities in the Yucatán Peninsula readily adopted the Catholic practice of Marian veneration: Maya notions of sacred materiality.

As such, this book directly engages with what some scholars are terming the "material turn" in the humanities and social sciences, an academic trend from which art history (save medieval art history) has largely (and strangely) been absent.[17] Since the trend's emergence in the late 1980s, various scholars have advocated for the centering of objects in historical and cultural processes and have offered a variety of paradigms, ranging from "social lives" to "biography" to "itinerary."[18] At various points in this text I engage with all these models, as the analysis of deity images, whether of precontact supernaturals or Catholic personages, provides an avenue where these seemingly distinct frameworks can peacefully coexist. In the historical theater of New Spain, much like that of medieval Europe, sculptures of Christ, Mary, and the saints have been understood as living and also peripatetic members of the community and so have a social or biographical aspect.[19] They are born, created, and discovered; they live their daily lives by overseeing feast days, hearing petitions, and so on; and in some cases they actually die (e.g., destroyed by fires) or are stolen. At the same time, they are not stagnant objects confined to a singular cultural context for all of eternity; they change homes through religious procession or, more violently, by being desacralized and forced to move into the new contextual reality of a museum gallery or private collection. These icons are biographically itinerant.

While the arguments I propose in this book were formed amid the scholarly web woven by dozens of scholars, two works deserve mention here, as they have contributed most significantly to my thinking. The first, Caroline Walker Bynum's *Christian Materiality,* served as my initial introduction to the concept of what she calls "holy matter," aspects of the physical world (sculpted icons, painted images, relics, etc.) deemed inherently animate by medieval Europeans. This was not a new concept to me, as a scholar of the precontact Americas, but Bynum's articulation of it within a wholly Christian context first caused me to ponder the ways in which Maya materialism influenced the Catholicism adopted in the Yucatán Peninsula. For obvious reasons, it should be clear that I am not proposing that these two social groups maintained similar forms of sacred materiality, but Bynum's emphasis on the role of matter offered an alternative understanding to the two traditional modes of analyzing the native adoption of Catholic tropes as described earlier.

Closer to my home field of Latin American art history, Stephen Houston's *The Life Within* provided a much-needed precontact frame for abstract concepts originally framed in a Western context—most significantly, the notion of materiality. Houston defines the term as a "cognitive engagement with matter." I found his subtle differentiation between matter and material to be particularly useful, as he argues, "Among the Maya, matter stores energy and latent potential. 'Matter' is what is there before the eyes; 'material,' embodying potential, implies an intent to work such stuff. The first underscores the physical and the palpable, the second beelines to purpose, to what humans and other beings think can be done with it." As an epigrapher, Houston accessed the linguistic world of the ancient Mayas, providing a textual source base richer than that of my own area of study, the colonial period. His synthesis of Maya notions of the sacred, particularly, as they relate to the term *k'uh* (god), impelled my own thinking about the survivability of this ideological system into the early years of the evangelical period.[20]

The title of this book, *Idolizing Mary*, an admittedly opportunistic pun, gets at the heart of the matter because the veneration of matter is at the heart of this book. I argue that what the Europeans responsible for the conversion efforts recognized in their neophytes was a publicly acceptable adoration of Catholic icons, but they deemed this veneration acceptable only because of their own misunderstanding of its nature. If these men of the cloth had amassed a more sophisticated understanding of Maya conceptions of the sacred, they likely would have deemed early modern Marian devotion a textbook definition of idolatry, the worship of the physical aspect of a "graven image," as forbidden in the Decalogue. What they failed to understand, and what I explain in detail later, is that Amerindians operated in a much more nuanced system of belief, one in which the activation of an icon's materiality was the actual object of veneration, the ability and capability of making the transient divine materially corporeal, an embodied sense of the supernatural.

Using the Virgin of Itzmal as a case study, I account for the successful implantation of dozens of Marian cults and the Maya acceptance of the Virgin Mary as a powerful protector deity.[21] While several evangelical strategies certainly assisted with this process, primary among them the training and indoctrination of young elite children in monastic schools, none can wholly explain the appeal of Catholic material practices to Maya communities. Larger forces than an overzealous church were at work. It just remains to be properly understood what those forces consisted of and how they were perceived, adopted, and ultimately self-consciously appropriated by the indigenous communities.

The chapters that follow place images at the forefront of this religious transformation, recognizing that for most of the colonized population, it was icons, not weapons, priests, or soldiers, who were the purveyors of Spanish colonization and Catholicism. In the place of precontact "idols" rose a veritable army of sculpted Catholic objects, diminutive and also life-size effigies of the Virgin Mary, Jesus Christ, and the various saints, rendered with what some modern viewers take to be an alarming degree of veracity. These objects were also represented in two dimensions in the form of panel paintings, but more commonly in woodblock prints or engravings, to more (cost-) effectively spread the growing network of Catholic veneration, bleeding into the domestic spaces of newly converted Maya families. This process was slow but perpetual, as the adoration of local religious statuary still defines native religious practices today.

This figurative discourse was, in Serge Gruzinski's view, composed of "images at war."[22] And perhaps this allusion to a military battle is apt, echoing Ricard's conception of the "spiritual conquest." Missionaries deployed the visual world as an instrument of Iberian Hispanization, more primary than the introduced Spanish language. In so many ways images were more appropriate tools of the colonial regime and ultimately more successful than texts in Spanish. I do not wish to diminish the role of language in these cultural processes, but one only has to remember that most indigenous peoples did not readily adopt Spanish as a kind of colonial lingua franca. Most communities continued to speak their native languages into the modern era. It was the Spanish clergy who, as William Hanks has shown for Yucatec Mayan, appropriated indigenous languages, gradually transforming them into tools of cultural conquest.[23]

Running parallel to the Mayas' own tale of material conversion is the European struggle over the meaning of Christian images, defined in the various meetings of the Council of Trent. While European theologians defined the orthodox use of religious images, mendicants in the Spanish Americas were tasked with extirpating precontact visual culture and placing in its stead that of the Catholic Church. They assumed native neophytes had adopted orthodox forms of what modern scholars would term early modern "visuality," that is, an understanding of visual representations of sacred personages (Christ, Mary, or the various saints) as mere conduits to the unseen Christian Godhead.

But these years were studded with the continual discovery of supposedly converted indigenous populations that maintained traditional ceremonies and continued to produce related material culture such as Maya deity effigies. Spaniards conceptually unified these diverse practices under the umbrella term *idolatría*, which eventually evolved into a semantic field that spoke to, and ultimately exacerbated, an entire realm of colonial anxieties. A discovery of idolatrous practices immediately brought into question the supposed God-ordained legitimacy of Spain's entire colonial endeavor. If after decades of concentrated mendicant conversion efforts the indigenous population still engaged their traditional ritual activities, was this not evidence that the devil had a stronger hold on the continents of the Americas than God? The unearthing of idolatría brought to the fore doubts about the paternalistic relationship that the mendicants had spent decades to establish between themselves and their indigenous neophytes.[24] The friars' decades of suffering—toiling among their new flock in a strangely foreign land, learning challenging languages, living in relative cultural isolation—would have appeared to have come to naught.

With time, all the hopes and disgraces of the mendicant orders were inextricably linked to the indigenous veneration of images. It is not overstated to say that in some senses the very success of Spain's colonial campaign came down to whether the indigenous populations could be made into proper Catholic vassals, and the most obvious index of this was the public display of Catholic religiosity expressed toward the sculpted world. For the mendicants responsible for the missionary endeavors of New Spain, nothing spoke more clearly to their internalized failure than the discovery of pagan material culture. These humbly sculpted deity effigies became semantically complex receptacles for all members of the colonial interchange.

Following the lead of scholars such as John D. Early and Mark Christensen, I argue that the Yucatecan mission system provided a venue for the development of a distinct form of early modern Catholicism, possible only because of cultural, geographic, and temporal particularities of this unique historical context.[25] The intellectual and religious interchanges that occurred within Yucatán's mission churches resulted in the creation of a fully operative nexus of meaning, based solidly within orthodox teachings of the (usually) Franciscan friars but equally and profoundly rooted in the spiritual beliefs of their Maya neophytes. As the generations of friars and Indians expanded, the emerging religious ideological web was continually reformulated, responding to changing needs and altered social and political contexts. It was the very fluidity of semantics, particularly in regard to the use and veneration of sacred imagery, that allowed for the survival of Catholicism among nominally converted Maya populations.[26]

My quest here is to determine to what end ideologies of the material world affected indigenous conceptions of and responses to Christian icons in the conflictive domain of early colonial Yucatán. At the same time, I also query to what end the seemingly simple appropriation of Iberian religious practices, specifically the procession of sculpted icons, colluded with these ideologies, affecting how not only the native population but also the Spanish population conceived of such events.

I seek to illuminate the web of ideas within and around which this visual material circulated and participated, querying how the objects themselves came to compose a distinct set of colonial actors. In the end, this is a book about the "power of images," power in terms of the religious sculptures' own sacred and numinous abilities, but also the power that their appropriate veneration had over complex cultural and sociological processes.[27] I posit, in fact, that beyond differentiations of race, ethnicity, language, and gender, in many ways, how people interacted with statuary became the primary and defining mode of categorization in the colonial Americas. In particular, cults of the Virgin Mary provided an avenue through which diverse colonial actors could rally around a common religious power; she was able to bridge cultural and linguistic divides because the ritual practices that arose around her had equal roots in both Europe and the Americas.[28]

A related concept to materiality, corporeality, is also paramount to this particular art-historical research. At no other time in human history has the simultaneous mixing of so many entities of the human and natural worlds occurred.[29] When all is said and done, this may be the defining characteristic of the Latin American experience, as studies of the emergence of the modern nation-state have attested.[30] Add to this stew the unseen, but undoubtedly more problematical, biological agent of infectious disease. Before many Amerindians had even set eyes on European bodies, their own corporeal lives were undergoing profound physical attack. Scholars have debated the quantitative reality of the waves of epidemics that swept through the American continents, but regardless of one's conservative or generous estimation, the result of this biological encounter was disastrous for the native population. The very somatic substance of indigenous society was compromised, undoubtedly resulting in a reimagining of seemingly stagnant conceptual categories such as *body, corporeality*, and even *materiality*. Thus, notions of contagion and susceptibility enter into the realm of colonial consciousness for all members of New Spain. Theories of contagion inform how images and their unorthodox use, idolatry, were understood to function in this dangerous, unpredictable, and temperamental colonial landscape. As such, this is also a book about bodies, disease, health, and the maintenance of the corporeal status quo.

Organization of the Book

The book is divided into five main chapters; each houses its own interrelated lines of argumentation, which unite the text's seemingly disparate topics into a cohesive whole. The first chapter, "A Virgin's Procession," highlights the case study that originally prompted me to think about the larger methodological issues described earlier, the Virgin of Itzmal's procession to Mérida during the yellow fever epidemic of 1648. This particular epidemic began in the port city of San Francisco de Campeche in the early spring, quickly spreading to Mérida and beyond, perhaps killing as much as half of the region's population by the summer's end. Unlike the peninsula's earlier epidemics, this particular plague claimed the various ethnicities of the province in equal number, causing Spanish authorities to completely reconceptualize their public responses to what they deemed was God's wrath meted out in direct proportion to their communal sins. After all other recourses of public health had been attempted (quarantine, medicines, washings, burnings, and the like), Mérida's civic powers reasoned their only hope to be the appropriate petitioning of the region's singular confirmed miracle-working statue, the Virgin of Itzmal. After gaining license from the Maya confraternity (an act that is itself a fascinating moment of colonial negotiation), the virgin was processed forty-five miles to Mérida to perform a nine-day vigil. This procession was the first time the virgin had left her home sanctuary in nearly one hundred years, and it marks the first Spanish-Maya communal healing procession ever enacted in the peninsula. I argue that this event suggests a profound shift in Yucatecan religiosity, one that continues to define regional devotion today.

The book's following chapters work in concert to provide readers with the conceptual threads necessary to make sense of the virgin's 1648 procession. The next chapter, chapter 2, "Maya Effigies and Material Sacrality," offers a revised understanding of Maya conceptions of religious statuary as means to contextualize native understandings of Catholic icons. I turn to the archival sources that purport to describe indigenous Maya religion, the words and testimony that survive in the thousands of folio pages produced as part of the Franciscan order's inquisitional queries of the sixteenth and early seventeenth centuries. Launched to root out the ever-present threat of idolatría, these archival sources contain accounts, written in both Mayan and Spanish, that describe how the indigenous population utilized their sacred sculpture. Pejoratively termed *ídolos* by the inquiring Spaniards, these objects were clearly much more than simply revered simulacra.

My analysis sheds light on how the Mayas of postclassic and colonial Yucatán understood sacrality to be housed within the materiality of the sculpted image itself, an aspect that the Franciscans should have aligned with idolatry. This ideology was particularly evident in practices devoted to physical healing. But the Franciscans were unable to comprehend the subtle nuances of this belief system, and their inability would have consequences for the indigenous veneration of Catholic icons that was to follow in the seventeenth century.

In chapter 3, "The Itzmal Icon," we return to this Maya town to trace the origins of its resident Marian icon. I reconstruct her original appearance, necessary because the statue venerated at Itzmal today is a replacement icon substituted for the sixteenth-century original after she was destroyed in a church fire on April 17, 1829.[31] I argue that in addition to her engagement with traditional Maya modes of locative sacrality (the accrual of sacred power in a singular locus over the course of centuries), the virgin's atypically mundane creation, commissioned from a well-known Guatemalan sculptor at the bequest of Itzmal's resident Franciscan, Diego de Landa, differentiates her from other early modern miraculous icons, which were generally deemed *acheiropoieta* (not made by human hands). Devotees to these other acheiropoieta conceived of their numinous abilities to be directly derived from mysterious godly intervention, but for the Virgin of Itzmal, other forces were at work. Primary among these is the fact that in his selection of production technique, Landa intentionally engaged with ancient Maya traditions of image making in an attempt to ease the reception of this icon among the native population, making her particularly appealing as an icon tasked with healing sick populations.

Thereafter, in chapter 4, "Maya Religiosity and Material Contagion," I turn to Spanish conceptions of disease and idolatry and the ideological conflation of these two spheres of colonial experience. As the singular chapter that isn't solely dedicated to the Yucatán Peninsula (although large portions do examine this context), this chapter may seem like the odd person out. But taking the wider view is necessary, as it throws into relief the cultural magnitude of the 1648 procession to Mérida. Using evidence taken from both Mexico City and Yucatán, I argue that within the first decades of the evangelical campaign, religious and secular colonial authorities understood sacrilegious acts and their underlying ideological systems to be contagious entities. Time and time again, Spaniards articulate in text and in administrative acts the belief that mere contact with offending practitioners had the potential to infect spiritually healthy individuals with the "disease" of idolatry. Given that the Creole population deemed any indigenous religiosity as a possible threat to orthodox Catholicism, their petitioning of a Maya Mary, as described in chapter 1, suggests a complexity of colonial Yucatecan religion that has not been suitably explained.

The final chapter, "Maya Conceptions of Mary's Birth," details the first scholarly analysis of Maya Mariology. I begin by translating and then analyzing a midcolonial Mayan account of the Virgin of Itzmal's sixteenth-century arrival, extant in "The Book of Chilam Balam of Chumayel." This historical rendering frames the Catholic deity's appearance as a cosmogonic event, her "birth" echoes other Maya creation narratives, signaling that the indigenous population conceived of it as ushering in a new era of human history. I go on to argue that Maya neophytes adopted Mary as a new god, accepted on her own terms. This line of argumentation requires a close analysis of Mayan-language documents that reference either Mary the abstracted religious actor or physical statues of her, such as the Virgin of Itzmal. I argue that these usages, rather than a mere Maya appropriation of Spanish terms such as "Santa Maria" or "Nuestra Señora," demonstrate the nativization of Mary. Tracing the chronological development of Mary's appellations reveals that the Spanish virgin was remade into a distinctly Maya deity, not a simple replacement for a single precontact goddess but rather a newly formed deity, capable of countering the colonial challenges posed to the indigenous community. This notion largely pivots on the indigenous incorporation of the Mayan term *suhuy* into her appellation, a term that in the precontact period and beyond referred to the ritual purity of a sacred body, material object, or ceremonial act. I end this chapter by visiting the mural cycle associated with another of Yucatán's miraculous Marys, the seventeenth-century Virgin of Tabí, to demonstrate how these concepts were appropriated by this town's ethnically diverse population and the devotees whom their icon inspired.

I conclude the book with a short epilogue that unites the separate threads of analysis presented in each of my discrete chapters and examines a revered icon that gained popularity in the century after the yellow fever epidemic, the Black Christ of Sitilpech. Until today that Maya village, located a mere five miles east of Itzmal, engages in an annual cycle of linked public worship, whereby the Black Christ enters into a month-long conversation with the Virgin of Itzmal to renew and thus maintain his own sacred potency. This contemporary practice of lived devotion shows how practices of materialized sacrality, first manifested and publicly expressed during the repeated health crises of the early colonial period, continue to define popular Catholicism in the Yucatán Peninsula today.

Source Material

To construct my argument of sacred materiality, my source base is necessarily broad. This is primarily owing to the poor level of preservation of both textual and visual documentation in the peninsula, especially when compared to other regions of Spain's colonial empire, most obviously the cosmopolitan centers in Mexico and Peru. A devastating series of both human and nonhuman disasters and factors (various wars, hurricanes, the tropical environment) have coalesced in this region to result in the mass destruction of hundreds of lines of historical evidence. But there is an upside to this story: the paucity of textual and material remains forces scholars to be interdisciplinary; to conduct sound research that convincingly tells anything about this historical time and place, we must use any and all evidentiary lines that have survived until the modern era. Archival sources become just as valid for visually minded scholars, such as art historians, as they are for the more textual fields of history, ethnohistory, and religious studies. The very lack of a substantial source base makes our jobs perhaps more difficult, but the results are more profound, as they speak to the various levels and complex intricacies of the lived reality of colonial experience.

The bulk of my visual evidence can be found in printed books and sculpted icons created in the first century of Spanish colonization. I try to reconcile two sides of an ideological exchange, and, as such, I rely on European- and Maya-authored visual material, which often represents contrasting sides of colonial processes. European engravings, such as those produced by Diego Valadés, are particularly revealing, as they present in snapshot form an idealized view of coeval Franciscan understandings of their own evangelical efforts. Similarly, Maya imagery included in native-authored manuscripts and also precontact artifacts and codices provide similarly ethnic-based views of colonial society. To study the cult dedicated to the Virgin of Itzmal, I rely on two panel paintings (figs. 3 and 28) and three prints (figs. 21, 22, and 27).

While the topic of this book is obviously visual, textual sources provide the armature of my argument. These sources come in a variety of forms, in four languages (Spanish, Italian, Latin, and Mayan) and include early modern printed books, archival documents, and colonial manuscripts written by indigenous actors. They are held in about a dozen libraries and archives scattered in both Europe and the Americas.[32] While searches in some of these repositories yielded only a few records that specifically related to Yucatán's colonial experience (and so are not cited here specifically), their collections frequently provided a much-needed view into contemporaneous regions of New Spain and beyond.

The method of my research is thus located at the nexus of art history, religious studies, ethnohistory, and the history of medicine. Perhaps this forced interdisciplinarity is serendipitous, as it reunites the humanities with the sciences and therefore re-creates an ideological reflection of this early modern moment, when these two poles of intellectual query were not violently divorced by Enlightenment thought. Regardless of the method's origins, it is one that turns to printed and inscribed words, recorded actions, and related ideas of a variety of colonial actors, European settlers, Franciscan friars, Maya neophytes, indigenous leaders, Spanish administrators, and African slaves alike to tell this story.

As much as I would ideally have equal representation among all these various people, the reality of the archival record is that Spanish colonists are disproportionately present, and of these all are male and most come from the very highest levels of the colonial social hierarchy. Thus, the bulk of the story is told from the perspective of the peninsula's administrative and religious authorities, the governors and higher-ranking members of the church, typically bishops and the heads of the Franciscan order. These men wrote lengthy accounts, intended for the Spanish Crown or the Audiencia de México (to whom Yucatán was jurisdictionally subject) and are thus preserved in the national archives of both Mexico and Spain. Typically, these take the form of *visita* accounts, tours of the province that bishops were (ideally) supposed to make each and every year. In reality, they occurred far more infrequently, but when the bishops deigned to enter the wilds of the peninsula, they recorded in great detail information of both a cultural and a religious nature. Occasionally, the words of lesser-ranked priests are preserved in other notarial genres, most frequently in the *probanzas de méritos*, written to the Spanish king as testimony of services rendered in an attempt to secure a royal stipend. All the Spanish sources are problematic in their own individual ways, primarily because they operated within a colonial system that rewarded hyperbolic language and the exaggeration of one's actual contributions to the emerging colonial society.[33] The challenge for scholars is thus to carefully and responsibly wade through the self-aggrandizing inflations to extract nuggets of reliable information.[34]

To do so requires the contextualization of these texts, a recognition that, like all objects produced by human beings, they are artifacts of the world in which they were created, in this case the political and religious world of the Spanish Empire. I am thus taking a very critical stance toward these sources, whenever possible utilizing their manuscript copies and not more easily accessible (and also more legible) translated and printed editions. In the following pages readers will find a close examination of the bibliographic biographies of each source, all aimed at convincing my audience that, much as they have been used by academics in the past, these texts are not neutralized journalistic reports that espouse a concretized "truth." This is most apparent in my use of Bishop Diego de Landa's supposed monolithic text, "Relación de las cosas de Yucatán," a manuscript that scholars typically assume to be solely authored by him (a problematic assumption) and also written as a cohesive document (an impossible scenario, given the bishop's own biography).[35]

Resurrecting the Maya side of my tale is more challenging, particularly in regard to their responses to Catholic images, my primary interest here. While dozens of Mayan-language documents have survived, at the highest level of colonial correspondence these are succinct petitions to the king of Spain and are suspect, as they seem to directly engage with known desires of the Franciscan order, such as the need for more priests on the peninsula. As such, scholars are unsure if these are coerced records or not.[36] Beyond these traditional notarial genres, two other lines of access are possible. The first is a handful of Maya manuscripts known collectively as "The Books of Chilam Balam." Repeatedly written, rewritten, and transcribed through the course of the colonial period, these books (nine in total are extant) are collections of Maya texts that do not easily lend themselves to systematic categorization. They are composed of histories, ritual prognostication, medical treatises, astronomical records, and annals, parts of which seem to have been directly copied from precontact hieroglyphic codices.[37] While Maya scribes composed "The Books of Chilam Balam" primarily in Yucatec Mayan, they frequently incorporated newly introduced Spanish and Latin loanwords. In addition, some of these texts retain redactions of Christian accounts, Islamic tales, and direct transcriptions of European printed works, both textual and visual. Of importance to my argument is the fact that these manuscripts were written by and for the use of Maya elders and as such offer a privileged view into indigenous conceptions of religion and the contemporaneous society in which they were created.

The third form of Maya material does not contain this emic perspective, as it is the "Inquisitorial Record." I have included the scare quotes around this genre's title to denote the fact that from 1571 forward indigenous persons were not technically under the direct jurisdiction of the official Inquisition (only people of European and African descent were). But this is not to say that the Mayas' sometimes unorthodox or heretical religious acts were not severely castigated. In some cases, bishops and even lower-ranking friars or seculars took it upon themselves to hold unofficial and certainly not legally sanctioned Inquisition-like trials, reaching a verdict and then meting out punishments as though by Spanish law. The probanzas de méritos described earlier frequently include copies of testimony from these events, as zealous priests used them to prove how they had sacrificed for the Christian God and successfully persecuted "idolatrous" Indians. Occasionally, we are fortunate enough to have Maya ethnographic details included in the official Inquisition trials of additional colonial actors, frequently Afro-Yucatecans. As many scholars have shown, the religion of colonial Yucatán reflects the fluidity of Maya and African practices.[38] When idolatries were discovered that included both Maya and African petitioners, the Africans would be tried by the Inquisition in Mexico City, while the Mayas would be dealt with by their local parish priests or perhaps, if the act was considered especially grievous, by the bishop. Interestingly, the accused Mayas were sometimes summoned to provide evidence of an African's participation; in these cases we have the very rare occurrence of a native person describing their own heretical act.

While the geographic expanse of this study is rather constrained, my hope is that the diversity of textual and visual sources allows for the ideas presented here to be applicable to other native populations of Mesoamerica and perhaps to the larger American continents. In doing so, I am not attempting to provide a universal ideology of images that can be applied to all Amerindian groups of either the precontact or early modern eras. Rather, my hope is that, taking my micro art history for the province of Yucatán, other scholars will be able to ask how the material, spatial, and corporeal ideologies of native and Creole populations alike contributed to the emergence of localized forms of Latin American Catholicism.

A Virgin's Procession

Today, when a pilgrim or tourist visits the town of Itzmal, it is impossible to disconnect the religious import of this small Maya town from the regional history of the larger province of Yucatán. Since at least the middle of the seventeenth century, city planners have worked to make this link visually manifest, punctuating various points of the urban landscape with commemorative plaques that describe in relatively concise detail the role Itzmal has played in Yucatán's spiritual redemption. Figure 4 is an example of this practice, a series of carved stones inserted into the matrix of an arcaded building that inhabits the eastern edge of the town's *plaza mayor*. Visitors are likely to view these plaques, raised as they are about fifteen feet above plaza level, as they descend down the monumental ramp that leads to the great church of San Antonio de Padua, the personal sanctuary for the Virgin of Itzmal (figs. 2 and 5). While the distance from the ramp to the plaques would impede their legibility—they are located across the small plaza located at the base of the monastery—their presence visually interrupts the bright-yellow field of the painted wall, drawing attention.

The group of plaques shown here enumerates the virgin's trips to the provincial capital of Mérida, located forty-five miles west, where she has been processed since 1648 during moments of health crises.[1] In doing so, the physicality of her material form serves to connect the Maya town of Itzmal to the Spanish seat of colonial authority. With her body the virgin charts an axis from periphery to center and back again, imbuing the diverse ethnic and religious geography of the peninsula under the sacred rubric of a singular religious system.

In this chapter I trace the development of this tradition, detailing the virgin's original peregrination during the 1648 yellow fever epidemic. I treat her voyage and subsequent events as a microhistory; in combination, they function as lenses through which to examine the ideological intricacies of colonial Yucatecan crisis response. This chapter opens by briefly setting the scene of colonial Yucatecan history for uninformed

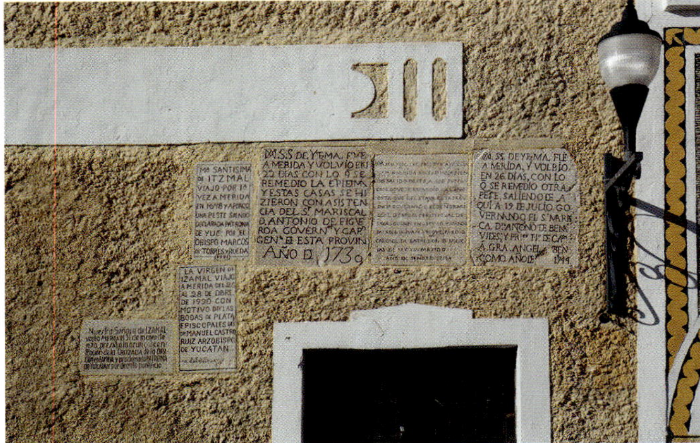

FIG. 4
Commemorative plaques posted on the public porticos of the main plaza, Itzmal, Yucatán. Photo: author.

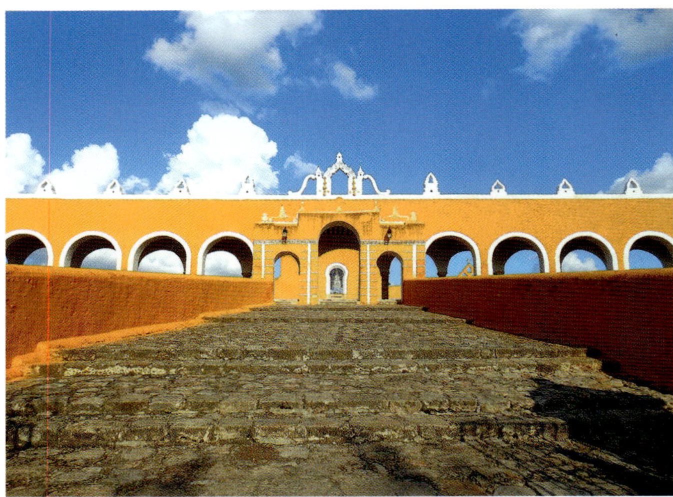

FIG. 5
Ramp leading up to the atrium of the San Antonio de Padua Monastery, completed circa 1580, Itzmal, Yucatán. Photo: author.

readers. I then jump forward in time by a century to retell the epic tale of a first encounter of another kind, the peninsula's initial brush with yellow fever. Our most detailed account of the event is included in Fray Diego López de Cogolludo's (1613–1665) *Historia de Yucathán*, composed in 1655 (but not published until 1688). In 1648 López de Cogolludo was resident in his brotherhood's Mérida monastery and so was poised to witness firsthand the horrifying event and its aftermath. He also nearly succumbed to the disease, being one of the province's luckier survivors.[2] The friar devotes an exhaustive seven chapters to the plague, paralleling in length other pivotal historical moments in peninsular history, such as particular events of the sixteenth-century conquest wars. Given the devastating impact that this pandemic had on the peninsula's diverse colonial population, it is striking that very few accounts of it are extant.[3] López de Cogolludo directly engages the literary tradition of plague tracts, which by this point in the early modern period had become a discrete and standardized genre of historical accounting.[4] Granted that fewer were published in the Iberian world than in England and France, a healthy corpus of Spanish examples circulated, providing models for how López de Cogolludo could approach this particular historical episode.

Like their Spanish forefathers, the Creole population of seventeenth-century Mérida blamed their sins against God for the plague and in response enacted processions of public prayers and mortification of the flesh. On the surface, at least, it appears that localized Yucatecan Catholicism was operating within the centuries-old Iberian tradition, understanding material icons as somehow community intercessors poised to petition on their behalf. However, in this chapter, I take issue with what I deem an overly simplistic interpretation of American appropriation of European religious traditions, as it fails to account for the material and processional traditions of the precontact indigenous population.

Setting the Scene

The Catholic evangelical campaign in Yucatán was an extension of the central Mexican endeavor, which itself expanded the Reconquista of the Iberian Peninsula. The province's first friars were fortunate to build on centuries of missionary experience among unconverted "pagan" peoples. The Crown granted the Franciscan order sole ecclesiastical jurisdiction over the peninsula's thousands of Maya souls.[5] Singular secular priests (and occasional bishops) influenced the development of Yucatecan Catholicism, but, unlike other areas of the Spanish world, here a single branch of the mendicants dominated indigenous conversion and religious life. A brief synthesis of the Yucatán's early colonial religious history serves to contextualize the cultural landscape that is analyzed in the pages that follow.[6] This missionary story is one of stops and starts, successes and failures, headway and backpedaling, two steps forward and one step back—in sum, an arduous process that mirrored the difficult complexities of the physical conquest of this region as well.

Europeans encountered the peninsula early in the history of Caribbean exploration, despite Columbus's having just missed it on his 1502 voyage to Honduras. Diego de Nicuesa led a disastrous expedition launched from Cuba in 1511, resulting in a shipwreck that deposited a handful of Spaniards onto terra firma, most of whom perished.[7] Between 1517 and 1519 the governor of Cuba, Diego Velázquez de Cuéllar, organized three distinct expeditions. Francisco Hernández de Córdoba led the first of these formal *entradas*, but, despite making landfall on Isla Mujeres, the expedition failed to leave a lasting Spanish presence, owing to the fierce resistance encountered from Maya militias. Juan de Grijalva headed the next, sailing from Cuba in April 1518, and met with similar disaster.[8] The third entrada, led by Hernando Cortés in 1519, would become better known to the world, as it eventually resulted in the European discovery of the Mexica Empire. Beyond depositing a handful of Marian images and crucifixes in Maya temples, Cortés's short-lived presence in the peninsula did not have a lasting cultural impact.[9]

In the wake of these failed early attempts, Yucatán's physical conquest rests squarely on the shoulders of Francisco de Montejo and his son and nephew, both of whom are also named Francisco; the former is frequently referred to as "El Mozo." In 1528 Francisco the Elder received a royal decree from Charles V to conquer the peninsula, and in 1530 he launched his first ill-fated expedition. This first entrada targeted the Yucatán's eastern coast, but Maya warriors repeatedly thwarted the Spaniard's efforts, like those of his predecessors. Montejo attempted to establish an outpost on the western coast in the following years, with multiple failed attempts between 1531 and 1535. It wasn't until his son attempted from the western shore in 1540 that Europeans maintained a permanent foothold, founding the port of San Francisco de Campeche and, two years later, Mérida, on top of a precontact city locally known as Tiho (map 1).[10]

It should be apparent that the military conquest of the Yucatán Peninsula was an outrageously protracted event; in fact, the southeastern region was never fully controlled by Spanish forces at any point in the colonial era.[11] The settlers soon began to understand the political organization of the peninsula and, like their contemporaries in central Mexico, used ancient political rifts to their advantage.[12] For the two centuries prior to European contact, the northern region had been divided into more than a dozen "kingdoms," individually ruled by a singular patrilineage (a *chibal* in Mayan) or, in rare cases, elite oligarchies (termed *multepal*).[13] These polities centered on traditionally designed Maya towns, whose ceremonial centers were simplified versions of the more monumental ones that had graced the peninsula in the early classic, classic, and postclassic periods (250–1250 CE), such as those of Cobá, Chichén Itzá, Uxmal, and Itzmal. Because of these political complexities, Spanish administrators focused their attention primarily on the northwest corner of the peninsula in the areas surrounding the Spanish port and fort at San Francisco de Campeche and the provincial capital at Mérida (map 1); it was in this region that they found expedient allies in the Xiu and Pech lineages who controlled these territories. Colonial outposts were also maintained in the province's inland center at Valladolid and along the eastern coastline at Bacalar.

Interspersed between these four Spanish strongholds were dozens of reduced native towns (*pueblos reducidos*) designed specifically for the Christianization and Hispanization efforts. A handful of Catholic priests had intermittently arrived in the peninsula (including the now-famous Jacobo de Testera, who was in the region perhaps as early as 1535 and so before the establishment of a permanent Spanish settlement, and also Bartolomé de Las Casas, at some point between 1544 and 1545).[14] But the true fathers of these Yucatecan mission towns were two distinct groups of Franciscan friars who arrived in 1547.[15] In that year Yucatán was a fledgling colonial province rife with administrative, juridical, financial, and agricultural woes, but the Franciscan order was able to successfully navigate this political turmoil, recognizing the missionary potential. As early as February the region's first *comisario* (commissioner), Juan de la Puerta, described his new mission as "very healthy where having good order every day the people will multiply and will be more in the favor of your Highness."[16] In this initial decade he was perhaps a bit overly optimistic. But in the next 150 years, it is undeniable that Puerta and his fellow Franciscans established one of the most ambitious religious-building programs that world had ever seen, constructing nearly three hundred monasteries, churches, and visita chapels by 1700. Some of these were made wholly new from the ground up, but most were grafted onto preexisting Maya urban developments, such as pyramid mounds and traditional range-style buildings. The unique design of precontact Maya towns easily lent themselves to Spanish refashioning, or transfiguration, as they were oriented around quadrilateral plazas delineated by mound structures, an orientation that serendipitously mapped the idealized and later legally instituted design for colonial Spanish settlements.[17]

The first wave of pueblos reducidos targeted the environs surrounding Mérida where Spanish civil authority was secure; Maní and Conkal were established in 1547, and Itzmal two years later, in 1549. The procurement, retention, and in some cases survival of religious personnel plagued the diocese from these very early days. As a result many of the monasteries hosted only one or two resident priests, making effective oversight of the indoctrination process challenging, to say the least.

In this overtaxed mission, friars not only oversaw the religious conversion of upward of five thousand individual Mayas but were also responsible for the education of elite children, the physical construction and upkeep of their imposing monastic complexes, and, frequently, the legal, financial, and in some cases physical protection of their indigenous neophytes from abusive *encomenderos* (Spanish colonists to whom the Crown had granted the right to extract indigenous labor and tribute from a designated spatial territory). This isn't to say that some Franciscans themselves were not responsible for taking advantage of the Maya population in various ways: the archival record is studded with indigenous petitions against their resident friars, accusing them of a wide variety of infractions ranging from cruel personal servitude to molestation and sexual exploitation. Clearly, the relationship between the various colonial actors participating in America's evangelical theater was not as idyllic as the early print culture would have one believe. For example, in an engraving of 1579 (fig. 6), the Franciscan friar Diego Valadés, who spent more than a decade evangelizing in the Otomí region of central Mexico, depicts an idealized version of this process, whereby a native interpreter introduces an unincorporated indigenous group to a Franciscan friar "armed only with an

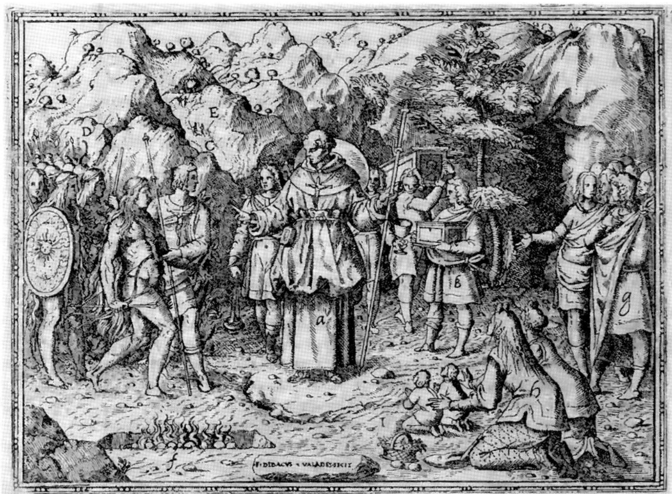

FIG. 6
Valadés, engraving from
his *Rhetorica christiana*,
224.

image of the Crucifix."[18] The native neophytes are pictured to the right of the image, behaving appropriately according to Christian decorum, with men helping to carry the sacred objects of the Catholic Church and the women offering gifts of sustenance to the priest while teaching their children how to correctly greet him.

Of course, this romanticized account of conversion certainly glosses over what can only be diplomatically described as the "cultural confusion" that must have actually occurred. What is clear, however, and perhaps somewhat counterintuitive is that in the following decades the friars did make substantial headway in their mission, creating indigenous towns whose inhabitants, at least publicly, appeared solely devoted to the Spanish Godhead and his earthly mortal representatives. Spanish and Maya sources speak to the welcoming acceptance of some aspects of Christianity, whereby native peoples appear particularly attracted to the most communal aspects of the new religion: public feast days, the construction of community churches, and the establishments of confraternities. The rest of this book seeks to explain an additional Catholic tradition readily adopted by indigenous communities, the veneration of Marian icons.

The Yellow Fever Epidemic of 1648

As López de Cogolludo described in his 1655 account of the 1648 pandemic, the horror began with a series of ominous signs. The first portent was a simple cloud, a cloud that floated over Mérida but stretched from Cozumel to Tabasco, blocking out all sunlight. Then every afternoon an intolerable stench swept inland from the northern coast, penetrating the homes of every inhabitant.[19] In April and May a handful of citizens died from unexplained causes, and fires broke out in the Maya neighborhood of Santa Ana and the African parish of Santa Lucia. On May 12 a disastrous run-in occurred between a Spanish vessel and a French corsair; a cannon aboard the Spanish ship misfired, causing all of the ship's stocked gunpowder to explode. Only thirteen badly disfigured sailors survived and made it to the peninsula's western shore. For López de Cogolludo and his contemporaries, these fateful omens signaled the true tragedy that was still to come.

By the beginning of June, a deadly plague hit the port of San Francisco de Campeche when dozens began to fall violently ill. Historical epidemiologists recognize this outbreak as the first occurrence of yellow fever on the American mainland.[20] Earlier that year, ill humans or *Aedes aegypti* mosquitoes carried the disease to Yucatán.[21] López de Cogolludo was not present in Campeche during its initial phase, but he was able to read a firsthand account sent to one of his Franciscan brothers in the Mérida convent. This anonymous correspondent hauntingly described the devastation by utilizing an early modern adage: "Soon one will say: here was Campeche, as it is said in the proverb, here was Troy."[22] The friar's verbiage reveals the desperation of the Campeche public during this moment: only a comparison with the most infamous battle in human history could accurately convey the port city's absolute devastation.

Letters such as these immediately ignited a panic in the capital city. Following typical European protocol, Mérida's *cabildo* (town council) closed the *camino real* (royal road) to Campeche, hoping that this tactic of quarantine would keep the disease at bay (as modern readers, we are well aware that the very fact that letters reached the city before the official quarantine precluded the avoidance of an outbreak). They also called on the supernatural authorities; citizens enacted public prayers and penitential processions of flagellants during the unnerving month of July. López de Cogolludo surmised, "The illness was punishment for our sins."[23] He likened Mérida to the ancient Assyrian city of Nineveh, where God had sent Jonah to preach against the inhabitants' wicked ways.[24] For López de Cogolludo, this Old Testament tale resonated with the ongoing crisis in Yucatán, since early modern theology directly linked the initial occurrence of devastating disease on the sins committed by the people of Mérida.[25] In the end, none of these strategies kept the disease at bay, as López de Cogolludo succinctly concluded: "When the Lord doesn't watch over a city, what does human due diligence matter?"[26]

By the end of July, a handful of people in Mérida had fallen ill and subsequently died, but it wasn't until the very beginning of August that it was clear these deaths were the result of the Campeche plague. Suddenly, "with great speed and violence [the illness] struck the old and young, the rich and poor, and in less than eight days almost all of the city was sick at once." The epidemic's death toll was so catastrophic that local cemeteries became overcrowded with the bodies of the deceased, forcing the excavation of mass graves in the surrounding countryside. López de Cogolludo maintained that the city had not seen such misery "since the Spanish nation conquered this land."[27]

In desperation, the cabildo approached the provincial of the Franciscan order, Bernardo de Sosa, to see if he would allow the summoning of the miraculous virgin from Itzmal so Mérideños could enact a nine-day oration, a *novenario*. This was an innovative tactic, since a Marian icon that was primarily venerated by a Maya population and lived in a mission town had never been processed in Mérida. It is especially intriguing since the province's Spaniards had their own resident Mary, who was housed in the Franciscan convent, the Nuestra Señora de la Navidad. Mérida's European inhabitants did not appear to have faith in their own icon; at this point in the peninsula's history only the Maya icon had proven to be miraculous.[28]

Incredibly, the Franciscans granted the cabildo license, and its members held an election to determine the most deserving person to oversee her transportation. They narrowly selected the lieutenant general, Don Juan de Aguileta, despite the fact that he already exhibited early symptoms of the sickness. Not trusting such a perilous task to a mere layperson, the provincial accompanied the military entourage on the forty-five-mile journey to Itzmal. The ill Aguileta reportedly "put his trust in the most holy Virgin, and pray[ed] that she would grant him health."[29] Miraculously, as he neared the sacred icon, his health improved..

Before their arrival in the pueblo, the colonial rumor mill had started to churn. By the time the Spanish cohort entered Itzmal, resident Mayas had already planned a strategic attack, using the Spaniards' own tradition of public petition to express their concerns.[30] At another point in the text, López de Cogolludo reveals that he had spent some time composing his tome while working within the Itzmal monastery. It was certainly during this time that he was able to access the only surviving copy of the Itzmal Maya petition (see appendix A); he quoted the petition in Spanish translation from its original Yucatec Mayan. These Mayas worried that the Mérida Spaniards would keep their icon for their own church. To avoid this threat, the petition first demanded that they accompany and guard their Marian icon for the entire journey. It also stipulated that she be absent from her home sanctuary only for a total of seventeen days, four for the trip there, nine days for the novenario, and four more for the return trip. And, finally, in what seems like their most gutsy move, they insisted that the provincial be held in her stead, that is, resident Mayas from Itzmal would hold Sosa hostage inside the convent as human insurance, to release him only upon her safe return.

It is clear from the petition's listed names that its authors represented Itzmal native elites, those of its inclusive barrios, and the town's dependent visitas. All of these Maya men had been granted the title of *don*, and all held political positions in their respective pueblos: "Don Juan Ek governador of the town of Izamal, Don Bartolomé Cauich of that of Pomolche, Alonso Canche, Gaspar Pech Alcaldes of Santa Maria. Don Matias Canche Governador of the town of Citilpech, Don Pedro Chim of Pixila, Don Bartolomè Uitz of that of Xanaba, Don Francisco Ke of Kantunil, Don Francisco

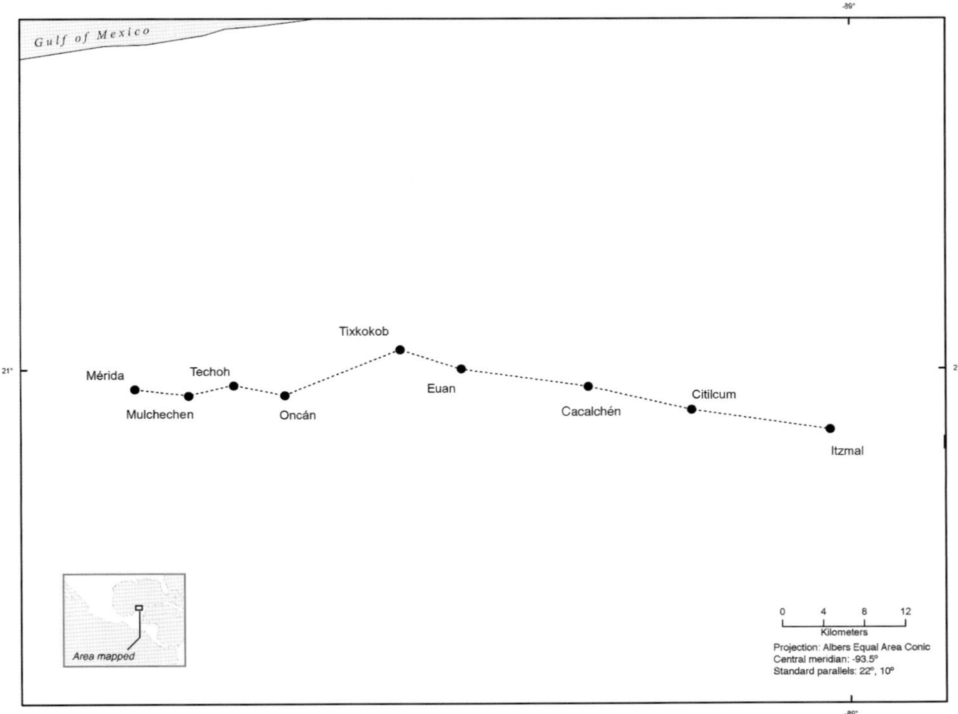

MAP 2 Probable processional route from Itzmal to Mérida. Map by L. J. Gorenflo.

Ve Governador of Zuzal, Don Sebastian Mena Governador of that of Chalmte, Don Bonifacio Zul of Uizi, and Tocbaz with all the Mayors, Councilers, and Elders of this Guardianship and town of Izamal."[31] Although it is never explicitly stated, I posit that these men constituted the body of the virgin's confraternity. The political importance of these Maya men is evident in the fact that the Spaniards acquiesced to all of their demands, signing a contract guaranteeing her safe return. Thus, a deal was made. These diverse colonial actors exchanged the material Virgin of Itzmal for the physical body of the Franciscan provincial.[32]

According to one of Itzmal's resident priests, Francisco Martínez, when the group tried to remove the virgin from her altar, "she had a flushed and angry face; she seemed to be frowning and angry" (upon her return, she was "cheerful and smiling"). Her entourage carried her out of her sanctuary and through the streets of Itzmal and left town on its western road. They processed westward toward the indigenous pueblos of Citilcum, Cacalchén, Euan, Tixkokob, Oncán, Techoh, Mulchechen, and then possibly Pacabtun (map 2). The icon's mood certainly improved en route to Mérida, since during the course of the journey she was continually honored by candles, songs, dances, and vigils. All along the country roads, the healthy Yucatecans came out to see her,

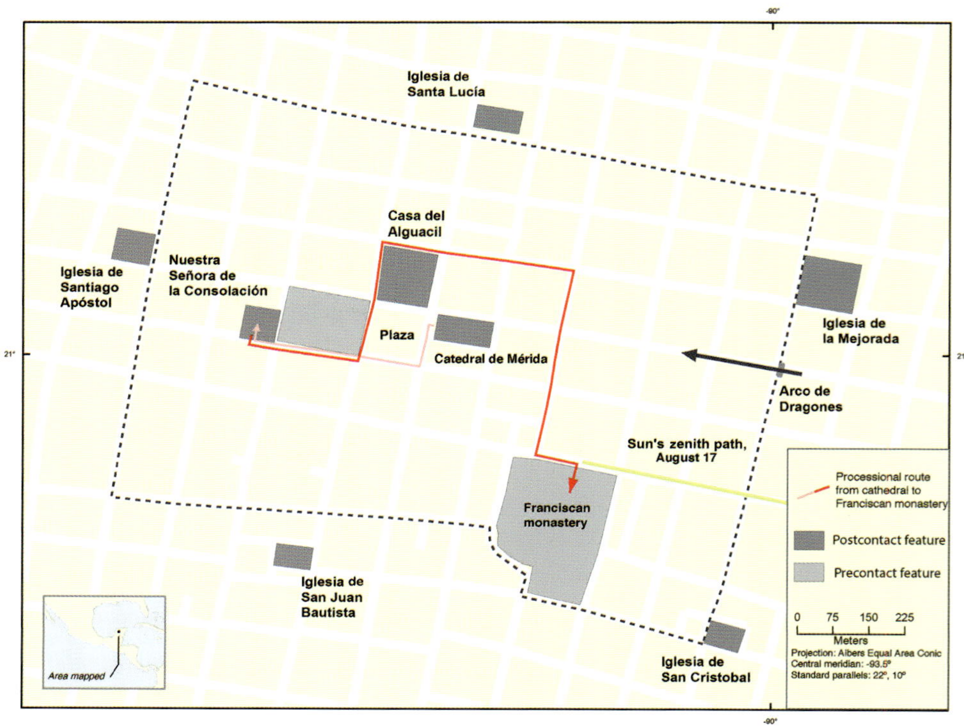

MAP 3 Seventeenth-century Mérida with parishes, *traza* limits, and 1648 processional route highlighted. Map by L. J. Gorenflo.

frequently assisting or carrying the already afflicted: "The towns on the roads that the Sacred Image passed went all out with dances and festivities to receive her. They had been blessed to see her in their village, and they venerated her with many wax candles the whole time she was there. People from the neighboring villages came to see and venerate her; it was in order to give a thousand thanks to God to see the faith that they had for the Most Holy Mother."[33]

Unfortunately, many of the Maya villages that once stood on the urban extremes of Mérida's city boundaries have been swallowed up by modern sprawl, forcing me to be less precise with my charting of the procession the closer she moved to the city. In the seventeenth century Mérida was still racially and ethnically segregated, defined by a *traza*, a delineated (but not physically demarcated) urban outline that marked a boundary, outside of which people of color were legally obligated to reside. A series of monumental "gates" punctuated the traza, physically and metaphorically protecting—through a kind of social quarantine—Spanish civility from the supposed Maya and African barbarity that dwelled beyond. The lived reality of colonial life made such a strict division impossible, particularly because members of the various *castas* (castes)

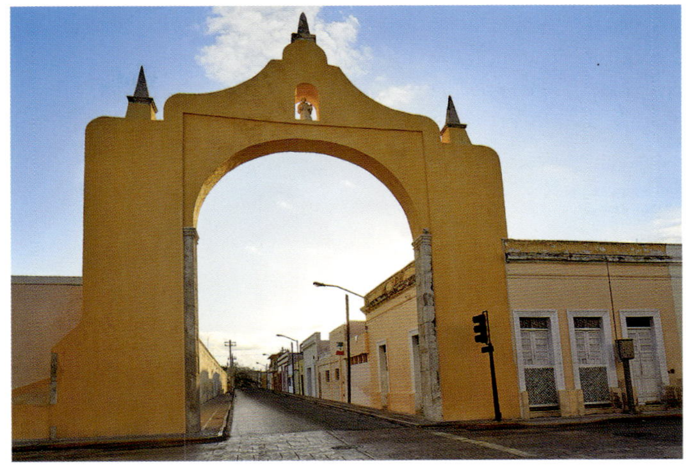

worked as domestic servants in the wealthiest of Mérida's households. While technically still part of "Mérida," five Maya barrios and a single African parish stood beyond this civic barrier, functioning as discrete villages complete with their own impressive churches (map 3).[34]

Following the four-day-long procession to Mérida, the Itzmal icon finally approached the perimeter of the Spanish traza, the eastern edge of which terminated along what is now Calle 50.[35] The colonial road from Itzmal into Mérida is today known as Calle 61. The intersection of these two roads marked the eastern edge of the Spanish town and was visually punctuated by a humble city gate, which was replaced at the end of the seventeenth century, when the imposing Arco de Dragones was erected (fig. 7). Both gates registered the formal entrance into the city, made all the more viscerally apparent with the later version's impressive size and elaborate baroque design. It is still capped with a colonial-era statue of San Antonio de Padua, and one can clearly see two of his diagnostic traits: the held bell and small Christ child. For the Spanish citizenry San Antonio therefore functioned as a spiritual guardian, visibly delineating the heathenized space of rural Yucatán with the fully Christianized urbanity of Mérida.

López de Cogolludo remarks that Mérida's social body greeted the Virgin of Itzmal prior to her formal entrance: "The morning she was to enter the City, they came out to receive her, not only those who were still healthy, but more so the sick, who couldn't walk, they were carried to the road by where she came, and some of them were healed, those who had the divine mercy."[36] The well members of the "two town councils, the ecclesiastical and the secular" also joined the throngs outside the city walls, approaching the virgin's procession with bare feet as an outward sign of their deference and humility. The enactment of these bodily proscriptions, coupled with the virgin's entrance beneath Mérida's southeastern gate, would have signaled a kind of triumphal entry, paralleling rituals enacted in the Old and New Worlds.[37] It also suggests that, like these similar processions, this public pageant made visually manifest the prominence of Mérida's Spanish population; the human populace of Mérida and the surrounding Maya and African parishes would have been organized according to their placement within the complex colonial social hierarchy.[38]

The participants then carried the Marian icon beneath this loaded social barrier, crossing into an urban space that was intended as the exclusive purview of the Spanish population. They processed her through all of Mérida's "principal streets." Here López de Cogolludo's description is too vague to chart her route with any certainty, except to assert that the path was likely confined within the traza walls and thus solidly placed within the capital's Hispanicized space. "The sick in the houses that she passed, even those who were taking some air, had thrown open the windows, entrusting their health in order to see her."[39] Presumably, given the thorough and exacting nature of López de Cogolludo's account, if the virgin had been processed to the indigenous and African barrios, he would have mentioned those ritual moments.

Having completed the Virgin of Itzmal's public procession, the entourage carried her into the cathedral, located on the eastern edge of the central plaza. Here the local dean recited mass. She was then transported through the cathedral's main entrance door and was taken across the central plaza, exiting by moving westward on Calle 63. A block beyond found the virgin at the city's only monastery of nuns, fittingly dedicated to Nuestra Señora de la Consolación, where close to forty "spouses of her most holy son received her with their glorious hymns and canticles."[40] López de Cogolludo describes the scene as such: "What was the most tender, and caused the most devotion, was upon entering the interior of the cloister, all of them removed their blue mantles, using them to make a throne, where they placed her, prostrating on the earth. They sang a hymn to her, asking her for health because they badly needed it, like the whole City, with such sickness and death that it had."[41]

Thereafter, her devotees hoisted the virgin back onto Calle 63, retracing their steps to move eastward, turning left onto Calle 62 and then right onto Calle 59 to make their way to the city jail, located on the back side of the administrative building, the Casa del Alguacil, that adorned the northern side of the plaza mayor. Here "the Magistrates don Juan de Salazar Montejo and don Juan de Ribera y Garate . . . opened up the doors of the City's public jail when the Sacred Image passed before it. Out of whose reverence and respect they liberated all of the prisoners."[42] Finally, they left the jail, headed east on Calle 59, turned south onto Calle 56, then continued east onto Calle 65, and eventually entered the primary chapel of the Franciscan convent, which perched on the summit of a precontact pyramid—an identical architectural tradition as the icon's home monastery.[43] She was placed on a throne adorned with as much grandeur as was possible, and there she remained for nine days: "All day and night, the doors of the Church remained open because there was constantly a great crowd of people that attended to her, the healthy who could come and also the sick who were carried."[44]

On August 19, in a move that would make permanent the desire of the cabildo to forever express their gratitude, the Spanish men of Mérida formalized a vow to the Virgin of Itzmal. The remarkable nature of this declaration is evident in the fact that never before in Yucatecan history had the Spanish settlers come to depend on the favor of an indigenous pueblo. So significant is this decree in the religious and social history of Yucatán, I have included it as appendix B. Not wishing to upstage the local Maya confraternity and to mark the exact day when the virgin was resident in Mérida, the cabildo chose to financially host the feast day of the Assumption (August 15), not the Virgin of Itzmal's advocation of the Immaculate Conception (December 8). I think we are looking here at a historical moment in which Spanish patrons accepted the favor a miraculous Mary had previously bestowed on an indigenous community and thus did not want to upset that divine balance. In so doing, they had to subjugate themselves to a Maya religious brotherhood, shifting the usual orientation of colonial hegemony.

During the course of the novenario, the Virgin of Itzmal became a wealthy woman. Numerous elite citizens of Mérida donated precious stones, pieces of jewelry, and clothing in the virgin's honor as a form of thanksgiving or private petition; many of these gifts were imaged in her portraits (figs. 3 and 26). At the end of the nine days, she was processed back to Itzmal, retracing her initial journey but now carried with even more "pomp, veneration, and accompaniment."[45] The magistrate who had drafted the initial petition, Don Juan de Salazar Montejo, oversaw her homeward trip, arriving in Itzmal four days later to reinstall the sacred image and in so doing release Provincial Sosa from his captivity. López de Cogolludo recounts that Itzmal Mayas and the resident Franciscan who had accompanied their icon into the capital city returned to the village infected with the disease; most began to succumb to the illness within a few days.[46] Unfortunately, history has not recorded how the indigenous pueblo internally responded to their infection.

Why would a Maya community, seemingly unaffected by the illness, have been willing to lend their venerated icon to the Spanish population of Mérida, the epicenter of contagion? Beyond the obvious likelihood of political coercion, a possible answer might lie in a Maya theory of disease, one that links the seemingly unrelated tragedies of epidemics and natural disasters. As Ryan Kashanipour shown, unending cycles of disaster—biological, in the form of epidemics, and natural, in the form of droughts, floods, hurricanes, locust infestations, and the like—defined the first decades of colonization. So cyclical were these events that some disasters seemed to foretell ensuing doom. While Kashanipour gives many examples of these interrelations, most pertinent to my argument is his observation that epidemics frequently presaged peninsula-wide "natural disasters."[47] From a demographic perspective, this link is perfectly rational. True epidemics would have decimated the population, significantly lessening the number of able-bodied men and women who would have otherwise been alive to see to agricultural needs, such as sowing and harvesting. With decreased food storages, famine would inevitably result, furthering the population loss. Moreover, for the Mayas, the opposite relationship could also be applied: natural disasters could foresee epidemics as well. Within this rationale, if a community experiences a devastating natural disaster that results in a poor harvest or even a widespread famine, that population would certainly be more susceptible to bodily contagions. Certainly, once news of the Campeche and Mérida yellow fever outbreak reached Itzmal, the local population would have understood the pan-peninsular ramifications of this event.

It is also tempting to credit the Yucatec Mayas with a far deeper level of historical memory than is usually assumed, relevant in this context in regard to the physical organization of Mérida. Recall that Mérida had been built on the ruins of a Maya city called Tiho, a monumental precontact capital whose urban design featured the expected astronomically aligned pyramids, plazas, and raised causeways that defined so many Mesoamerican polities. Within Maya traditions of ritual protocol, populations enacted communal ceremonies during astronomically significant moments, typically using the built environment as a physical armature that charted meaningful solar events. The pyramid on which the Franciscan monastery sat and the street that fronted it, Calle 65, were two such precontact urban features. The street is atypically aligned with reference to the rest of the city's orthogonal grid (map 3). Mark Lindsay surmises that this street—along with Calle 67, which runs parallel to Calle 65 on the south—was one of Tiho's principal thoroughfares, *sacbeob* that radiated from the precontact pyramid on which the Franciscan monastery was built. The section of the *sacbe* that ran directly west and east of the pyramid-cum-monastery marked the zenith passage of the sun between August 8 and 17, overlapping the expanse of time when the Itzmal virgin was resident in the Mérida convent.[48] The Mayas who participated in the icon's peregrination to this locale thus likely engaged with very ancient modes of native religiosity. Unfortunately, the exact meaning of the 1648 event to indigenous devotees will forever remain just out of focus.

Conclusion

On the surface this event seems to be lifted directly from the religious protocol of southern Spain, as the processing of a Marian icon during public health crises had been a strategy of sacred petition since at least the medieval period. But there are a number of factors pertinent to the 1648 event that suggest a rereading is in order. For now let us recall that the yellow fever epidemic transpired nearly a century after the founding of the Itzmal convent in 1549, and it was the first time the virgin left her sanctuary to assist in the physical and spiritual healing of the peninsula's population. Since the Franciscan convent resided solidly within Mérida's traza space and was intended as a region reserved for the city's Spanish population, the social impact of the virgin's novenario must have been profound. This was only the second instance in the Yucatán's colonial history of ethnically and racially diverse public veneration—the first was the 1618 confirmed veneration of the Immaculate Conception.[49] It would be another thirty years before Spaniards, Mayas, and Africans reunited to petition their deities within the same architectural space and for the same desired effect. It is tempting to apply Victor Turner's notion of *communitas* to this historical event, as López de Cogolludo's description appears to perfectly mirror the moment "in and out of secular social structure, which reveals, however fleetingly, some recognition . . . of a generalized social bond" that Turner advocated during moments of civic ritual.[50]

In the next chapter we recede back into time to analyze how the precontact Mayas conceived of and produced sacred images. Such a regression is necessary if we are to understand how indigenous petitioners conceived of their newly introduced Marian icon. As I hinted in the introduction, ancient Maya modes of materiality fill an intellectual lacuna and help us better comprehend the indigenous willingness to so readily adopt a physical image of the mother of God as a community savior, particularly one credited with the corporeal protection of a diseased population.

❧ 2

Maya Effigies and
Material Sacrality

Nearly four centuries after the anecdotes described in the introduction, another European, the Englishman Thomas William Francis Gann, portrayed Yucatecan religious objects with an identical "understanding" of indigenous religious beliefs. While serving as His Majesty's district medical officer in the British colony of Belize between 1892 and 1923, Gann had ample opportunity to venture into the remote regions of Yucatán, contacting Maya villagers and documenting the artistic and architectural accomplishments of their ancient ancestors.[1] During one of his exploratory forays (that of 1926–27), he journeyed northward along the eastern coastline of the newly designated Mexican state of Quintana Roo, setting out to find archaeological ruins overlooked by earlier European adventurers such as John Lloyd Stephens and Désiré Charnay.[2] Along with his usual hired Belizean guide, Amado Esquivel, and another man simply called "Muddy," he boarded a small boat and crossed the border that separated the English and Mexican territories, picking up another local guide, Sabas Ojeda, along the way.[3] With Ojeda acting as ambassador, they spent the next several months exploring the small-scale Maya towns scattered along the Caribbean shore.

Gann published the account of his adventure in *Maya Cities: A Record of Exploration and Adventure in Middle America* the very next year. He selected as the book's frontispiece the photograph depicted in figure 8. In it Gann's pose mirrors that of a sculpted Maya "idol," which he looted from a Maya temple located close to Tulum, the postclassic site now so well known to Maya Riviera vacationers (map 1). For readers devouring the textual details of Gann's account, this image would have resonated with one of his more exciting anecdotes. According to Gann's recounting, within a few weeks of the party's departure from Belize City, they found themselves in the modern village of Tulum, requested by "special invitation" from the local chief, Canul. Although

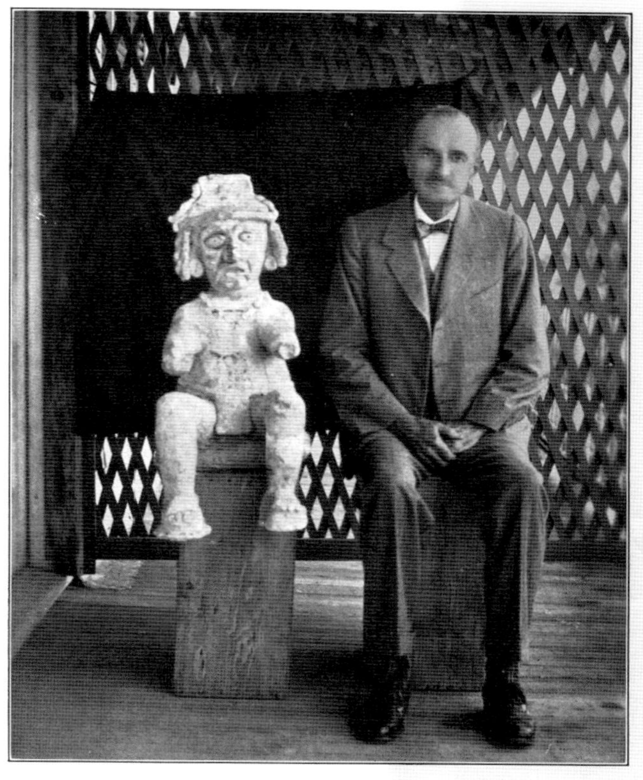

IDOL FROM THE TEMPLE SOUTH-WEST OF THE RUINS AT TULUUM;
WITH THE AUTHOR SEATED, SHOWING RELATIVE SIZE.

Gann's ultimate goal was to find the recently disappeared Chan Santa Cruz, the infamous oracular "Talking Cross" of the Caste War, he was instead promised a guided tour of an ancient structure that "no white man had ever seen." Led by Canul's son, the expedition set off the following morning, traveling three miles south and then taking a path that headed westward into the low growth of the Yucatán's tropical coverage. Peeking out through the dense foliage, a structure emerged, a "beautiful little oblong temple, standing upon a low stone platform composed of three narrow terraces." Gann stared through the diminutive doorway to be confronted with a material object his European episteme could define only as an "idol," a figurative humanoid form rendered in stucco modeling and vibrant polychrome paint. His description is worth quoting at length, given its atypical level of detail:

> It represented an individual, who, when standing up, could not have been
> much over three feet in height. He wore the stiff, formal head-dress—from the

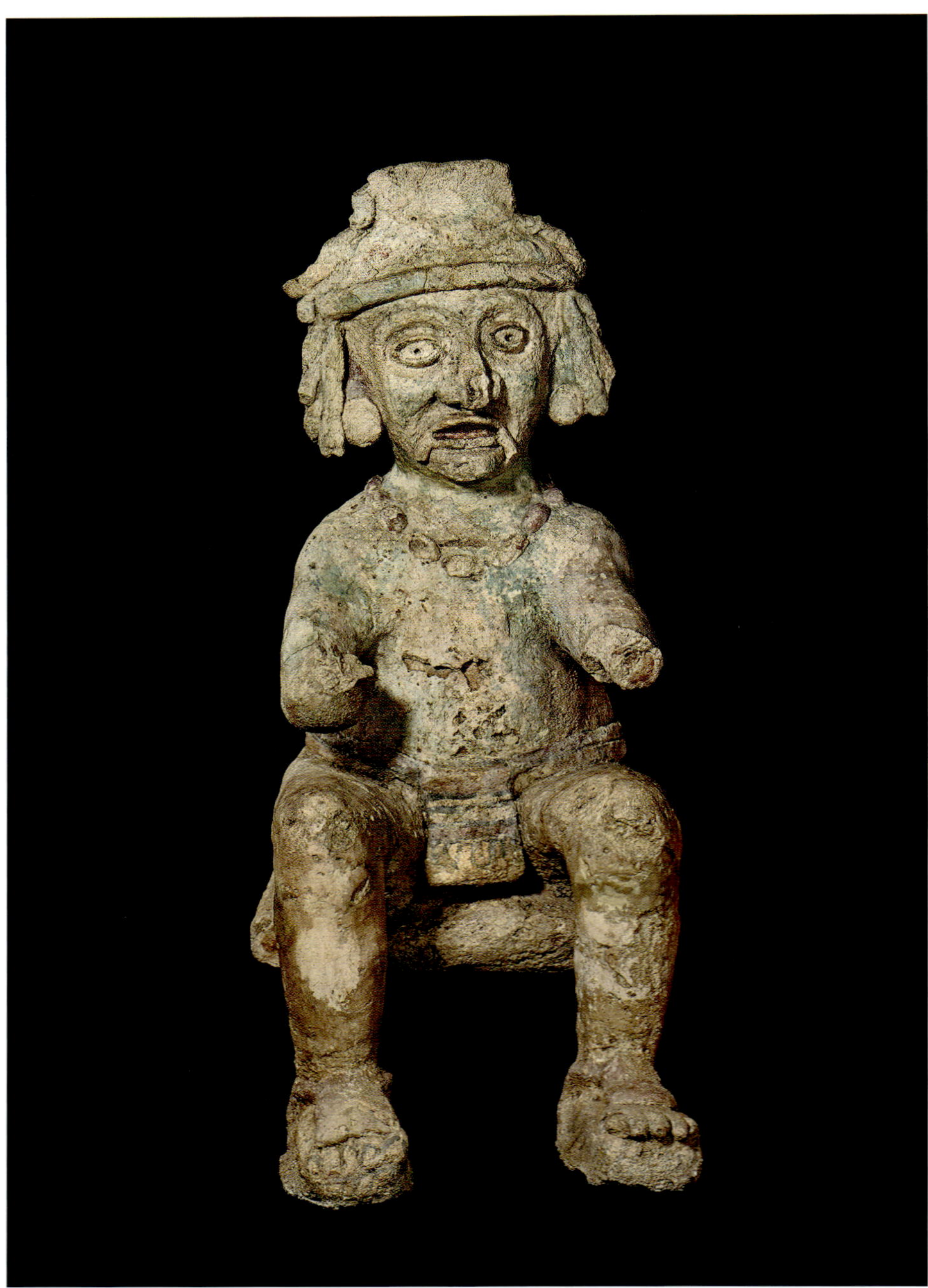

FIG. 9 Maya effigy sculpture, late postclassic period, approximately three feet in height. The British Museum, London. Photo © The Trustees of the British Museum.

bottom of which extensions reached outwards and downwards almost to the shoulders—so commonly found in appliqué on Maya pottery incense burners. In his ears were huge round *orejeras*, or ear-plugs, and round his neck a string of beads, coloured alternatively red and green, probably to represent shell and jade. Extending outwards from the head-dress to the waist were curious, stiff, wing-like ornaments, nicely carved and painted. The usual *maxtli*, or small apron, hung down in front, and crude sandals were worn upon the feet. The upper part of the idol was carefully modeled in pottery, covered with a wash or slip, of lime; the lower part from the waist down was made of cement, and much more crudely modeled. The whole figure had originally been painted, the colours used being red, green, yellow, blue, and plum colour, but a good deal had worn off.[4]

Gann further notes the presence of in situ offerings scattered in front of the sculpture, two incense burners, an obsidian knife, and three stucco turtles, triggering him to erroneously conclude that the figure represented the Maya god of "turtle-fishers." All set to confiscate the sculpture and its offerings, Gann ultimately decided to abstain, citing his own sense of history: "As the shrine and its occupant have been undisturbed in this desolate, uninhabited spot for five hundred years, it may be many more before they are rediscovered, and possibly removed, by some less sentimental archaeologist."[5]

Remarkably, this same sense of historical preservation did not keep Gann from appropriating the sculpture he would later pose with, which he was shown just a few days later (fig. 9).[6] In its scale, composition, and color, the effigy is remarkably similar to the one he previously encountered, suggesting that the small-scale temples located along the Yucatán's gulf coast were operating in a regional system of shared visual aesthetics and associated religious beliefs. The seated individual, now a resident in the musty storage rooms of the British Museum, spans nearly three feet in height and was once vibrantly painted in hues of reds, greens, and blues. He dons the familiar sandals, earspools, and loincloth that defined the other statue. Gann notes that this effigy was similarly found in an unaltered temple structure (undoubtedly late postclassic in date), but he did not include an account of its discovery. What is also missing from his analysis, steeped as it is in early twentieth-century notions of Amerindian civilized barbarity (the Maya "noble savage"), is an anthropological understanding of how the Mayas who created and cared for these remarkable objects would have conceived of them.

This chapter offers a rebuttal to Gann's designation of Maya deity effigies as idols by illuminating the ideological system that persevered in the Yucatán Peninsula in the centuries following Spanish colonization. My objective is to elucidate that potent world—consciously recognizing that it is impossible to fully resuscitate the religiosity that defined late postclassic Yucatán—as a means to more fully understand how

Catholic religious statuary would have been received in the following decades. I rely on a close visual analysis of sacred objects but then move beyond it, critically considering a variety of evidentiary avenues, including the European textual record, whose very homogeneity and intertextuality speak to its inevitable bias. In the pages that follow, I argue that during the precontact era (and beyond), a sensitively articulated framework of two related characteristics—materialized sacrality and absorptive potency—defined Maya religiosity. By coining these phrases, I do not mean that Maya worshipped the physical matrix of the icon—to do so would be to align myself with the conquistadors and colonial administrators who alleged idolatría. Instead, Maya "holy matter" (typically sculpted deity images) was part of a much more nuanced system of belief.

Abundant archival sources and modern archaeological investigations have proven that deity effigies continued to circulate among the peninsula's vast Maya population during the early colonial period, in some cases seamlessly blending with recently introduced Catholicism. Not surprisingly, decades after the beginning of intensive evangelization, material artifacts, either of traditional or Catholic personages, operated in much the same way as they had in the precontact period. While this has been widely recognized in scholarship, it has not been adequately explained. It is my contention that the indigenous adoption of Catholic statuary can be related to the Maya recognition that the divine could be made manifest in material artifacts, given appropriate ritual activation. While the Spaniards understood precontact practices as simply the adoration of physical objects that related to supernatural deities, the Mayas were actually venerating the ability of the supernatural to enter the world of the material; the physical world was merely a fitting receptacle for sacred powers. By the end of this book, I will show that although these Europeans fought to eradicate this form of religious belief, the Mayas utilized it as an avenue through which to pursue Catholic veneration.

The Material World of Maya Religiosity

Over the course of the first decades of evangelism, numerous extirpation campaigns targeted this visual world, resulting in the destruction of vast quantities of Maya religious statuary. Extant archaeological remains provide a fragmented view of what was once an undoubtedly diverse corpus of Yucatecan sacred effigies. Sculpted deity figures came in an astounding variety of forms, compositions, scales, and styles. The topic is too varied to offer more than just a mere overview here, but I'll give a substantive impression, describing a cross-section of representative types, ranging from elite effigy censers (*incensarios*) to their humbler "brothers" and "sisters," produced and used in commoner domestic contexts. This formal analysis reveals that, irrespective of class association, the Yucatec Mayas maintained a concretized religious ideology that understood the material world of the sacred to be actively participatory in the mundane existence of the human world.

To date, John Chuchiak has provided the most exhaustive tabulation of these kinds of ritual objects still used in the colonial period by analyzing hundreds of Spanish accounts, known as *probanzas de méritos*.[7] What I provide in the following pages is heavily dependent on Chuchiak's research, coupled with my own insights. But, in using similar documentary evidence, my goal is slightly different than Chuchiak's. He successfully demonstrated that the court tasked with eradicating indigenous idolatry, the Provisorato de Indios, actually "shaped and facilitated these reciprocal exchanges between the two cultures . . . help[ing] to preserve many of the very same traditional beliefs it hoped to eradicate."[8] Mine is a less historiographical inquiry; I'm not concerned with the creation of colonial legality per se. My engagement is more solidly based within the intellectual concerns of anthropology. In my use of these same sources, I seek glimpses of an articulated religious ideology, one subtly linked to a distinctly Maya (but perhaps pan-Mesoamerican) conceptualization of sacred materiality.

Early modern religious personnel did not waste time or energy familiarizing themselves with Maya "art history"—that is, they were disinterested to learn how their flock used, perceived, and conceived of their sacred effigies. Instead, they deemed all traditional native religion as *idolatría*, the veneration of graven images, and all associated material culture as *ídolos*. This immediate categorization for all religious practices other than orthodox Catholicism created an epistemic reality wherein an intellectual inquiry into the ideological contours of indigenous sacred traditions was not only unnecessary but could easily be deemed heretical. The exceptions to this were the officially sanctioned quasi-anthropological projects launched explicitly to garner information about native religion as a means to ease the processes of evangelism. Friar Bernardino de Sahagún's "Historia general de las cosas de Nueva España" is the most well-known and elaborate example of this missionary strategy; sections of Diego de Landa's "Relación de las cosas de Yucatán" likely fall into this same category, but the contexts of the project's commission have not survived.

Owing to this epistemological blind spot, the friars who were on the front line of their orders' extirpation campaigns, those who had perhaps the best firsthand knowledge of native religious art, are rarely helpful in the modern scholarly quest to re-create precontact conceptions of sacred images (although, as we'll see later, they sometimes provide accounts of the native rites themselves without analytical commentary or interpretation). They are particularly conservative in their descriptions of the formal qualities of Maya religious statuary, tending to mention only the media of sacred statuary. For example, writing in 1600 to the Spanish Crown to attest to his services rendered in the name of the king and God, secular parish priest Baltasar de Herrera boasted of finding more than four hundred "idols of terra cotta, wood, and stone" during the course of his tenure in the peninsula.[9] Only occasionally is this mere material description elaborated. In the 1589 testimony of Fray Andres Fernández de Castro, the friar comments offhand that "they embraced [the idols] as their gods."[10] In this abbreviated phrase Castro conflates the sign (the sculpted effigy) with the signified (the abstracted supernatural being), thereby defining Maya religion as a textbook example of idolatry and teleologically reifying the epistemic blindness described earlier in a kind of mental feedback loop. As a relational term, *idolatría* serves only to define Maya religion in counter distinction to early modern orthodox Catholicism and, as such, is not productive as an analytical category.

The singular exception to this rule is the manuscript attributed to Bishop Diego de Landa from the 1560s. The "Relación de las cosas de Yucatán" provides this more detailed treatment of the Mayas' sculptural universe: "They had so many idols that even their gods were not enough for them. There wasn't an animal or creepy-crawly thing that they didn't make a statue of. All were made to resemble their gods and goddesses. They had some idols of stone, rather few, and others of wood, voluminous and also small ones, but not so many as of clay."[11] Here, the Franciscan seems to suggest that the Mayas were decidedly *not* venerating the materiality of their sculpted effigies, given that he states they were produced simply to "resemble" their deities; they were not conceived of as the supernatural beings in and of themselves. In his continued use of the term *ídolo*, however, he maintains his order's party line, but, as I describe later, he uses the terms *estatua*, *imagen*, and *ídolo* interchangeably.

Thankfully, the archaeological record fills the documentary lacuna of the friars. Owing to issues of preservability, the historical proportion of wood and wax effigies are not accurately represented. But because Maya petitioners continually deposited objects into Chichén Itzá's infamous cenote of sacrifice from the terminal through late postclassic periods (1000–1521 CE), a handful have been preserved for systematic study.[12] The initial dredging of the cenote began in 1904 under the direction of Edward Herbert Thompson before the development of scientific archaeological techniques.[13] Thus, many of the recovered objects lack contextual information such as original provenience, dates of production, and the like. It is therefore impossible to provide a developmental sequence for the sacrificed effigies; I have to treat them within the temporal vacuum of early twentieth-century salvage archaeology.

Sadly, very little remains of the wooden objects, given the medium's susceptibility to organic decay; as the second most abundant in the entire corpus, this is especially tragic. Landa records that "the idols of wood were held such that they were bequeathed and kept by the principal heir of the inheritance," and he also documented in detail their mode of production.[14] The original appearance of the deposited wooden effigies is difficult to reconstruct, but a close visual analysis reveals that Maya artists carved them from singular blocks of wood or conglomerates, typically a larger brick-shaped

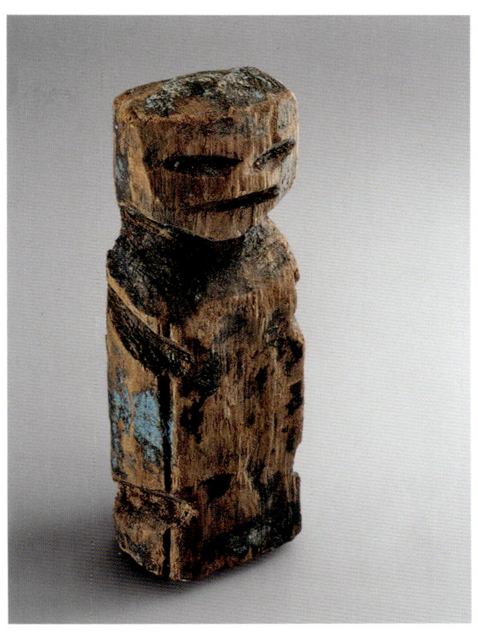

FIG. 10 Foundation for human effigy in wood and rubber. Peabody Museum of Archaeology and Ethnology, Harvard University, Cambridge, Massachusetts. Photo © President and Fellows of Harvard College, Peabody Museum of Archaeology and Ethnology, PM# 07-7-20/C4795.1.

piece for the torso and then separate plinths for the limbs and heads. As can be seen in figure 10, the extant wooden torso exhibits distinct grooves on the left and right sides, to which the Maya artist would have affixed separate arms and legs composed of rubber, presumably using a kind of glue.[15] Resin was then applied to the raw wood, which was then fleshed out using a gesso or plaster substrate. We cannot overlook the role that polychrome pigments played in the finalized product's overall aesthetic, resulting in increased visual detail that enhanced the mere compositional form of the effigy. Most of the Chichén Itzá artifacts retain traces of paint that was used to decorate each object, in addition to Maya blue, which was liberally applied just prior to the work's deposition in the cenote (and which can clearly be seen on figure 10).[16]

In other examples, the wood performed more of a compositional role than simply functioning as the internal buttressing system of the finalized effigy; the wood itself was carved to represent a naturalized deity figure. Perhaps these terribly eroded examples from Chichén Itzá's Sacred Cenote once (roughly) approximated their sixth-century comrade, produced centuries earlier in the Guatemalan highlands (fig. 11).

In addition to these wooden effigies, Spaniards also mention the production of wax (*cera*) effigies, whose preservation history is even more problematic. The "wax" to which these Europeans refer is either the copal resin (*pom*) that is ubiquitous as offered incense in Maya ritual, or it is beeswax, an abundant natural resource in Yucatán. The seventeenth-century archival record mentions these kinds of objects, specifically

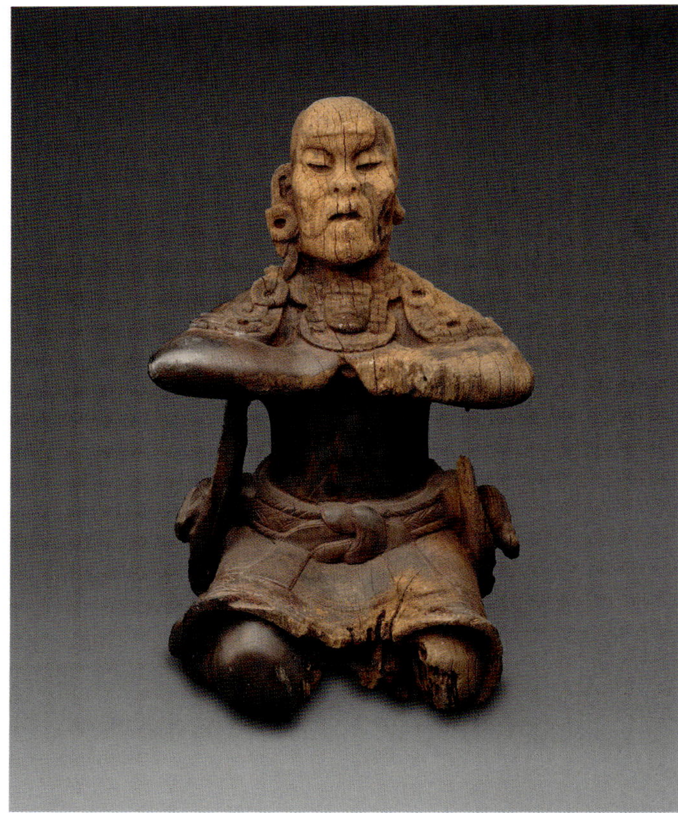

crafted from copal resin, and they also appear in later nineteenth-century accounts, in the context of healing rites.[17] The preservation of these objects is so badly compromised that an illustration in this text is not warranted. For many, the basic contours of a crouching, humanoid form donning earspools and an emphasized beaded necklace can be discerned. In their original form they approximated the composition of the object imaged in figure 12, a ceramic effigy of God M, the Maya merchant deity. In other visual examples (extant sculptures, mural paintings, and the various codices), this deity is typically rendered with dark skin, a protruding lower lip, and a prominent "Pinocchio" nose.[18] While these three diagnostic elements have eroded on most of the Chichén Itzá examples, an additional attribute of God M, the presence of a tumpline wrapped around his forehead, is often still discernible.[19] Given this deity's associations with travel over distant territory, his effigies were fitting offerings in the far-flung pilgrimage city of Chichén Itzá.

According to Landa, ceramic objects were the most commonly produced "idols," and numerous scholars have contributed to our larger ethnographic understanding of

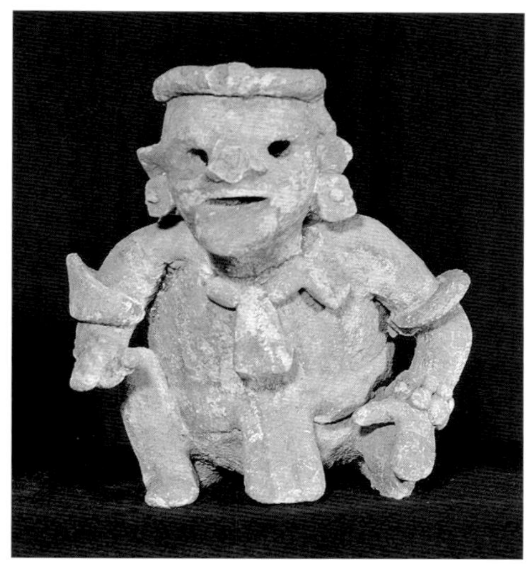

FIG. 12 Ceramic effigy of God M. Peabody Museum of Archaeology and Ethnology, Harvard University, Cambridge, Massachusetts. Photo © President and Fellows of Harvard College, Peabody Museum of Archaeology and Ethnology, PM# 58-34-20/60320.

them.[20] Indigenous artists rendered ceramic effigies in dozens of distinct types, from sculptures modeled completely in the round (like Gann's object imaged in fig. 9) at various scales to diverse pieces that feature a hollowed cavity to host incense as a form of sacrificial offering. For my purposes these censers are the most illuminating as a means to elucidate precontact ritual traditions, as their base composition presupposes active human engagement. Archaeological deposits at all levels of the social hierarchy and throughout the course of Maya history reveal that censers were continually integral to native religious practices.

The Mayas conceived of censers as receptacles, and artists used the exterior walls as blank expanses on which to attach the free-formed representations of deities or ancestors. Figure 13 images this vessel type and displays the genre's most basic composition; a vase form on which rudimentary components of a human face have been applied.[21] A Maya crafter rendered the visage using crude gouges for the eyes and mouth. The nose is depicted using the simplest protrusion of clay and plain semicircular pieces are attached to the side, doubling as ears and lug handles. Because of the vessel's eroded state, it is impossible to ascertain if additional ornamentation was applied to the rim, but others display a flaring headdress that cantilevers from the vessel's rim. In all the examples that I examined, however, the vessels' attributes conspire with the physiognomic generality of their visages, making it impossible to wager a sound identification of a particular Maya supernatural. Although this vessel was undoubtedly used at the household level, its facial generality links it directly to coeval censers intended to represent deities, similarly lacking in diagnostic iconographical indicators (fig. 14).[22]

Contemporaneous with this practice, however, are additional examples of the genre in which sound identification is clearly intended on the part of the Maya artist

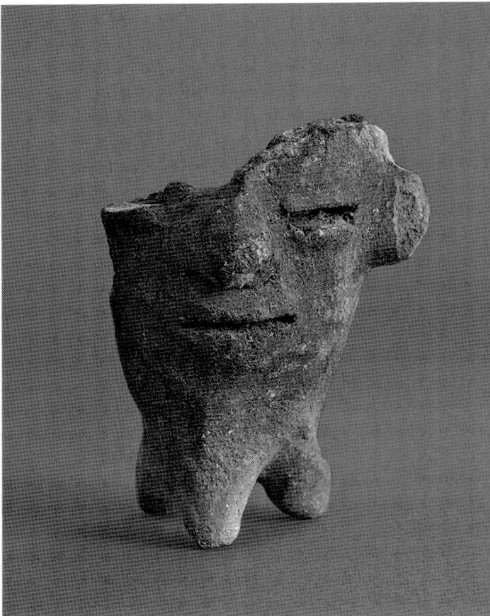

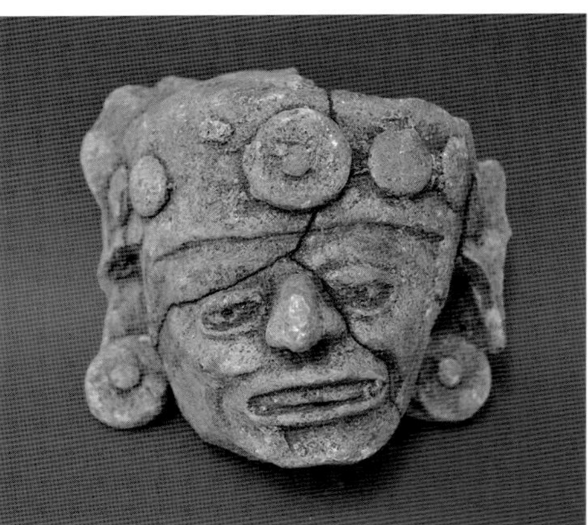

and the vessel's user. More elaborate decoration allows for indicative traits to be recognized, such as those in figures 15 and 16. Figure 15 is an even more elaborated example of a similar practice; it is a member of the Chen Mul Modeled Complex, produced in postclassic Mayapán. Susan Milbrath and Carlos Peraza Lope have argued that this ceramic type ushered in a new kind of ritualized veneration in Yucatán, evidenced by the archaeological contexts of the censers' deposition, which include "burial cists, ceremonial middens, and caches found in ceremonial structures." Although rare, censers were also found in a handful of residential structures. Much more frequent was their use in association with altars erected in "colonnaded halls, shrines, round structures, and pyramids," in other words, a variety of nondomestic sacred architectural types.[23]

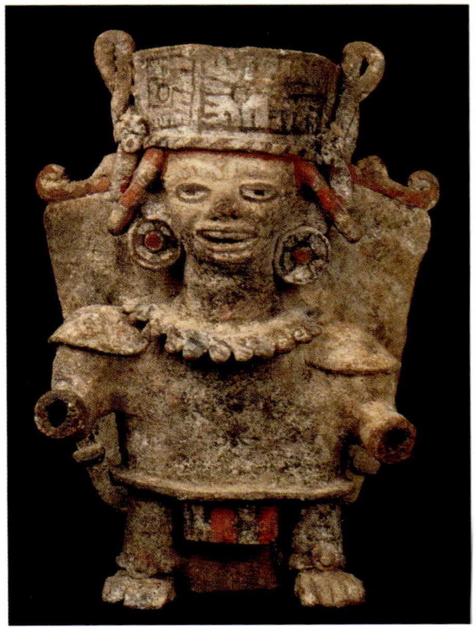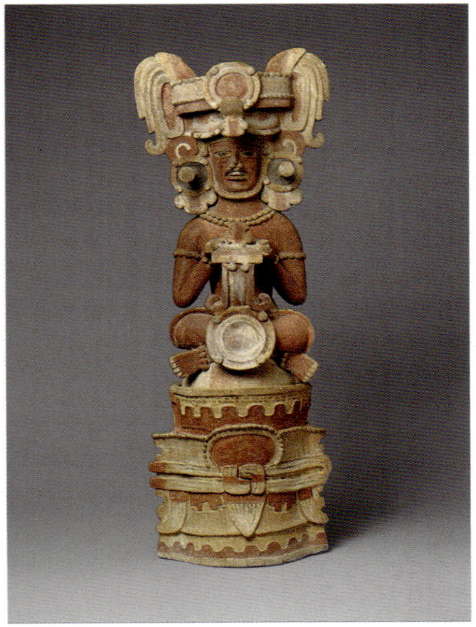

FIG. 15 Effigy censer, postclassic period, Mayapán. 29.5 × 22.2 cm. Peabody Museum of Natural History, Division of Anthropology, Yale University, YPM ANT 260321. Photo courtesy of Yale Peabody Museum of Natural History, http://peabody.yale.edu.

FIG. 16 Seated king censer, fourth century, Guatemala. 80 × 31.1 cm. The Metropolitan Museum of Art, New York. Gift of Charles and Valerie Diker, 1999, 1999.484.1a. Photo: The Metropolitan Museum of Art, www.metmuseum.org.

Although not directly related in terms of formal evolution, earlier examples of effigy censers from other Maya contexts, such as figure 16, which dates to early classic Guatemala, suggest a long-standing cultural tradition of rituals associated with the censing of known figurations. Perhaps the best-known examples from the classic period come from Copán, where humanoid effigies have been excavated from Structure 26-L. Here they were placed directly in front of the tomb reserved for the body of the represented ruler; they are thus effigies of specific historical actors. The vessels were fed incense; the rising smoke they produced was understood as speaking. It carried verbalized petitions upward, serving to summon and petition the ancestral presence that came to embody the vessel. That these ceramics were deemed animate entities is evidenced by the fact that they were ritually killed in the context of the funerary monument's subsequent building phase.[24]

What is intriguing about the censer genre of ceramic vessel is that despite their relative simplicity or complexity, they all assume an animated quality. The depiction of the eyes, and in particular the mouths, lend these objects a sense of enlivening. Their

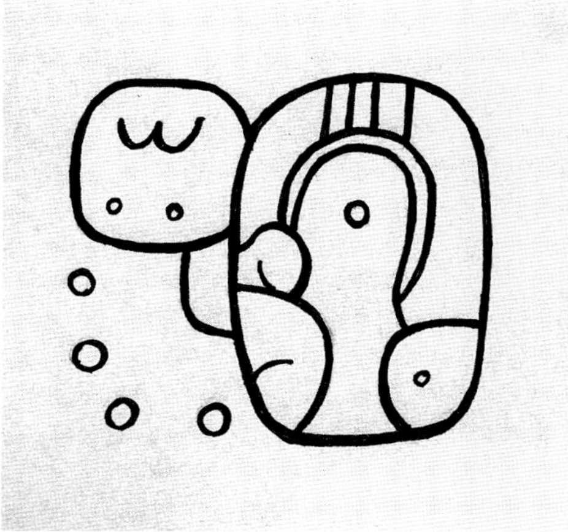

slightly parted lips evoke the ability of speech, as though they have a presumed oracular function.[25] In this way they approximate the compositional traditions executed elsewhere in the Mesoamerica, most obviously the famous "masks" of Teotihuacan, whereby artists intentionally enlivened otherwise static forms by rendering gaping mouths and eyes inlaid with precious stones to evoke the anatomical reality of irises and pupils.[26]

Beyond this artistically achieved animism, these diverse forms are also unified by their artists' insistence on interiority—they maintain an interior cavity, which is essential and primary to the composition of the piece. In the more simplified versions (fig. 17), their cavities are "seen" before the identity of the figure is recognized. These cavities speak to a religious ideology in which ritual objects necessitate metaphorical feeding, accomplished by placing ritual substances inside and thus ensuring the permanence of a sacred presence. Feeding was integral to these objects' sustained care, and their holes, cavities, divots, and spaces were receptacles for offered substances, be they incense, food, drink, or perhaps even autosacrificed blood. One can easily imagine the constant attention and care given to these objects, which were maintained as living members of the household.

But a substantive difference exists between the effigies whose generic facial attributes defiantly refuse a correlation with a distinct ancestor or known Maya deity (fig. 13 and possibly 14) and those that obviously represent a known deity or historical actor (figs. 15 and 16). This frequent generic aspect of the humbler icons is of interest to the "ideology of images" for which I am arguing; perhaps it is as revealing as their formal qualities. In many cases, particularly in the more modest context of commoner domestic spaces, where resources could not be garnered to procure multiple deity effigies, the very lack of secured identity was exactly the point.

A clue to this practice of flagrant nonidentity can be located in the associated hieroglyphs and images of the late postclassic Mayas. By conducting an extremely close analysis of the so-called discrepancies between hieroglyphic text and depicted images in the Madrid and Dresden Codices, Gabrielle Vail has argued that, rather than being attributable to "scribal error," these apparent mistakes were actually intended. Maya scribes worked safely within their own conceptualization of the sacred, a complex system of belief that scholars have been incapable of fully comprehending, given our own assumptions about pantheistic religions. Vail suggests that one of the deity glyphs (T14.1016c, fig. 17), previously assumed to be a distinct god, God C, may actually symbolize sacrality in an abstract sense, *k'u* (or *k'uh*). That is, the glyph is a generic qualifier that serves to modify nouns (numinous objects or gods) referenced in associated glyphs; it "may represent any of the dozen or so deities worshipped by the precontact Maya."[27]

It is my belief that this notion of a generalized qualifier can be applied to the physical world as well. The generic vessels that don't appear to represent a particular deity were receptacles for divinity in an abstract sense. Or, and perhaps this is more likely, these generic vessels could be transformed into a variety of deities, a sort of "one size fits all" approach to religious statuary. This notion of *k'u* resonates with Stephen Houston's understanding of the concept for the classic Mayas, for whom the term "operates both as a transcendent quality and a specific identity. It is a general, unitary principle and an animate force that alights and merges with the particular and the tangible. Segmented into beings with personality and predisposition, it adheres to particular objects, places, effigies, even units of time."[28]

Additional visual evidence from the Madrid Codex verifies this unification of generalized sacrality and the material world. The bottom register of folio 100d (fig. 18) images two deities, Itzamna and another unidentifiable god, as ritually interacting with two ceramic vessels. These vessels are squat tripod urns, topped with inverted vessels of similar form that function as a sort of lid and are intriguingly inscribed with an inverted *ahau* glyph (thus signifying either "ruler" or a month name from the 260-day calendar). The T14.1016c glyph—what Vail identified as the generic qualifier for sacrality, *k'u*— is imaged as a simplified profile face on the upward-facing vessel. In these images the tripod vessels have been marked as generically sacred; their identity and related numinosity can be made manifest only through the appropriate ritualized action, enacted by the two deities imaged to their right.

Modern anthropological studies supplement the evidence provided by the archaeological record and the Madrid Codex. For anyone looking for an illumination of precontact religion, the Lacandones are an obvious first step. Although they currently inhabit a far-flung region of the Petén (the same area that is studded with classic period cities), it is likely that they emigrated from northern Yucatán between 1560

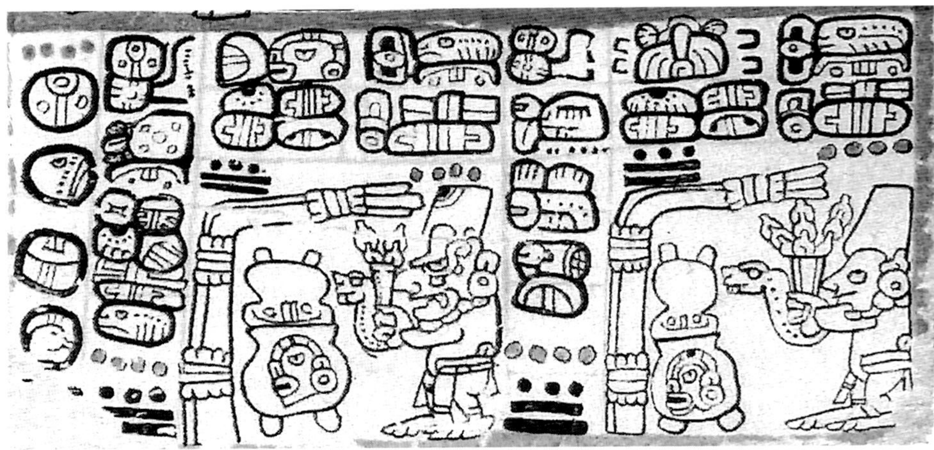

FIG. 18 Artist unknown, Madrid Codex, detail, fifteenth to sixteenth century, fol. 100d. Museo de América, Madrid. Photo: author.

and 1600, escaping Spanish colonization and adamantly maintaining traditional life-ways among the chaos of colonialism and subsequent modern nationalism.[29] Sustained ethnographic work of anthropologists such as Jon R. McGee and Joel W. Palka have verified a remarkable degree of similarity between the Lacandon religion and the material remains of earlier Yucatecan sacred traditions.[30]

Lacandon ritual life revolves around material artifacts termed "God pots" (*lak-il k'uh*). These vessels are simple bowls, often resting on a ceramic pedestal foot, which host figurative faces affixed to their fronts. In general, they are small in scale, about ten inches in height, and are rendered with a fairly simple mode of representation (fig. 19). As noted by McGee, the God pots function as generic receptacles for the offering of sacrificed goods, both edible and inedible. The most common of these is copal (*pom*), conceived as transforming into tortillas as it burns for the deity's consumption. Additionally, *balché* is given, along with a kind of ritualized water (*sak haa'*), liquefied chocolate, and tamales. Leaves of particular species, a palm (*xate*), figure prominently in these rites, as they are used as ritual accoutrement, a kind of spoon to "feed" balché to the pots and also as a kind of matting on which edible offerings are placed. Significantly, despite the outward signs of animation, the Lacandones do not conceive of these vessels as the object of veneration. Rather, "They are an abstract model of a human being, and the medium through which an offering is transmitted to the god for its consumption."[31]

Given the formal similarities between the God pots and precontact Yucatecan effigy vessels and the obvious resonance between this ethnological detail and colonial anecdotes, the Lacandon ritual practices provide a lens through which to better under-stand the sculptural traditions of their ancestors. Late postclassic practitioners similarly

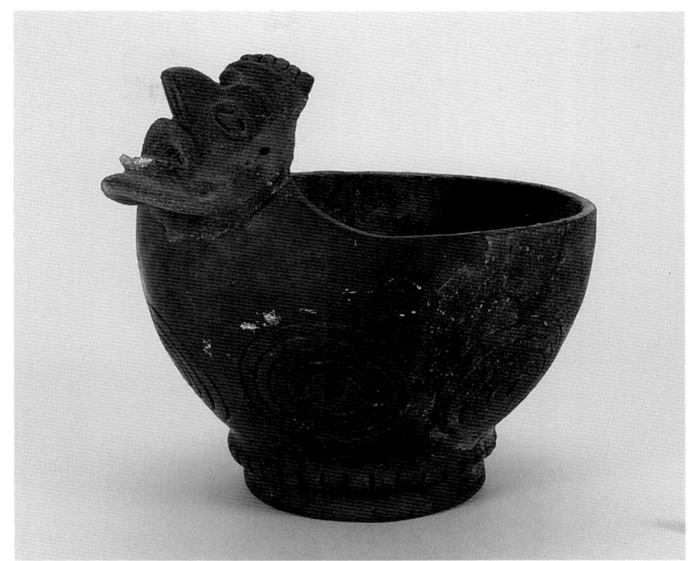

conceived of their hollowed-out effigies as receptacles for the generalized divine and ensured the presence of those supernatural forces with a designated set of ritualized care.

So rather than being the "idolatry" that the Spaniards feared, colonial and modern Maya object veneration was not of graven images per se, the adoration of the materiality of the object for the sole sake of the material substance (clay, wood, stucco, etc.). Instead, what defined this religiosity was a veneration of the sculpted world as material stand-ins for a divine aspect. The physical world had the potential to become part and parcel of the spiritual world, and in so doing the physical universe, this army of deity sculptures, was evidence of the divine presence on earth. Rather than acting as a kind of conduit, as in the decreed Catholic mold, these images of deities, whether they were distinct personalities or more generalized sacralities, spoke to the fused nature of the human and divine realms, of the physical and the spiritual universe. As such, these were animated and active members of communities, participants in ritual events that ensured the cosmic health of its earthly inhabitants. To ensure their proper involvement in the human world, however, Maya people believed that the birth of these objects was just as significant as their continual upkeep. As we shall see, sacrality began at inception, as it were.

Making the Sacred

The reconstruction of Maya modes of image production is a challenging endeavor, to say the least. Beyond the analysis of extant physical objects, as attempted earlier, a handful of Europeans left us a sense of how artists in ancient Mesoamerica practiced their craft. Of these, words traditionally attributed to Bishop Diego de Landa are by far the most effusive, and in fact in Yucatán he is our sole source that illuminates native practices of effigy crafting. Rather than a cohesive text with a definitive linear progression, the mid-sixteenth-century "Relación de las cosas de Yucatán" is actually a random collection of documents that describe various aspects of the peninsula: its precontact history, artistic and architectural achievements, history of the Spanish conquest, and lengthy descriptions of the Maya calendric systems and their associated ritual activities.[32] According to scholarly lore, the Franciscan composed the text after he was summoned to Spain to account for his illegal administration of an auto-da-fé in the Maya town of Maní during the summer of 1562.[33] The resulting manuscript was supposedly used to buttress Landa's defense. The accounts of Maya calendric rites in the "Relación" are the most ethnographically rich of the entire manuscript, suggesting that we are looking at a discrete intellectual project, one that an indigenous informant, quite possibly the well-known Maya intellectual Gaspar Antonio Chi, could have singularly authored.[34]

Regardless of the manuscript's own production history, it is rife with references to the Mayas' sculptural world; the term *ídolo* appears a total of fifty-three times in the manuscript's eighty-nine folio pages.[35] But the manuscript's later section uses more precise descriptive language, deploying more specific terms to reference precontact effigies, such as *imagen* and *estatua*. Here the author's level of cultural specificity provides proper appellations for each of the described sculptures. For example, while describing the ceremonies enacted to commemorate and welcome the new year, starting with the day Ix, it was necessary to "incense [the image of Zacuayayab] as is usually done, decapitate a fowl, and place the [year's patron's] image on a wooden stand called Zachia."[36] So when the identity of a particular deity is known, the "Relación" author was less likely to utilize *ídolo* as a descriptor. He subtly differentiates between a statue being "called" a particular deity name and a statue "being" a particular deity.[37]

It is also embedded within this ethnography of Maya ritual that we encounter the most detailed account of image making extant in the archival record. Here, in the course of describing ritual proscriptions for the twenty-day month of Mo, the author includes a description of the conventional production of wooden effigies.[38] We can assume that the manufacture of effigies made out of alternative media, such as the wax and ceramic pieces described earlier, was similarly complex. The summary of the "Relación" is exceedingly rich, and, given its detail, I quote it at length:

> One of the hardest and most difficult things was how they made idols of wood, which they called "making gods." They had the following way to make them, during a special time, and it was the month of Mo or another time, if the priest said it would suffice. Those who wanted them made first consulted

the priest, who brought his request to the official of the ídolos.[39] It is said that these officials frequently excused themselves because some of them had some cases of death, or withering illnesses had come to them [as a result of this process]. Having accepted, the *chacs* [personifications of the rain deity; for this they were also elected], the priest, and the official started their fast, and he who commissioned the idols was sent into the *montes* [the uninhabited wild zones of the peninsula] for the wood to make them, which is always cedar. He returned with the wood, and they made a little hut of thatch close by in which he put the wood and a kiln in which to make the idols. There they were trapped while [the idols] were being made. They placed incense that burned to the four demons called Acantunes, which they included and put on the four corners of the world. They put in with that blood taken from the ears, the weapon to carve out the black gods. And with these preparations the priest, *chacs*, and official locked themselves in the hut, and they started their godly work, frequently cutting their ears and joining with the blood those demons, and burning incense. Like this they stayed until they had finished them; they were fed only what was necessary, and they did not know their wives nor think of anything; no one left [the choza] to go anywhere.[40]

From this description we can surmise that several steps were deemed necessary if a sacred icon was understood to ultimately function as a receptacle for the manifested divine. At the most basic level, this was a material production that required appropriate personnel; not anyone could simply carve or create an image and expect it to be potent. The author suggests an intimate relationship between at least seven players: the person commissioning the object, the town's principal *ah-kin*, the "official" of the effigy production, and finally the chacs, four elected community members who participated in this and other religious ceremonies throughout the annual cycle. While scholars have been able to provide insight into the role of ah-kins and chacs in indigenous communities, the artists' social functions remain elusive, particularly in the late postclassic period.[41] During the classic period, we know that artists employed in Maya royal courts held privileged social positions. Their patrons valued artists' creative talents and the intellectual capabilities that visual production necessitated. The closest Mayan term for "artist," *ah ts'ib*, alludes to this complex set of semantic fields: it is usually glossed as "he of the painting/writing," hinting at the multinatured aspect of courtly classic Maya craft production. By the late postclassic period, and certainly within rural Yucatán, it is difficult to argue if the same connotations existed, but the manuscript's distinction of *el official de los ídolos* suggests a singularly privileged social and religious position.

The party of seven corporeally prepared for the sacred rite. In concert, they enacted proscribed protocols that ensured their bodily purity. As we'll see later in chapter 5, the avoidance of spiritual contamination was an integral part of precontact and later Catholic ceremonial decorum. For an image-making ceremony, the men refrained from sexual relations and consumed only the bare minimum to ensure survival during the course of the ritual.

This notion of physical purity was also ascribed to the raw materials the men used as well. We learn that cedar was used exclusively for these objects, presumably given the wood's challenge to quick decomposition and natural resistance to insects.[42] It is also significant that the wood had to come from the monte; that is, deity effigies could not be manufactured from a previously used or recycled piece of wood. Instead, the statue's medium needed to come from a forested area that was clearly delineated from the lived spheres of human interaction, the urban space of a town, or the agriculturally cultivated zone of worked fields.

In a similar vein, the physical space within which the production ritual occurred needed to be distinct from that used for mundane life. The group established a privileged locale, a specialized site of craft production, housed in a thatched building, a simple choza. They erected the choza "close by," but it was clearly intended as a structure whose sole purpose was the production of sacred icons. As such, it would have been understood as a space apart from the daily reality of the living community, a space imbued with particular powers. That this space was intended to be cosmologically charted, and thus understood as a ritual space within the Maya worldview, is attested to by the required incensing of the Acantunes, the vertical upright posts located at the four corners of the choza. In nearly all of Landa's descriptions of ritual spaces, including those for children's coming-of-age rituals and the new year's festivities, ritual space was required to be cosmologically mapped against the four cardinal directions (as has been argued elsewhere), in an attempt to make the ritual stage a microcosmic representation of the larger Maya world.[43] It seems that within the context of image production, the same cosmologically directed spatial ideology was at play. We know from other contexts that these posts were meant as metaphorical representations of the pillars that stood at the four corners of the world, the place where the Bacabs stood holding up the Maya celestial realm. The group offered sacrificial blood from their own ears to the Bacabs and also anointed the knives used to carve the icons with this bodily fluid.

The party finished the production space with facilities to cure the wood. The nineteenth-century copyist of the "Relación de las cosas de Yucatán" included the term *tereja* to describe the object in which the statues were "put" (*echar*), but, as speakers of Spanish will recognize, *tereja* is not a term that appears in modern or sixteenth-century Spanish.[44] Instead, I believe the transcriber erred here, instead intending the term *tejera*, a kind of kiln, most frequently used for the baking of clay tiles. While firing is obviously not recommended for the production of wooden effigy statues, modern Yucatecan

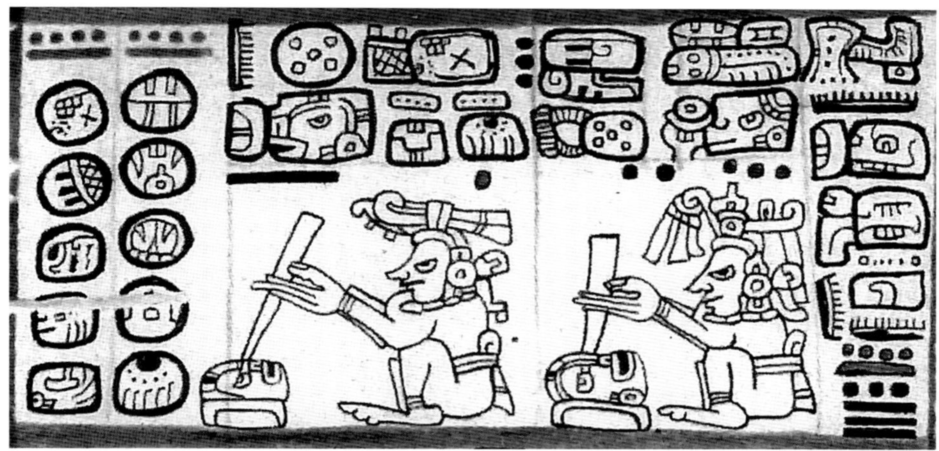

FIG. 20 Madrid Codex, fifteenth to sixteenth century, eastern Yucatán. Museo de América, Madrid, fol. 101b.

carvers treat wood, even cedar, to ensure the medium's longevity by exposing it to high temperatures. It is to this part of the production process that the manuscript refers.

An earlier visual and textual source, the Madrid Codex, provides further insight into the meaning of effigy production in the Maya world. Mary Ciaramella conducted a close reading of the texts and images in its "idol-making" pages (fig. 20), specifically analyzing a series of crouching figures in the process of effigy crafting. The sculptors hold various carving implements above small, humanoid mask-like objects that rest on short platforms. In her reading of these pages, Ciaramella succinctly correlates a variety of evidentiary lines, using comparative anthropology and an English transla-tion of the Landa manuscript to argue that the figures on folio 101.b are engaged in an "eye-opening" ceremony, the final moment of image production that effectively gave "life to an idol." Ciaramella notes that the glyph located in the position of C2 (posi-tioned immediately above the sharpened instrument held by the right-most figure) phonetically reads *le-b(i)*, or *leb*, signifying the verb "to open or conjure something that is easily opened."[45] She understands this as the ultimate act of creation, the moment that ritualizes a form of life giving, bestowing on the material world enlivened animation.

Although the description provided in the "Relación" does not end with a similar moment of ritual, the visual and textual evidence provided by the Madrid Codex attests to the final act necessary for ritual completion. These images of "eye-opening" cere-monies resonate with Molly Bassett's brilliant illumination of Mexica (Aztec) "ritual manufacture." Using contemporary linguistic ideologies of Nahuatl-speaking popula-tions in Zacatecas, Bassett has analyzed how ceremonial practitioners transform the mundane—whether it be a natural resource or even a human body—into sacred enti-ties. Her complex argument pivots on the use of two Nahuatl verbs for "to be" and their application in a variety of linguistic contexts. Of paramount importance to this sacred alteration was the entity's "ability to see (and be seen)."[46] In the case of Bassett's example of "localized embodiments," humans transformed into animated deities for ritual performance, this aptitude for vision was inherent within their title, *teixiptla-huan*, which incorporates the root word for eye, face, and surface, *ixtli*. Clearly, the Maya material world, with its crafted emphasis on eyes, coupled with the documented "eye-opening" ceremony, demonstrates the pan-Mesoamerican applicability of Bassett's central observations. For Maya effigies to be ceremonially effective they too had to see.

Moreover, Bassett maintains that these divine embodiments retained animacy because they "participate in the life-world of their devotees."[47] This cultural practice also has parallels with Maya traditions, in particular with the ways in which deity effigies were ritually sustained following their production. To ensure continued intercession, Maya practitioners engaged in a variety of what can be deemed caring or maintenance rituals, all designed to keep their sculpted effigies healthy. These typically involve the feeding of sacred sculptures. It is here where the formal qualities of the ceramic corpus and their ritual use coalesce. Intriguingly, the Spanish clergy repeatedly home in on this notion of "feeding," highlighting it as one of the primary offences to the Spanish Godhead.

Foodstuffs were continuously given to deity statues as a kind of offering, but I believe the presentation of consumables hints at a much more nuanced relationship between the Mayas and their sacred objects. Only specific kinds of foods were given; in witness testimonies these are sometimes named. For example, in 1582 the Mexico City Inquisition tried an African slave, simply referred to as "Cristóbal," for participating in Maya religious rituals in a Maya village called "Xecechekan" (Hecelchakán), located just north of Campeche.[48] During the course of the event, the local *maestro de los ídolos* (master of the idols), Andres Cuyoc, presented the "old idols" with *ch'uyul ha*, a ritual beverage, and one hundred kernels of *k'an*, a type of mature yellow maize.[49] Thereafter the effigies were incensed with copal.[50] An additional case from 1604 recalls Mayas giving "copal incense, precious stones, and cacao."[51] In a later case from 1613, a Spanish encomendero, Juan Vela de Aguirre, is brought up on charges of idolatry and witchcraft. Similar to Cristóbal's case, testimony (provided by Maya informants) details the offerings of *tutul uah* (*tutul wah*) and *huisil haa* (*wisil haa'*) (both are kinds of ritual beverages) to sacred sculptures and their subsequent ingesting.[52]

Fortuitously, other colonial sources provide additional ethnographic details of similar caring rituals. For example, in 1600 the secular priest Baltasar de Herrera included a case in his *probanzas de méritos*.[53] It detailed the 1598 quasi-Inquisition of Francisco Pech, a Maya resident of the Maya village of Peto, where Herrera served as the local priest. As Francisco Che, another Maya resident, describes the scene, "Francisco Pech worshipped idols, he was an idolater.... In his milpa [we] found a clay idol. It had been offered copal or incense and was placed on green leaves from the tree they call *bolon-colob*."[54] They had been recently placed there because "they were still green."[55]

This practice of placing effigies on particular leaves, essentially providing them with appropriate ritual furniture, resonates with additional colonial sources. In the calendrical treatise in the "Relación," the author describes a similar practice multiple times. During the month of Uo, the town's religious specialists honored the deity of sacred knowledge, an "idol" named "Çinchau Ytzmná," likely a muddled version of "Kinich Ahau Itzamná." The priests reveal their accordion folded books and "spread them on the fresh leaves they had prepared to receive them." During a later ritual performed during the month of Xul, "idols" were similarly set "on leaves of trees brought for this purpose."[56]

This discussion suggests a complex system of belief within which the sculpted world of the Mayas operated. Rather than venerating the materiality of sculpted icons, native practitioners activated their religious statuary through a series of sacralized rites that began with the first moments of the effigy's production and continued through the life cycle of that object.

Absorptive Healing in Maya Ritual

Once the material artifacts were ritually activated, Maya practitioners utilized them within the context of complex ceremonies devoted to healing; "holy matter" could ease the physical ailments of individuals or the entire community. This ability pivoted around the objects' capability of absorbing unwanted material or spiritual entities.[57] Healers understood certain artifacts as fitting receptacles for negative energies (manifested as disease or discomfort). These objects embodied the power to absorb human suffering, interiorizing it into the matrix of their compositions as a means to dramatically alter one's corporeal response.

The earliest mention of the rites that involve such material is Don Bartolomé José del Granado Baeza's lengthy account from the early nineteenth century.[58] Responding to a request sent by King José I's royal physician, Dr. Don Pedro Agustín Esteves, in 1813, Baeza wrote an extensive letter describing the Maya inhabitants of Yaxcabá (map 1). The friar responded to all thirty-six of the king's queries, detailing local demographics, ecology, and a smattering of indigenous beliefs. The longest of Baeza's sections is chapter 5, which details the *supersticiones* of the local population. He informs the king that although these beliefs were rampant when he arrived in the province fifteen years earlier, they had now been "silenced" (*en silencio*) because of the harsh punishments that he meted out to offenders. It is also important to note that Baeza understood these practices to be the result of a "pact with the devil" (*pacto del demonio*), administered by deceitful imposters who tricked ailing Mayas into believing in the rite's curative properties.[59]

Baeza describes a healing ritual within the context of Maya divinatory practices that necessitated a transparent crystal, termed a *zaztun*, "through which they can see occult things and the origin of illnesses."[60] When summoned by the family of an ailing person, healers oversaw a three-day ritual in which the household held constant vigil with the aid of *aguardiente* (moonshine) or *pitarrilla* (honey and bark mead, likely balché), food, and lit candles. Once the healer determined the illness's cause, he used the zaztun to locate a spot on the house floor and he began to dig. In full view of the family, the healer removed a dark-colored waxen figurine concealed under the house floor.[61] Once the humanoid effigy had been revealed, the healer informed the family that it had caused the illness—evident in the fact that a thorn protruded from the same body part that pained the ill human.[62] With herbs the sick person became fully healed.[63]

Despite Baeza's continual editorial asides that convinced his Spanish readership of his incredulity, his account does provide some insight into Maya notions of materiality. It is clear that to some degree physical artifacts were understood to function as corporeal proxies during moments of pain or illness. This same notion is further emphasized in his following section, when he recounts a similarly intriguing rite, the *keex*, which he defines as "change." His description is abbreviated; the ritual involves hanging particular food and beverages around the sick person's house. These offerings are given to Yuncimil, which Baeza translates as "the Death Lord."[64] By sacrificing these precious foodstuffs, the deity would intercede and spare the inhabitant's life.

Serendipitously, Robert and Mary Park Redfield's much later seminal texts on medical practices in mid twentieth-century Maya villages include an intriguing anecdote that significantly contributes to our understanding of this same *k'ex* ritual. Similarly, Evon Vogt, working among the modern Zinacantan Mayas of Chiapas, has described a related healing rite termed *k'esholil*.[65] The Maya ceremony derives its names from the noun used in Yucatec Mayan and Tzotzil Mayan that signifies "change," or "exchange"—a fitting name, as this ritual involves the metaphysical swapping of an illness from a diseased human body to a physical object, most typically foodstuffs or, more infrequently and significantly, small sculptural icons.[66] The noun *k'ex* can also refer to the diminutive trinkets referred to as *exvotos*, which are still placed on altars in remembrance of a specific miracle worked by a larger religious icon. Within all the observed Maya communities, the rite's title refers both to the ritual accoutrement used and the ritual process itself.

According to the Redfields' informants in the Maya villages of Chan Kom and Dzitás (map 1), there appears to be some internal debate and difference in how the k'ex should be performed.[67] According to the Maya informants of Chan Kom, illness entered a human body by hitching a ride on a "wind," which typically derived from a water source or perhaps a cave.[68] The presence of winds as a cause of disease is also mentioned in the earlier colonial Maya text "The Book of Chilam Balam of Kaua."[69] Once an unsuspecting human came in contact with one of the "evil" winds, that person was infected; bad airs were deemed contagious entities that, while intangible, had the ability to carry with them the very palpable effects of bodily disease.[70] The only possibility for renewed health was the removal of these winds from the body through the assistance of a local *yerbatera* (one knowledgeable about healing and herbs) who enacted a k'ex ritual.[71] Significantly, Maya residents maintained that the k'ex was performed only when there had been no ritual breach (another potential cause for illness); it was the healing rite (among others) deemed most effective when the illness was not caused by an upset deity who had summoned the diseased wind to enter the unsuspecting human.

For my purposes, the Redfields' analysis is paramount for the illumination of the Maya belief that elements of the physical world were capable of material and metaphysical absorption. Structurally, the k'ex involved the creation of a tripartite system to be established between the patient, the evil wind that had affected the patient, and a material object, which could take a variety of forms. It seems that the most common mode of performance involved the exchange to occur between the patient and specially prepared foodstuffs.

To summarize, an ill person or their family would summon a healing specialist, typically when all other potential cures had been deemed ineffective. The healer hangs a serving of *zaca* (*sakha*, or "white water," a ritual beverage composed of cold water and ground corn, whose ceremonial use is well documented in modern anthropological literature and is mentioned by early Franciscans during the colonial period) on the choza rafters.[72] The healers request "permission of the winds and the three santos [the Virgin of the Assumption, Saint Lazarus, and Saint Roque] . . . to offer them their dinner at some future day named."[73] The zaca is understood to entice the attendance of the deities and the winds to be present during the aforementioned day. When that day arrives, the healer presents food previously cooked by the house's owner, typically three pints' worth of corn, one of ground squash seed, and a live turkey or other kind of bird. The bird is presented to the winds by being strangled while held above the patient's head. Family members collect a variety of herbs and thirteen *kax* fruits, which have been hollowed out by wild birds or insects. According to Redfield and Villa Rojas, since these hard fruits contain an interior space, they are imagined as the "*homa* [gourd container] of the winds." At midnight the healer offers food to the three saint images, who stand on a table, and places the specially prepared foods for the winds: body parts of the previously sacrificed bird, the hollow *kax* fruits filled with a bit of the zaca mixed with rum, and a bottle of rum with a glass beneath it. The healer then prays as a means of giving the offered foodstuffs to the saints and the winds. Thereafter, the winds' food is carried far from the home and discarded. The healer concludes by stating "that thereby the winds, that have come for their dinner, are returned again to the sea."[74]

As evocative as all these anthropological details are, what is most significant in light of my argument is the Maya conception of ritually prepared food as having the ability, as sacrificial offerings, to quite literally absorb illness by enticing the cause of that illness, the winds, to vacate the body of the suffering human. While most of the Redfields' research was based in the small Maya village of Chan Kom, additional field-work from Dzitás suggests a variant of this rite, but it maintains the same structural components. Most significant, one informant revealed that in some cases, a small-scale figurine (or doll) would be created to serve as a metaphoric stand-in for the ill person and is used in the place of the food.[75] This variant seems most closely related to the tradition of using wax figurines described a century earlier by Baeza. At the conclusion of the ceremony, the figurine is deposited, not on the edges of the village as in the above-mentioned performance but within the village. In so doing, illness has been effectively transferred to the surrogate and has killed the figurine instead of the living human. In another case, at the ritual's end the surrogate figurine was placed next to the community's Marian icon, housed within a local chapel. A transfer of illness was also deemed to occur, carried within the materiality of a household religious figure, only to be delivered to a more powerful community icon and thereby defeated.

The use of representational figurines in healing rites is also present in an older colonial source, this one authored by Maya healers themselves, the manuscript that Ralph Roys deemed the *Ritual of the Bacabs*.[76] This text's present transcription dates from the eighteenth century, but it is certain that the dozens of incantations contained within its covers certainly date to a much earlier time in Maya history. In a handful of these ritualized healing proscriptions, material artifacts are used to alleviate disease, such as stones, particular plants, and so forth. For my purposes, specifically in regard to the future development of a Maya Catholicism based on a communal veneration of human-oid saint figures, what is most interesting is the use of figurative sculptures of humans. These appear in only fifteen of the incantations, but in nearly all they are responsible for the eradication of disease.[77]

These incantations are extremely esoteric; they record the words muttered by Maya healers as a means to exorcise particular diseases from inflicted bodies. The sculpted entity is typically referred to as the "wooden man" (*uinicil te*) or the "stone man" (*uinicil tun*), either mentioned singularly or as a linguistic couplet.[78] The Maya healer most frequently engages the material artifact by sprinkling it with prepared liquids derived from ritually significant local flora. As Roys's incantations are mere textual record-ings of vocalized words, they don't contain explanatory asides that could lend explicit insights into exactly *how* materiality operated. It is my contention that these figurative icons are the same the Redfields' informants spoke of and, as such, are paramount in the successful absorption of deadly entities; they are the physical entity by which the k'ex is accomplished.

For now, suffice it to say that these sources, strewn throughout the expanse of the peninsula and across at least three centuries, clearly evidence that a Maya conception of absorptive materiality endured and continued to direct religious and healing practices. Physical objects, whether they be crafted ceramics, hastily made "dolls," or prepared foodstuffs, functioned as an outlet that linked the human and supernatural worlds, delivering the human population's thanksgiving or, alternatively, harmful substances to the deities who had within their powers the ability to eradicate them through absorption. This ideology of the potentiality of the material world would come to define how Catholicism was itself "absorbed" in disparate Maya communities.

Conclusion

In this chapter I have proposed a Maya ideology of images. To do so required a careful reading of extant archaeological remains and a formal analysis of the Mayas' diverse sculptural world, but also a rereading of the very same sources that unthinkingly use the term *idol* to describe every piece of Maya artwork, irrespective of cultural, religious, or social function. Precontact religiosity involved a notion of the physical universe as capable of activation. In the case of healing ceremonies, mundane change came from the icon's capacity to absorb into its physical matrix the illness that plagued an individual or an entire human community. Interestingly, this link between "idols" and disease was not uniquely limited to the indigenous population of New Spain. As we'll see next, these notions of sacred materiality and absorptive potency would be paramount to how the Maya population at Itzmal came to accept introduced statuary. In the pages that follow we turn to the first decades of the colonial period, to examine the "birth" of the Virgin at Itzmal.

3

The Itzmal Icon

In the middle of the seventeenth century, the Jesuit Francisco de Florencia took readers on a cartographic journey of religious devotion. In his encyclopedic voyage of text and images, which would later be published as the *Zodiaco mariano*, the Jesuit traced the territorial expanse of New Spain and Guatemala through descriptions of localized Marian icons.[1] Given the date of Florencia's authorship (post-1688) and his residence in the central Mexican city of Puebla, we would expect his odyssey to begin in the viceregal capital of Mexico City.[2] Legend maintained that the Virgin of Guadalupe had revealed herself there over a century earlier, and the icon's popularity in these years exploded due to the 1648 publication of this miracle.[3] Instead, Florencia's itinerary began in the provinces of New Spain, in the middle of the Yucatán Peninsula, detailing the miraculous abilities of the Virgin of Itzmal, forcing to center stage a Catholic icon certainly unknown to his cosmopolitan readership.

This decision was intentionally rhetorical. Florencia mapped the conquest history of New Spain, as his narrative trajectory takes the reader from Yucatán to Central Mexico, Oaxaca, and then into Guatemala, loosely following the routes of sixteenth-century conquistadors. The Jesuit was explicit about his choice, declaring that Yucatán was the natural place to begin, since "it was the first place where veneration for the Most Holy Virgin was planted [by Cortés] against idolatry, in the [pyramid] of Cozumel."[4] It was also a location where Mary seems to have been desperately needed. According to Florencia, the Mayas of this province "maintain the bad habit of idolatry, which they have inherited from their ancestors." Many had absconded to the monte, where they "venerate many idols . . . [giving] to the Demon the adoration that should be given to the true God." He maintained that although some of the idolatry had ceased, because of the "preaching and vigilance of the Apostolic Ministers, it would have been more difficult to extinguish it in all of them if God, through the intercession of his beneficent mother, had not so moved [the Indians'] hearts."[5] In saying this, Florencia positions the Virgin

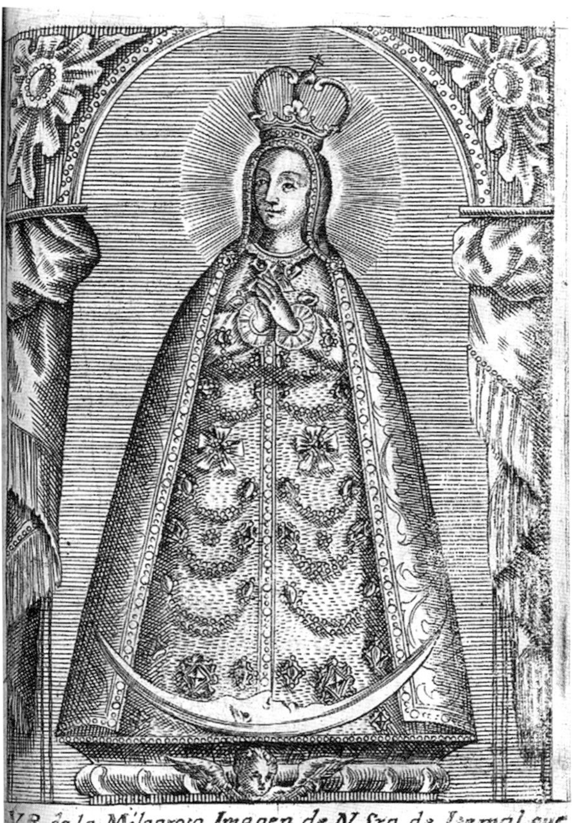

Mary as a kind of spiritual cleanser, a soldier directly enlisted by God himself to assist in the evangelical endeavor by appropriating the adoration indigenes once reserved for their precontact deities.[6] She was poised as the agent who made Spain's Christianization of the Americas possible.

Florencia's posthumous text was wildly successful when it was first published in 1755. It certainly spurred Marian devotion to Mexico's secondary shrines, leading to the later publication of various devotional texts, such as that reproduced in figure 21. On the front page of this 1764 *Novena de la santissima Virgen*, devotees are offered a compositionally standardized view of their venerated icon; the Virgin of Itzmal is shown sumptuously dressed, standing on a pedestal held aloft by an angel with a crescent moon at her feet. Rays of holy sanctity radiate from behind her lavishly gemmed crown, as she piously clasps her hands at her breast in prayer. A serene smile graces her face. The solidity of her physical form, and thus her status as a statue and not simply a representation of the living Mary or her apparition, is evident in the icon's placement within the Itzmal church's high altar; her form is framed by the wooden arch and drawn, tasseled drapes of her flowered niche.

This chapter presents a detailed view into how the Virgin of Itzmal developed from a localized Maya icon in the sixteenth century to a statue of such widespread repute that she warranted the publication of a novena and the production of a sophisticated engraving in Mexico City more than two hundred years after her installation. As such, I offer a condensed history of a singular icon, similar to Jennifer Scheper Hughes's treatment of the Crucifix of Totolapan, in Morelos.[7] I begin by briefly overviewing extant sources of this history, then visit Itzmal's early colonial history and its transformation into a mission town. I argue that in the early years of the pueblo's precontact existence, religiosity was defined by a kind of "locative sacrality," a sense of sacredness derived from the unique formulation of Itzmal's topography and ancient history. I then reconstruct the icon's biography, her procural and installation in the early years of the Itzmal mission, by providing a chronological overview of the colonial sources previously described. These various accounts detail the statue's procural from the Guatemalan highlands and its material production and finally summarize her miraculous acts. These sources describe the icon's transition into a miraculous icon, offering a view into mid-seventeenth-century Yucatecan religiosity, when we start to see her emerge as a pan-Yucatecan deity venerated by all members of colonial society, Mayas, Spaniards, and Africans alike. The chapter concludes with a visual study of the icon's extant representations, offering an analysis of her original appearance.

Sourcing Religious History

Before I begin, a few words are necessary to illuminate the atypical methodology I use to reconstruct Itzmal's early history. As is true of all Yucatecan indigenous villages, Itzmal's archival record is extremely scant. Beyond a confirmation of an *encomienda* (grant of land and labor) to Rodrigo Alvarez and a probanza de méritos of a later seventeenth-century ecclesiastical judge (which is sadly lacking in local detail), there are very few early colonial documents composed in or in reference to Itzmal.[8] The most flagrant exceptions to this are two responses to Philip II's "Relaciones geográficas" project, one written by the Itzmal encomendero Juan de la Cueva Santillán, and the other by neighboring encomendero Joan de Paredes, but both are strangely fantastical and abbreviated.[9] Beyond these, two seventeenth-century printed sources survive: Fray Bernardo de Lizana's *Historia de Yucatán: Devocionario de Nuestra Señora de Izmal y conquista espiritual* of 1633 and Fray Diego López de Cogolludo's *Historia de Yucathán*, composed in 1655 but not published until 1688. Both men attest to consulting now lost archival documents in Itzmal's convent archive and flesh out their accounts using local folklore, provided by indigenous informants.[10] López de Cogolludo also derived a great portion of his text from Lizana's earlier account. Francisco de Florencia relied on these texts when he composed his *Zodiaco mariano* toward the end of the seventeenth century.

Despite the similar titles (*Historia de Yucatán* and *Historia de Yucathán*), Lizana's subtitle, *Devocionario de Nuestra Señora de Izmal y conquista espiritual*, verifies their absolute difference of literary genre. Lizana's earlier work is actually a fragment of a larger text, which today is divided into two parts. The first he dedicated to the history and miracles of the Virgin of Itzmal; it reads like a very conventional early modern book of miracles, as Lizana details wonders worked by the virgin that he had witnessed firsthand or were "well known" (fig. 22).[11] The second half is the earliest surviving ecclesiastical history of the province. Despite this section's historical veracity, it serves as a hagiography of the first two generations of Franciscans who established the Yucatán mission. In particular, Lizana dedicates half of the text to the life of Diego de Landa, glossing over his questionable actions during the 1562 auto-da-fé. The rest is a chronological summary of the other notable Franciscans who had worked in the province; tellingly, they are nearly all referred to as "saints."

By the time of Lizana's writing, the miracle stories recalled in his first section had been cast as verified local history, and they had entered into the communal memory of Itzmal's own biography. As such, I do not concern myself with the historical veracity of the events the friar recounts, as I am not using this source to solidly construct "what really happened" but rather to analyze what seventeenth-century Yucatecans believed to have happened. As with all narratives that circulate within the realm of religious conviction, "truth" has not a single claim. Belief is its own beast, certainly not weighed down by verifiability; what really happened to the icon during her earlier colonial history is actually of little accord. To that end I follow William Taylor's wise words: "To historians of my time, these texts are valuable primary sources, especially when they established a standard, official story and shaped devotion, but the information in them about popular belief, practice, and past experience is not transparent."[12]

Between the two decades that separate Lizana's text from López de Cogolludo's composition, the archival record is absolutely silent.[13] Rather than being squarely in the realm of the wondrous, López de Cogolludo's text more closely approximates what modern scholars would term a social and institutional history; it is an extremely dense retelling of the region's colonial period, drawn from primary and secondary sources available to a religious working in mid-seventeenth-century Yucatán. López de Cogolludo composed the majority of the text while in residence in Mérida's Franciscan convent and thus had access to the monastery's archive and library. Today the tome also serves as a kind of inventory, shedding light on the now lost book holdings of this

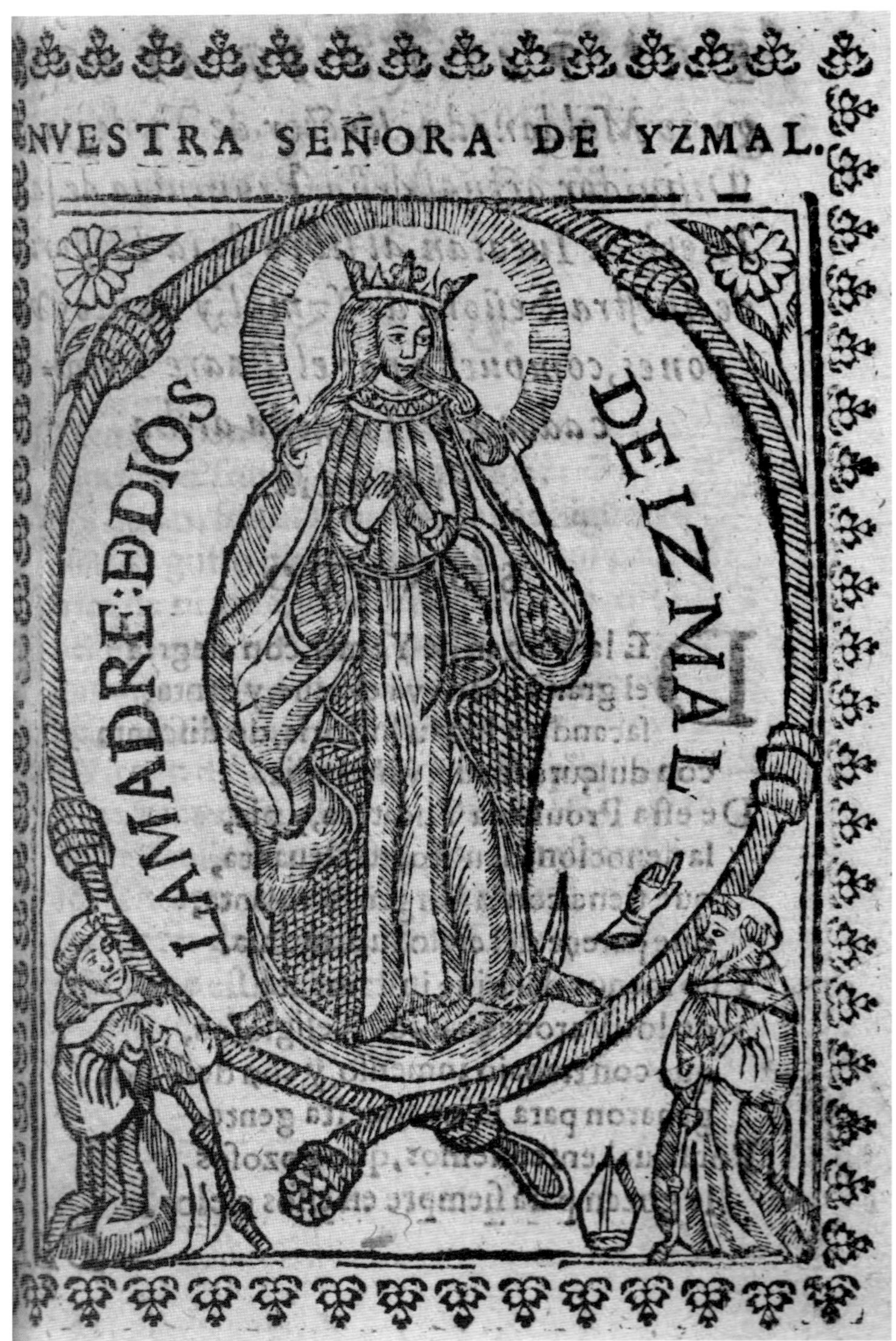

FIG. 22 Devotional print from Lizana's *Historia de Yucatán*. The British Library, London. Photo: author.

religious institution. To write the regional history that predated his arrival, López de Cogolludo consulted various sixteenth-century authors, all of whom are repeatedly called out (with chapters and page numbers) in printed marginalia or mentioned in the body of the text. For the peninsula's earliest moments of contact the friar consulted Antonio de Herrera y Tordesillas's *Historia general de los hechos* (1601), Juan de Torquemada's *Monarquía indiana* (1615), Antonio de Remesal's *Historia de la provincia de San Vicente de Chiapas y Guatemala, o Historia general de las Indias Occidentales y particular de la gobernación de Chiapa y Guatemala* (1619), and Bernal Díaz del Castillo's *Historia verdadera de la conquista de la Nueva España* (1632). López de Cogolludo also had access to the region's various parish archives and so was able to incorporate entire transcriptions of papal bulls and letters from the Audiencia de México, the Spanish Court, the Consejo de Indias, and the like. For Yucatán's slightly later religious history, the contents of these archives were supplemented by Pedro Sánchez de Aguilar's *Informe contra idolorum cultores del obispado de Yucatán* of 1639 and a manuscript draft of Francisco de Cardenás Valencia's "Relación historical eclesiástica de la provincia de Yucatán" (also completed in 1639). As would be expected, López de Cogolludo relies on his own memory and those of his living compatriots to detail the most recent history of the seventeenth century; in these sections the author did not cite external sources. His style for retelling the Yucatán's "modern" history and contemporary events is much more literary, as he provides succinct details not available for the earlier historical eras.[14]

Itzmal's Precontact and Early Colonial History

Yucatán's history of conquest was a tumultuous affair that could never be described as complete. Given such difficulties, the Franciscan order's perseverance is extraordinary, physically manifest in the multitude of religious structures that still dot the peninsula's landscape and remain the vital center of most indigenous communities today. This is perhaps most evident in the central Yucatecan town of Itzmal, home sanctuary to the infamous Virgin of the Immaculate Conception. The early colonial history of Itzmal has been addressed in much greater detail elsewhere, but here I provide a simple overview.[15]

The experienced Friar Lorenzo de Bienvenida and the then young novice Diego de Landa established the Itzmal mission in 1549, when the region's Second Custodial Council tasked them to find an ideal location east of Mérida to begin the expansion into the peninsula's interior. They settled on Itzmal because of its impressive archaeological remains. It had once stood as one of the region's largest precontact cities, expanding to nearly three square miles, and it was connected to neighboring cities by a sophisticated series of raised paved causeways, stretching as far as thirty-seven miles. Ceramic analysis has revealed the site's occupation since at least the preclassic period (700–150

BCE), but its extant architectural remains dated to the early classic period (250–650 CE), with stylistic modification extending into the postclassic period (1200–1500 CE).[16] The presence of the modern town on top and within these ancient structures has made thorough excavation impossible; much has to be surmised from extant colonial accounts, as problematic as this method may be.

The industrious friars established the mission on August 6, the feast day of the Transfiguration of Christ. They recited the first mass in a small *capilla* (chapel), newly built on top of the site's largest ancient mound, first recorded in 1581 as the "Kinich Kakmo" pyramid by Joan de Parades, encomendero of neighboring Cizil and Sitilpech.[17] Undoubtedly, this chapel was composed of wooden posts and a thatch roof, no match for the Yucatán's strong winds, which promptly and supernaturally swept the chapel from the summit of the Kinich Kakmo right at the conclusion of that first mass. Taking this as a bad omen, the friars decided to move their base of operations to the second largest mound, the Ppop Hol Chac, ultimately a smart decision since the architectural design of this structure fortuitously replicated European monastic cloisters.[18]

Shortly thereafter Landa ventured farther eastward, spending the next four years among unconverted Mayas in the monte. It was during these years that he learned to speak Yucatec Mayan fluently, was educated about the Mayas' hieroglyphic system, and also observed several of the communal rituals enacted by this indigenous group. His homecoming occurred in 1552, when Mérida's Franciscan council elected Landa as guardian of the Itzmal convent. In his absence Bienvenida appears to have done little to establish a permanent architectural presence; in all likelihood he had been residing and conducting his early conversion efforts from the preexisting Maya structures. Perhaps Bienvenida had constructed a very simple ramada chapel, but neither the textual nor the archaeological records provide evidence of this construction. That same year Bienvenida returned to Mérida to serve as the order's *custodio* (custodian), vacating the Itzmal post. Landa was left solely in charge of the mission, now armed with an entire arsenal of cultural insight and remarkable language acuity.

Local Mayas informed Landa that Itzmal had been a popular pilgrimage destination for centuries, hosting pilgrims who petitioned the assistance of Itzamnaaj, the Maya deity of healing and sacred knowledge. In fact, when Bienvenida and Landa had arrived at the massive ruin in 1549, the site was inhabited by only a handful of religious specialists, who remained to oversee the administration of Itzamnaaj's cult and to tend to pilgrims. So Landa knew of the site's numinous qualities and centuries-long history of healing. Much later, in his seventeenth-century text, Lizana maintained that, before the arrival of the Spaniards, sick Mayas would journey to Itzmal to contact specific ídolos: "They said that when they had mortality, or epidemics, or other communal maladies, everyone came to it, men as well as women, bringing many presents that they offered to them."[19]

Both men were also aware of where Itzamnaaj's power lay—in the supernatural properties of the local topographies itself. Archaeologists have located, directly underneath the largest mound, the same Kinich Kakmo that hosted that first but ultimately doomed mass, a naturally occurring cave that had been augmented by human hands in ancient times.[20] According to Lizana, the temple at the top of the mound had been used as a sanctuary for Kinich Ahau, the Maya sun deity and spiritual avatar of Itzamnaaj, his *nahual* or *way* (spirit companion), who was directly linked to Itzamnaaj's shamanic and healing abilities. The massive bulk of the pyramid served to monumentally mark the location of the cave, a portal to the underworld and thus an ideal location to commune with the metaphysical presence of the Maya gods.

In the seven years following Landa's return to Itzmal, he accomplished what his predecessor had not: the construction of the most impressive monastic complex that would ever grace the Yucatán (fig. 2). Engaging the assistance of the poorly understood architect-turned-friar Juan de Mérida and thousands of Maya laborers, Landa remade the entire city of Itzmal into an idealized, Hispanicized town, utilizing the ancient Maya urban plan as a template on which to graft Iberian notions of *policia*, the idea of living in a civilized, urban, Christian manner.[21] He retained nearly half of the precontact plaza, reshaping it into the colonial square, and also used the five radiating *sacbeob* as the primary gridlines of his newly established orthogonal plan. Most impressive, the friar utilized the sixteen-foot-tall base of the Ppop Hol Chac to support his monastic complex, incorporating the finished stonework of the building's upper terraces to complete the masonry nave, cloister, and processional walkways of the church's massive atrium. This monumental forecourt was the world's largest until Gian Lorenzo Bernini's redesign of Saint Peter's Piazza in 1667.[22]

The Birth of the Virgin

Unfortunately, the archival record does not provide sources that would shed insight into the early years of the virgin's life. Strangely, the extant writings of Landa himself fail to mention the presence of a Marian icon at his much-loved monastery, San Antonio de Padua.[23] The next logical source for the virgin's biography should be the *Relación* penned in 1581 by encomendero Juan de la Cueva Santillán, but amid his detailed description of the convent and its evangelical functions, he also neglects the miraculous statue.[24] The earliest account of her physical arrival at Itzmal is Lizana's 1633 text; the tale I present here is derived from his account.

According to the friar, in 1558 Landa journeyed to Santiago de Guatemala. That same year the city hosted a custodial; Landa was likely resident in an official capacity, representing his order's interests in Yucatán. Lizana's text, in its expected hagiographic mode, leads readers to believe that the trip was intended solely for the garnering of a statue of Mary, which the native residents of Itzmal had requested. None of the historical sources tell us of his exact route, but it is most likely that his journey there and back relied on a circuitous itinerary, certainly suggested by his mentor, Bienvenida, who had taken a similar path some years earlier.[25] Landa set off from Itzmal, headed southeasterly into the monte to eventually arrive at the small Spanish outpost of Salamanca de Bacalar. Here he would have hired a canoe and sailed along the southern Yucatecan coast (off what is today Belize), staying between the coastline and the barrier reef for protection from early British pirates.[26] At Gulfo Dulce, Landa disembarked and slowly made his was up into the highlands, eventually arriving at Santiago de Guatemala.

Lizana recounts that, once there, Landa commissioned the production of two icons of the Virgin Mary, categorically confirming the icons' status as non-acheiropoieta. López de Cogolludo confirms this, claiming that Santiago de Guatemala hosted a renowned sculptor, an "Artifice Escultor."[27] According to Florencia's even later rendering, the city "had always flourished in the art of sculpture, in which one sees many statues that compete in perfection and beauty with the most celebrated ones of Naples and Rome."[28] Following the completion of these icons, specialists constructed a special crate to ensure the virgins' safety on their journey back to Yucatán.[29]

For his return trip, Landa approached the peninsula from the western coast, as he stopped in Mérida before he arrived in Itzmal. Like his Franciscan forebears, Landa left Santiago de Guatemala heading north, toward today's Mexican state of Chiapas, passing through Palenque, Acalan.[30] Once on the coast at Champotón, he engaged a canoe to transport him northward along Mexico's Gulf Coast, where he disembarked at San Francisco de Campeche. From Campeche the trip was relatively simpler, as he traced the camino real directly into Mérida. An unrelated archival document from the following year recalls that such a trip typically took about forty days.[31] Once in Mérida Landa stayed in his order's primary convent and granted his Franciscan brothers first choice in selecting which of the two Marian icons they wanted for their chapel. According to Lizana, the friars chose the image they considered the most beautiful in the face (*mas hermosa de rostro*), described as "a devotional image with a Christ child in her arms with the title of his Most Holy Nativity."[32]

At long last Landa arrived home in Itzmal. At this point in the town's architectural history (1559–60), the monastic complex was nearly complete, so it is likely that Landa installed the icon on the church's main altar, undoubtedly a very simple wooden table. Soon thereafter it is probable that an elaborate mural was created to serve as a dramatic visual backdrop for the Marian icon. This mural cycle is today hidden beneath layers of whitewash and the baroque nineteenth-century *retablo* (altarpiece) that stretches to the nave's ceiling. But the recently uncovered murals of contemporaneous Maní (fig. 23) may serve as a visual stand-in for the once-extant Itzmal painting cycle.

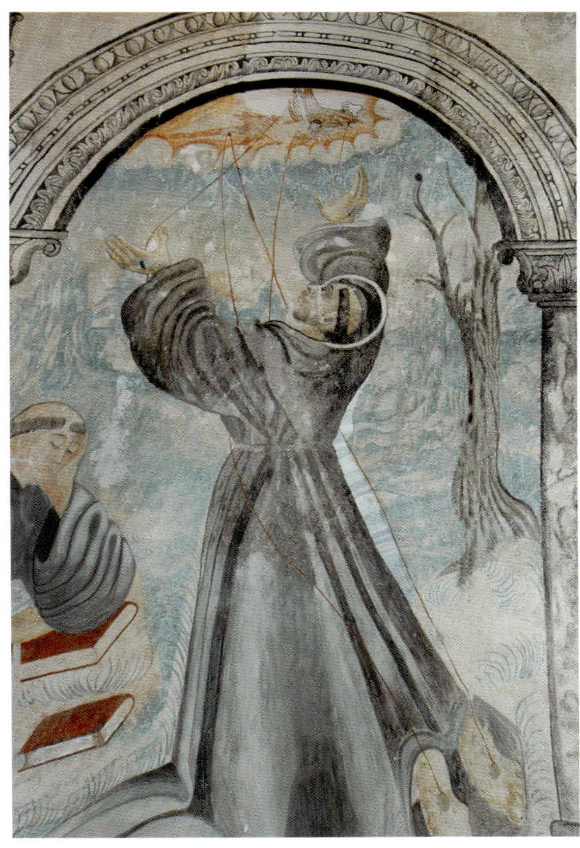

It seems that the Franciscans in Mérida chose unwisely. By the time Lizana recorded these events, it was widely accepted that, upon Landa's departure from Guatemala, one of the Marian icons starting working miracles, as witnessed by Landa and his Maya porters. The numinous statue of Mary was *not* the one selected by the Mérida friars; instead, it is the one that would eventually be installed in Itzmal. Her early performed miracles fall into the expected tropes imported from the European tradition of miraculous statues. The most significant occurrence was that during the course of multiple storms that plagued the group on their return journey, not a single drop of rain struck either the box that contained the virgins or their porters. This would have been quite a feat, given that the group inevitably trekked through the tropical forests of southern Mexico. Significantly, at this point in the virgin's biography, she is not credited with healing abilities. Her numinous talents were ascribed only once the Itzmal icon became firmly associated with that refashioned town.

By the seventeenth century, local lore maintained that the virgin self-consciously selected Itzmal and its Maya residents to be her devotees. At some point between 1561 and 1563 (dateable, as the event occurred under the custodial tenure of Francisco de la Torre), Spanish residents and Franciscan friars of Valladolid (the Spanish town located fifty-eight miles to the east; see map 1) conspired to kidnap the virgin for their own church, claiming that "it was unfair that this Queen of Heaven should be in a village that had been so shortly before worshipping the devil." These *vecinos* (residents) petitioned de la Torre, who (under understandable pressure) granted them license to remove her. According to Lizana's account, "Even though they were resistant, the Indians carried her [to the Spaniards], remaining so inconsolable that God was served; his mother didn't want to be moved or leave the pueblo because of the care that those who carried her had shown."[33] López de Cogolludo expanded the tale, adding the narrative detail that, when the Valladolideños came to remove the Virgin, "they didn't have enough human force to move her," and so she was "returned to her convent to the great happiness of the Indians and the admiration of the religious."[34]

For local Franciscans this legend proved the completed religious conversion of the Itzmal Mayas. Lizana eloquently summarized this sentiment when he proclaimed, "Oh, marvels of the almighty God, who in this way manifests his will, so that it seems it was that the Most Holy Image would hold onto her throne and place and would work so many miracles and wonders where the astute and infernal serpent had done so many tricks, that she would take as her own house this sacred Convent and temple . . . [the devil's] same house."[35] Over a hundred years later Florencia would echo Lizana: "The advocation of the Pueblo [of Itzmal] was the Immaculate Conception, with whose devotion the Indians have totally forgotten that which they once had for their idols."[36]

Thus, the earliest whisper of the virgin's existence that I have been able to locate dates to the very end of the sixteenth century; in this time lag we are either seeing three decades of archival silence or are confronted with the reality that Landa's conversion strategy took nearly thirty years to be effective.[37] In 1586, during their five-year-long visita though Philip II's American territories, the *comisario general* of New Spain, Alonso Ponce, and his secretary, Antonio de Ciudad Real, stopped in Itzmal for two days. During their visit they were made aware of the pueblo's icon: "In the convent's church, there is a life-sized image of our Lady, to whom the Spaniards, and even the Indians, are very devoted."[38] It is in this visita account that we find the very first hint that the virgin had acquired numinous abilities. Ciudad Real relates that "many [Yucatecans] come to say novenas before that image when they are sick."[39] The past thirty years had witnessed a series of devastating epidemics. Specifically, Kashanipour cites generalized pandemics (1566), smallpox (1575–76), measles (1580), and fevers (1580) as striking the peninsula. If central Mexico, with its better level of archival survivability, is any indication, there were far more health crises than are indicated in the historical record.[40] Given this period of intense illness, it should come as no surprise that the Virgin of Itzmal would appropriate the role of community healer once assumed by her forerunner, Itzamnaaj.[41]

Nearly thirty years pass before the icon appears again in the documentary record, this time as a passing reference in *Informe contra idolorum cultores del obispado de Yucatán* (Report against the worshippers of idols of the bishopric of Yucatán), composed sometime between 1613 and 1617.[42] Its author, Pedro Sánchez de Aguilar, was a Creole of Yucatán, had been educated and took orders in Mexico City's University of San Idelfonso, and returned to the province to minister to the Indian parishes in 1591, learning Yucatec Mayan and quickly becoming one of the region's foremost *lenguas* (translators).[43] In 1613, while serving as dean of the Mérida cathedral, the friar appears have begun a weighty tome as a response to a *cédula* (royal decree) of Philip IV, which asked local clergymen to account for the continued discovery of idolatry.

Within this context Aguilar informed his king of the religious situation in Yucatán, describing it as rather grim. Among many suggestions for its improvement, he recommended that visual culture be directed to play a more sustained role in evangelism. He remarked, "The [Mayas publicly] venerate sacred images of the sacred Virgin Mary . . . in particular in the pueblo and convent of Itzmal."[44] But he also explicitly advocated for the use of images in private devotion as a means to combat the province's incessant problem with idolatry: "The Indians should have altars, images, and crosses in their houses . . . because in this they are remiss, little devoted, and they don't imitate the Mexicans, each of whom has their own oratory. Also, they should wear rosaries on their chests."[45]

It is to this criticism that Porras and Lizana seem to respond when they wrote their king a decade later in 1624, as quoted in this book's epigraph.[46] The Franciscans directly charted the Maya use of visual culture as an index of their internalized Christian beliefs, reflecting the complex relationship that the order had with images. In the few years between Sánchez de Aguilar's departure from the province in 1619 and the 1624 composition of the Porras-Lizana letter, a massive sea change had occurred among the Yucatecan Franciscans, as they now appeared to accept the utility of Catholic images for their evangelical efforts.[47] This was also partly owing to the efforts of Bishop Gonzalo de Salazar, who throughout his tenure (1609–36) waged massive extirpation campaigns, which culminated in a public *auto-da-fé* and bonfire to destroy traditional Maya religious statuary.[48]

By the 1620s private, domestic Marian devotion mirrored communal veneration, which was becoming increasingly elaborate. The virgin's feast day, December 8, had already become a regional festivity. Porras and Lizana reported that on "the day of the feast of the Holy Conception, and all year long, incessantly, where the said Indians of all this land of Yucatán, Cozumel, and Tabasco, Bacalar, come to hold vigil with such spirit and faith that (they go) from the church doors to the main altar, where the image is, asking for health."[49] This was obviously a long, drawn-out event: "They have scarcely crossed the threshold of her sacred temple when they fall to their knees, their eyes glued to the sacred image, and in this way they crawl on their knees, moving, little by little, until they reach the altar of this most serene Queen of Heaven." Such overt devotion caused the friar to declare Itzmal the "New Jerusalem, built as a city where all the nations come to confess in the name of the Lord."[50]

The Franciscans also described a local *cofradía* (devotional brotherhood or confraternity): "They have a confraternity founded for the Immaculate Conception, and they support the savior and burials of those brothers and the masses that they say for Our Lady with lit candles in their hands that they placed with their devotion."[51] Given that the town harbored only a single Spanish family, that of the encomendero, it is indisputable that Maya elites composed the corporate body of the brotherhood, perhaps replicating the social trends that simultaneously occurred in other indigenous communities. Nancy Farriss and Matthew Restall have independently raised the possibility that in the colonial period cofradías became avenues through which Maya elites who had been dispossessed of the administrative and religious roles they held in the precontact period could reestablish their placement in the local social hierarchy.[52] It is likely that the Itzmal confraternity of the Immaculate Conception accepted the financial burden of her feast day as well. This is confirmed nearly a century later, when the leadership of the pueblo's confraternity was brought under an investigation that questioned the proper administration of their funds.[53]

Following the 1624 letter, in 1633 the virgin resurfaces, this time as the primary protagonist in Lizana's *Historia de Yucatán*.[54] He pronounces her an all-around powerful deity. The friar perhaps overspoke when he claimed that she was well known in Spain and in other "remote parts" by the miracles that God had worked through her (and promoted by Lizana's publication), but it is undeniable that by the mid-seventeenth century the Virgin of Itzmal had a sizable and diverse following. This was explainable by the fact that the virgin "had a remedy for every need, comfort for the sad, redemption for the captive, liberty for the incarcerated, riches for the poor, health for the ill, medicine for the wounded, life for the dead, light for the blind, the heart of charity for the half-hearted, and snow to cool the tempted." But, above all, she was "such a friend of the poor and humble" that she "obtained eminence with the Indians, for their poverty and humility," becoming the "cure and medicine of their sicknesses."[55]

Lizana enumerates the various miracles the Virgin of Itzmal had bestowed on the faithful (listed in table 1 and translated in appendix C).[56] Clearly, the virgin's miracle stories operated in the realm of folklore, and, as such, Marian apparition and miracle tales from the colonial period have tended to be ignored by historians for being ahistorical by definition.[57] The friar's miracle stories follow the usual tropes of miraculous Marys and resonate with localized versions of early modern Iberian Catholicism and published accounts of the virgin's miracles.[58] They display an interest in both the materiality of the icon herself and the numinosity of the sacred locus of Itzmal, regardless of whether the petitioner was Maya, African, or Spanish.[59]

TABLE 1 Collated selection of the miracles attributed to the Virgin of Itzmal

Protagonist	Ailment	Mode of remedy	Source
Maya boy (from Tixhotzuc)	Long-term physical disability, paralysis, "crippled" or "shrunken" since birth	Physical proximity for two days, monetary payment, perseverance	Lizana (22v–23v) Cogolludo (311) Florencia (12–13)
Spanish sailor	Injured, tongue excised by English pirates	Physical contact with her temple, prayer	Lizana (23v–24v) Cogolludo (311–12) Florencia (13–14)
Maya man	Long-term physical disability, paralysis, "crippled" since birth	Physical proximity, prayer, perseverance	Lizana (24v–25v) Cogolludo (312) Florencia (14)
Maya girl, five years of age	Death	Physical proximity; when she awoke she was fully Christianized and able to recite an Ave Maria	Lizana (25v–26v) Cogolludo (312–13) Florencia (14–15)
Maya woman (from Homun)	Long-term disability, mute since birth	Physical proximity, prayer	Lizana (27r) Cogolludo (313) Florencia (15)
Maya man	Long-term disability, deaf "for a long time"	Physical proximity	Lizana (27r) Cogolludo (313) Florencia (15)
Maya man	Long-term disability, blind since birth	"Intercession"	Lizana (27r) Cogolludo (313) Ignored by Florencia
African man (slave of Canon Alonso Rodriguez)	Sick, maggot infestation	Physical proximity	Lizana (27r) Cogolludo (313) Florencia (16–17)
Maya man	Long-term physical disability, paralysis, "crippled" "for a long time," happened in 1625	Physical proximity, prayer	Lizana (27r–27v) Cogolludo (313) Florencia (16)
Spanish man from Seville	Sick, internal burning, insomnia	Physical proximity for two months, prayer, subsequent vow, and recited masses	Lizana (27v–28r) Cogolludo (313–14) Florencia (17)
Spanish boy from Mérida (son of Francisco de Espinosa and María de Matos)	Injured, broken bones from a fall from a great height	Mother vowed to make a novena to the virgin	Lizana (28r) Cogolludo (314) Florencia (17)
Spanish woman (María de Sosa, wife of the local encomendero, Rodrigo Alvarez de Gamboa)	Sick, arthritis ("fire in her hand" that came with the waning of the moon, so painful she couldn't eat or sleep)	Physical proximity, donated an ornament for her altar, said novenas and nine masses; on the feast day of Expectation they hosted the mass	Lizana (28r–28v) Cogolludo (314) Florencia (17–18)

Protagonist	Ailment	Mode of remedy	Source
Spanish man (Capitán Domingo Galvan)	Storm at sea	Crew vowed to live cleaner lives and visit the virgin; after the event stayed for nine days and listened to nine masses	Lizana (28v–29r) Cogolludo (314) Florencia (18)
Maya men from Campeche	Storm at sea	Vowed to stop committing idolatrous acts and to go to the virgin and give her alms	Lizana (29r–29v) Cogolludo (314–15) Florencia (18–19)
Spanish man (staying at an inn in Itzmal)	Injured, gunshot wound to his stomach and groin	Upon impact, petitioned the virgin's assistance; subsequent physical proximity	Lizana (30r–30v) Cogolludo (315) Florencia (19)
Maya woman (from Mérida)	Sick, stomachache, torso exploded on the side of her navel	Physical proximity	Lizana (30v) Cogolludo (315) Ignored by Florencia
Spanish woman (in Madrid at the Court of Philip)	Sick, generic ailment (*dolencia*)	Prayers and vows to be her devotee and visit her	Lizana (30v–31r): painted at Itzmal chapel Cogolludo (315–16): painted at Itzmal chapel Florencia (19–20): painted at Itzmal chapel
Maya man (in Mérida, servant of a Spanish woman)	Injured, fell from the Spanish woman's terrace, broken arm and leg, nearly dead	Tactility: Spanish woman wrapped the arm and a leg with the packing papers she had collected years before when the virgins first came from Guatemala	Cogolludo (310–11) Florencia (12)
Sailors on the Spanish ship, Capitán Alonso Carrió de Valdés	Ran aground off the north coast twice within a short time, September 1634	Prayer recited aloud, promised and then gave her a silver cable	Cogolludo (316) Ignored by Florencia
Spanish woman (Jerónima de Laso y Castilla, wife of the governor, el Marqués de Santo Floro)	Sick	Prayer right before she was to die, gifts subsequently sent	Cogolludo (316): painted at Itzmal chapel Florencia (20): painted at Itzmal chapel
Spanish man (Diego López de Cogolludo)	Sick, but not deadly, great pains, October 1654	Vow to the virgin	Cogolludo (315) Florencia (20)
Mérida residents	Possible pillaging from many groups of pirates, especially from the famous pirate, Lorenzillo y Monsiur de Agramont, who wanted to steal the virgin's treasures	"The favor of the virgin"	Florencia (20–21)

Sources: Lizana, *Historia de Yucatán*, 22v–31v; López de Cogolludo, *Historia de Yucathán*, 310–16; Florencia, *Estrella del norte de México*, 12–21.

When López de Cogolludo took up his pen, he copied verbatim Lizana's seventeen miracle events and then added four more that must have occurred in the intervening years, so between 1633 and 1655 (listed in table 1 and translated in appendix D). Of López de Cogolludo's twenty-one included tales, eighteen (86 percent) are stories of the virgin's intercession to enact corporeal healing. These are divided into three distinct types: the easing of long-term ailments (such as a physical disability since birth), the healing of an acute illness, and, in one case, the raising of a Maya girl from the dead. Of these tales of miraculous healing, twelve necessitated that the suffering individual be in physical proximity to the icon, typically, kneeling before her altar or, in the case of a Spanish man who had his tongue removed by English pirates, placing his mouth on the floor of the Itzmal nave. Even in this midcolonial moment, Maya and Spanish Catholics alike were relying on a kind of locative sacrality, an understanding of the miraculous as particularly powerful within a potent topography, a place whose history was ripe with previous happenings of similar import. The "absent" petitioners were cured simply by praying to the virgin or vowing to visit her at a later date, sponsor masses for her, or grant her some kind of material gift.[60]

López de Cogolludo is the original source for the most intriguing of the healing stories, but he describes it in some detail.[61] According to this legend, which appears to have started circulating in the mid-sixteenth century, when Landa returned to Mérida with the two virgins safely housed in their traveling crate, some of the packing papers fell into the street. A Spanish woman gathered these up and kept them, only to use them years later, when her Maya servant fell from the house's roof, breaking his arm and leg. While they waited for the doctor to arrive, the Spanish woman remembered the packing papers and carefully draped them around the Maya man's broken limbs. When the papers touched the arm and leg, both were miraculously healed.

Florencia notes his consultation of Lizana and López de Cogolludo. He copied most of their stories verbatim, omitting three (one of the healing of a Maya man, one in which a Maya woman's bellyache was cured, and finally one of a Spanish vessel that was saved from a storm). His only original contribution is his final aside, in which he claims that many times over the icon had saved the residents of Mérida from pirates.[62]

In addition to the oral and printed circulation of the icon's miracles between the seventeenth and eighteenth centuries, two forms of visual culture also advertised these wonders. Before the construction of the *camarín*, a small chapel located directly above and behind the nave's main altar, following the 1648 epidemic, the interior walls of the Itzmal chapel functioned as a display space for figurative representations of singular miracles. Lizana, López de Cogolludo, and Florencia all recall an anecdote in which a woman at the Spanish court was cured from an unknown illness. As a form of thanksgiving, her family members sent a painted image of the scene so that it would become known on the other side of the Atlantic. Similarly, the wife of the governor,

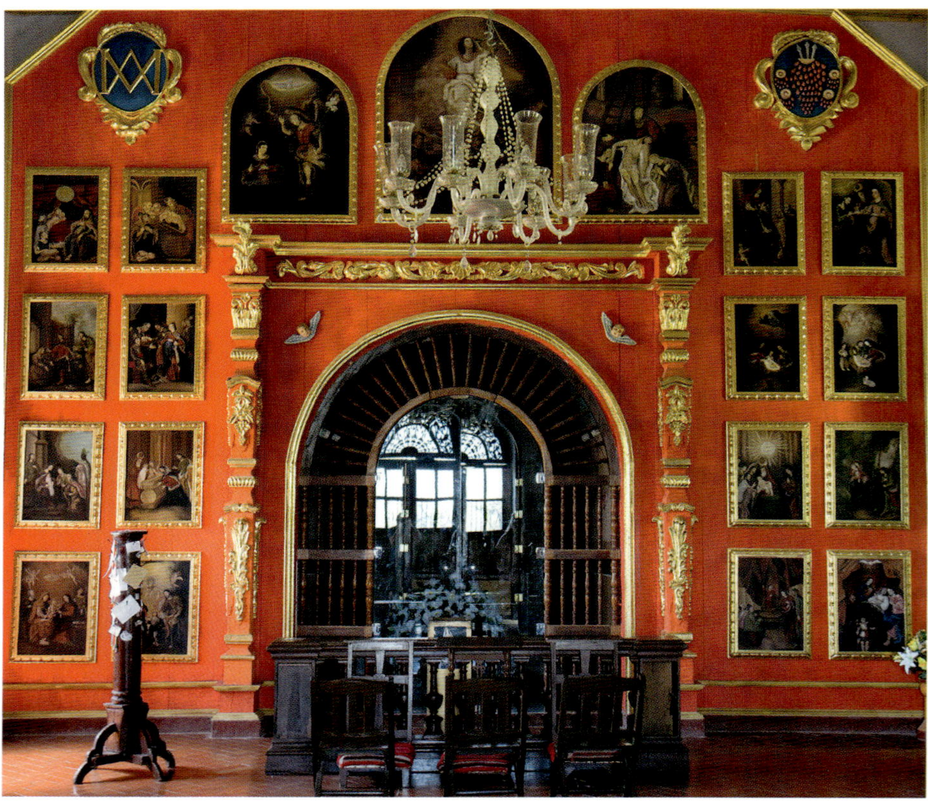

FIG. 24 Interior of the camarín of San Antonio de Padua Monastery, Itzmal, Yucatán. The sixteen flanking scenes depict miracles performed by the Virgin of Itzmal. Photo: Lightworks Media/Alamy Stock Photo.

Jerónima de Laso y Castilla, commissioned her miracle story to be recorded on a *lienzo*, a large-scale canvas, which hung in the icon's camarín. Unfortunately, all these paintings were destroyed in the 1829 fire but were remade into devotional images for the reconstruction of the camarín (fig. 24).

Smaller-scale material culture also functioned as mnemonics, forever reminding viewers of the icon's numinous powers. Writing before the construction of the camarín devotees, Francisco de Cárdenas Valencia claimed that on the nave's walls hung "entire bodies of wax, arms, legs, heads, crutches, cables, candles, and other various things, with muted voices publicizing the blessings of this supreme princess."[63] These objects undoubtedly prefigure the metallic trinkets that adorn holy shrines throughout Latin America. López de Cogolludo expanded this: "Furthermore, she has on her altar silver lamps, and in the church many tokens of the miracles that have been done, that it has been necessary to remove many of them, because they overflow the walls."[64] Today this practice is still maintained on the walls of the icon's camarín and on a makeshift

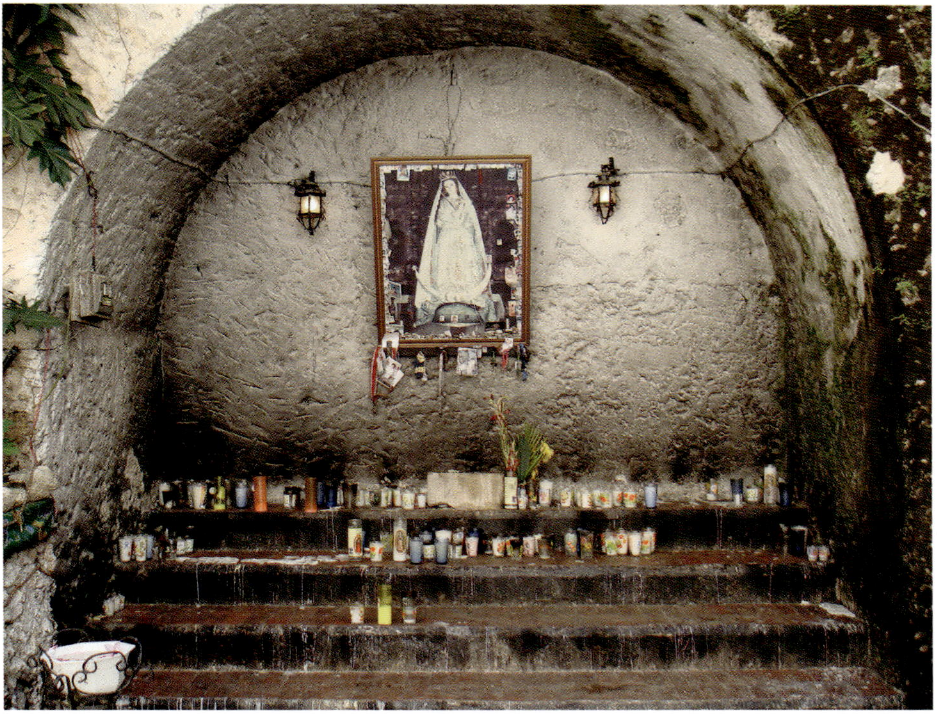

FIG. 25 Devotional altar, San Antonio de Padua Monastery, Itzmal, Yucatán. Photo: Linda K. Williams.

altar located just outside the nave's southern wall, where photos of the healed, votive candles, and various trinkets are publicly displayed (fig. 25).

The recorded tales attest that ideologies of sacred materiality were paramount to early devotion to the Virgin of Itzmal. Nearly three-quarters of her healing miracles occurred only when the ill or injured person was in direct physical contact with the icon or at least in physical proximity to her. As Jeanette Peterson has articulated, "Touching and seeing went hand in hand in authenticating the reality of an icon's force and in transmitting that energy, like an electric charge . . . from icon to pious believer."[65] Although seemingly derived from European traditions, this aspect of sacred tactility certainly had Amerindian roots as well. It is certain that for her Maya audience ritual proscriptions imbued the icon with a sense of the sacred.

Envisioning Mary

Because the original icon was destroyed in 1829, to reconstruct her physical attributes we are left with only four visual representations that predate the tragedy: two

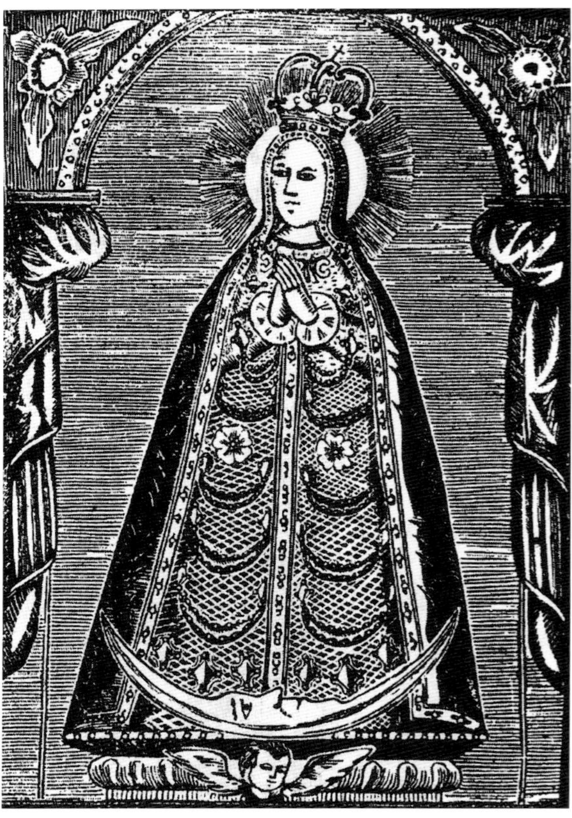

woodblock prints and two oil paintings.[66] Of these, only the paintings were created "from life," that is, directly in front of the sacred icon. The production contexts of the two prints suggest they are simply generic representations of icons of the Immaculate Conception. The Virgin of Itzmal's earliest image is Lizana's frontispiece (fig. 22), a relatively primitive woodcut likely created in Valladolid, Spain, the location of the book's printing. Perhaps Lizana provided the printer with oral descriptions of the icon's appearance, but this production technique makes it impossible that the 1633 rendering resembles the actual Itzmal icon. The next representation, the 1764 engraving described in this chapter's introduction (fig. 21), was produced in the colonial capital (Mexico City) and so was likely etched by an artist who similarly had never seen the Itzmal Virgin firsthand (but again, an oral description is possible). It was the prototype for a later (postfire) 1854 engraving (fig. 26), published as the frontispiece to an additional novena. It seems to have been printed from a heavily used woodblock (note the lack of clarity on the composition's hard edges) and so may have been also used earlier to create popular devotional prints that circulated among the peninsula's devotees.[67] Taken as a group to evidence the icon's original appearance, however, these images leave much to be desired.

Given the uneasy possibility that the earliest prints are simply generic depictions, a surer assessment of the icon's visual and physical form is provided by the two eighteenth-century oil paintings that survive. Both were commissioned during what scholars have termed the Great Famine (1765–73), the most devastating drought and resulting food shortages of the colonial period.[68] The earlier of the two (fig. 27) follows the expected composition of American devotional images, since its configuration is as standardized as her prints.[69] A textual cartouche reveals the context for the image's execution:

> A true portrait of the miraculous image of Our Lady of the Immaculate Conception with the title of Ytzmal. The Illmo. and Rmo. Sr. D. Fr. Antonio Alcalde of the Sacred Order of Preachers [Dominicans], the dignified Bishop of these provinces of Yucatán of his majesty's council, blessed her today on July 13, 1769. At the same time, he granted 10 days of indulgences to everyone who prays a *Salve Regina* to this Most Holy Lady. [This painting] was taken from the original [sculpture] on the day of his blessing, in public adoration in the church of the nuns in the City of Mérida, by two Dominican fathers.

The two friar artists completed the image to commemorate the icon's visit to Mérida in 1769. This procession, like that of 1648, was an attempt to alleviate a communal crisis, albeit of a different sort. The famine struck the province earlier that spring, initially caused by a massive locust infestation, and was only worsened by a disastrous hurricane that landed on the peninsula the following year.[70] According to the plaque installed in Itzmal's central plaza (fig. 4), the icon left the village on June 15 to spend fifty consecutive days in the capital city. During that time, Bishop Antonio Alcalde y Barriga blessed the image and offered all those who joined him in prayer with a ten-day reprieve from their destined time in Purgatory. Today the painting hangs in Mérida's Pinacoteca Juan Gamboa Guzmán, a small gallery that houses a handful of colonial-era paintings, but the image's atypical cropping hints that it was once part of a larger altarpiece: the edges of her triangular gown have been incised from the composition. The vertical struts of the frame dramatically bisect this garment, suggesting that the canvas was originally larger. Like so many other colonial paintings with similar fates, she was likely removed from a complex baroque altarpiece. I suspect that she once was utilized as a devotional object inside Mérida's singular convent of nuns, dedicated to Nuestra Señora de la Consolación, a religious institution that had maintained close ties with the virgin since her 1648 intercession.[71]

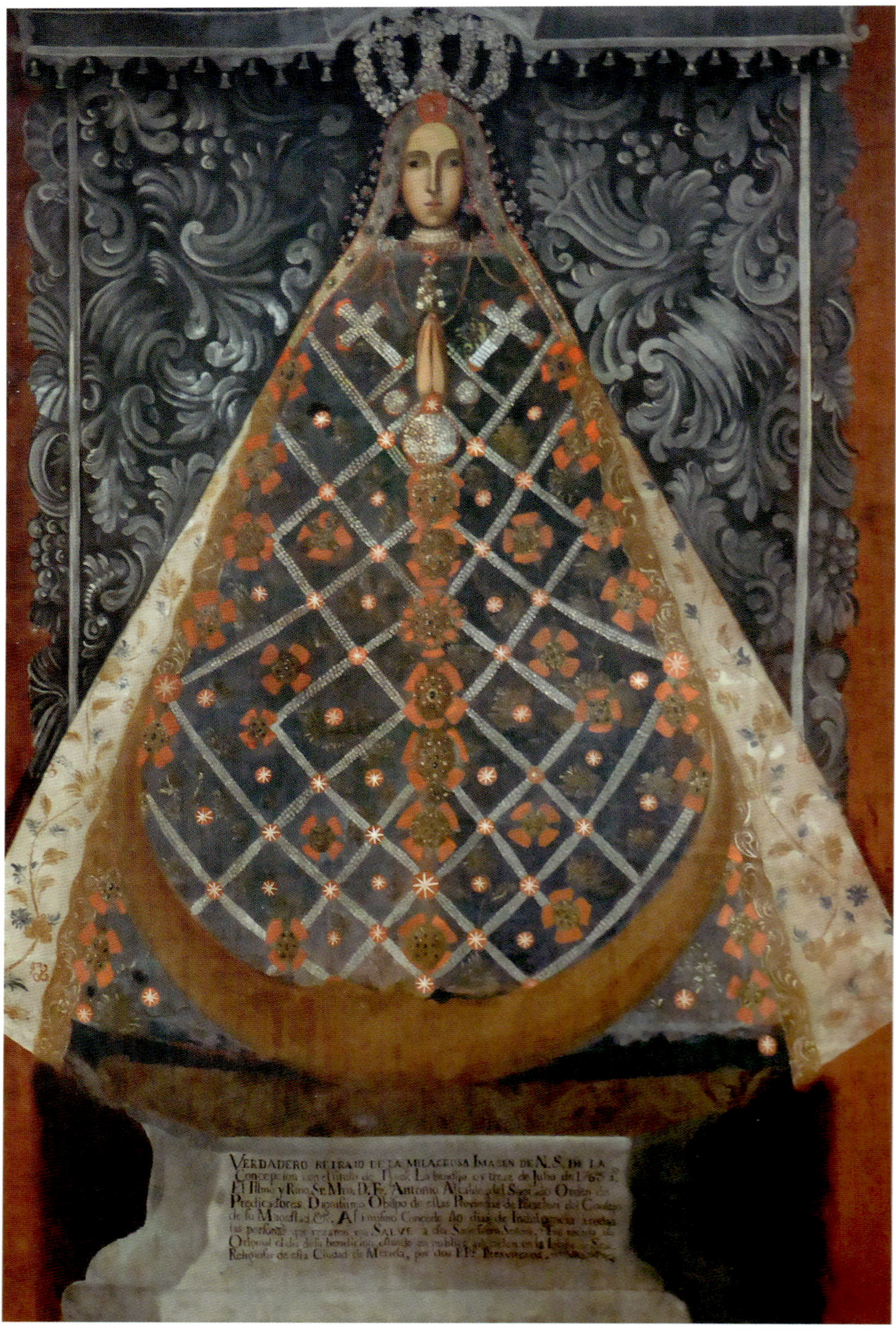

FIG. 27 Artist unknown, *Virgin of Itzmal*, 1769. Pinacoteca Juan Gamboa Guzmán, Mérida, Yucatán. Photo: author.

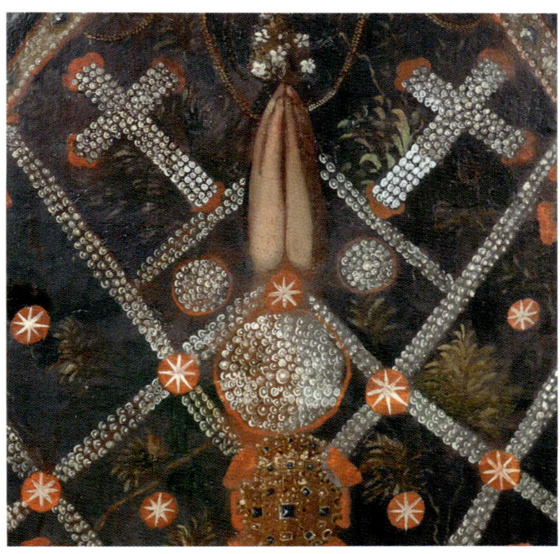

Regardless of the image's more recent cropping, the artists intended a very simple composition whereby viewers would not be distracted by unnecessary ornamental detail. She functions as an object of contemplation, a site of introspection and personal piety. The composition forces viewers to interact with this image directly; her artists represented a placid look on her face, in which the statue's eyes directly meet with those of her audience. Her scale replicates that of the original icon, suggesting that for viewers this image functioned as a stand-in for the actual icon, an image that could be prayed to and supplicated in modes similar to the icon itself. As such, it is likely that we are looking here at an artifact that, like its prototype, was understood not as a mere painting but as a holy object capable of sacred intercession.

To enhance this aura of religious intimacy, the artists used two visual techniques to tightly frame her. First, even prior to her excision from the altarpiece, she was imaged incredibly close to the picture plane, so her body inhabits the majority of the painting's expanse. Also, her artists placed her on a silver pedestal within the confines of a small litter that had been made for her a century earlier. According to López de Cogolludo, it was purchased with the jewels given to her following the 1648 epidemic. He described it as "a throne of very costly and meticulously applied hammered silver. Afterward a silver-plated litter was made, on which she is placed for the procession on her feast day."[72]

These same donations purchased the icon's elaborate costume.[73] Figure 28 reveals her elaborately embroidered gown to be studded with seed pearls, precious gems, and gold chains. For a viewer these valuable items functioned as an index of her successful intercession: it was widely known that her wardrobe was maintained by grateful (and wealthy) devotees, such as Padre Fray Antonio Ramirez, who bestowed a rich trunk of treasures from Spain on the icon earlier in the seventeenth century.[74]

Thereafter, the original Itzmal Virgin is imaged only once more, in the most grandiose of her representations, in the patron portrait of Dr. Don Agustín Francisco Echano, canon of the Mérida cathedral in 1769 (fig. 3).[75] In it, Echano kneels before the sacred icon, cap in hand, demonstrating his prostration. The artist imaged the sculpture with a three-quarter view, naturalizing the space she inhabits while at the same time referencing her status as an inanimate object. She wears the same gown from the additional devotional painting and is placed within the confines of an identical silver and crescent-framed litter, which itself has been positioned on a makeshift altar covered with a swath of white silk. A candle and flowers have been strewn around her temporary sanctuary. Unlike the earlier painting, a better sense of architectural context is given, as one can make out the base of a raised wooden column on the right side of the composition along with rich velveteen curtains, rendered in a deep red. Echano holds an elaborately carved wooden frame (or mirror), on which the artist has glossed an abbreviated account of the virgin's intercession in the 1648 yellow fever epidemic and the Mérida religious elites' reavowal of devotion that occurred on the plague's centennial anniversary.[76] Unlike the 1769 image, Echano's portrait is a commemorative piece, intended to remind viewers of the canon's personalized veneration of the icon and that of Mérida's Spanish citizenry.

These images reveal that, like her American sister Marys, the Itzmal icon does not perfectly replicate the strict iconography of any of the virgin's advocations; instead, artists hybridized her accoutrements.[77] We know that she was deemed an Inmaculada, given that seventeenth-century sources record her feast day as December 8, the Feast of the Immaculate Conception, but Immaculate iconography was only slowly concretized during the very long sixteenth century, firmly established by Francisco Pacheco in his *Arte de la pintura* of 1649.[78] In all her extant images we can see that the Itzmal icon regally stood with hands clasped in front of her chest, thus approximating a traditional Assumption, or Tota Pulchra. In a reference to the Woman of the Apocalypse from the Book of Revelation, she has a silver crescent moon at her feet. An opulent crown tops the virgin's head, and the weighty folds of her embroidered gown virtually encrust her solid wooden form.

In addition to these visual sources, seventeenth-century textual descriptions also provide insight into the icon's original appearance. One hundred years after her production, López de Cogolludo described her as a "life-sized statue with her robes in *estofado* of a height of five spans and six fingers," bringing her just under four feet.[79] López de Cogolludo's words evidence that her original dress was masterly carved into the wood of the statue's matrix. In this technique artists use single or multiple pieces of wood to sculpt the bodily form of the icon. Thereafter, multiple layers of gesso, clay slip, gold leaf, and paint are applied. Only then can artists gently carve through the outermost layer of pigment to reveal the glittering substance beneath, beautifully replicating the golden threads of embroidered cloth. This was a commonly used technique in contemporaneous southern Spain, speaking to the Guatemalan sculptor's probable training in the Spanish school.

Conclusion

On the surface the appearance and early biography of the Itzmal virgin appear to simply replicate the long-standing European relationship to sacred sculpture, which largely dates to the medieval period. Yet, despite the apparent similarities between the European and Yucatecan traditions, given the multiethnic society of sixteenth- and seventeenth-century Yucatán, I would argue that such an assumption is overly simplistic. It intentionally ignores the indigenous actors, who, perhaps more so than their Spanish overlords, actively contributed to the production of this emerging Yucatecan Catholicism, particularly in their role as stewards of public and private devotion. At best, it is irresponsible to overlook the preexisting belief systems of this sizable native population. Instead, it is more insightful to ask if López de Cogolludo's anecdotes don't in fact suggest that traditional Maya understandings of the sacred potentiality of the material world influenced Yucatecan Catholicism. Recall that for the precontact Mayas, sacred effigies that had been properly created and ritually activated through a series of "caring rites" enacted change in the human community. Moreover, the materiality of appropriate physical objects, deity effigies and later specially selected "stones," effectively absorbed into their matrix the cause of human suffering, such as corporeal ailments. In most of her miracle legends, this is exactly the same numinous quality that is associated with the Virgin of Itzmal.

The question that is left to be answered is how the Creole population conceived of material objects and their link to causal healing. One roundabout way to address this query is to examine exactly how they related religious belief and concepts of illness. In the following chapter I suggest that the Spanish reaction to the 1648 yellow fever epidemic can be anchored—perhaps counterintuitively—to how they conceived of native religious ideologies and their potential as contagions.

❧ 4

Maya Religiosity and Material Contagion

In 1571 the Franciscan friar Diego Valadés left his home monastery of San Francisco in Santiago Tlaltelolco, Mexico, for Europe. He disembarked in Seville, eventually making his way to Paris and then on to Rome. There, in 1575, he was elected procurator general of the Americas to the Holy See, only to serve in this capacity for a short two years.[1] During his tenure Valadés was able to hobnob with the intellectual elite of contemporaneous Europe and build a network of contacts that would eventually allow him to publish his magnum opus, *Rhetorica christiana*, in Perugia and Rome in 1579. This book represents Valadés's life achievement. It is a 394-page tome, replete with twenty-seven elaborate engravings, which appear to be the work of the author himself.[2] Although the friar's text is most frequently referenced as a form of early ethnography, the bulk is devoted to the art of rhetoric, derived from European precedents, but fully placed within its American context.[3] But Valadés provides readers with a detailed, if hyperbolic and fantastical, account, buried within part 4, of Mexica religious practices, with the aim of advocating for the successful use of Christian rhetorical devices to more effectively convert this native population. Here Valadés inserted an illustration, spread over two full pages, that in compositional terms is unique within the Franciscan's larger corpus (fig. 29).

At the most basic level, these two engravings illustrate the threat, possible avoidance, and then probable consequence of idolatrous speech. Valadés himself provides a guide to his complex images within the book's text, allowing his audience to visually and textually follow the friar's argument. The images illustrate an imagined indigenous universe, gallantly ruled over by none other than Satan himself, who sits enthroned at the very top of both images. He is depicted as an overly muscular form with reptilian serpents emerging from his head and open mouth. Smaller-scale devils flank and

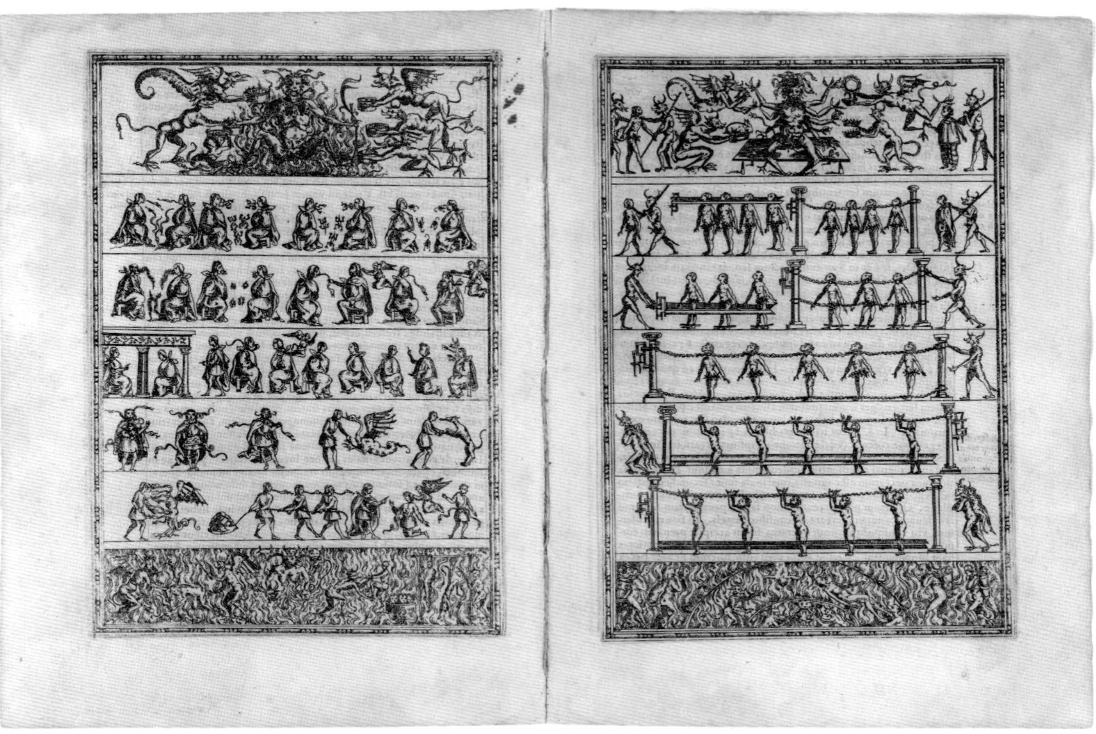

FIG. 29 Valadés, *Rhetorica christiana*, 216–17. Photo courtesy of the John Carter Brown Library at Brown University.

surround the beast, each offering up foodstuffs and precious objects to the grotesquely sexualized being, who sits with spread legs, advertising his animated genitalia. Flames surround him in the first image, immediately reminding viewers of the hellish landscape from where Satan comes. Below Valadés divided the composition into six horizontal registers. The bottommost of these depicts scenes from hell "where each one [of the sinners] receives their punishments in the body and soul."[4] We see devils torturing indigenous bodies, in the right image physically carrying the damned in backpacks to meet their fate.

As evocative and titillating as the engravings are in their entirety, what is most fascinating from my perspective are the middle registers of the left scene. The image can be understood as visualizing Valadés's philosophy of indigenous sin, singularly pictorialized as acts of speech.[5] The second and third topmost registers (fig. 30) depict pairs of indigenous people participating in blasphemous conversations. Valadés blatantly editorializes these exchanges, as he depicts the speech acts as revolting creatures emerging from the mouths of the speakers like vomit. Snakes, frogs, scorpions, centipedes, and

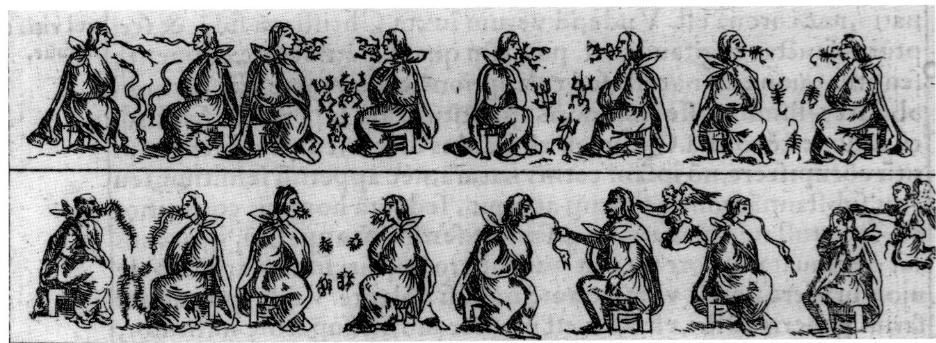

FIG. 30 Valadés, *Rhetorica christiana*, detail, 216. Photo courtesy of the John Carter Brown Library at Brown University.

other unidentifiable creepy-crawlies squirm their way out of their mouths. He states that these false words "leave our mouth like snakes and other pestilential animals for our destruction and of those who listen to us." This theme continues in the third register, where "one can clearly see how death enters through the mouth in those that have said false words."[6]

In this chapter, I use Valadés's engravings as an avenue to explain the permeation of the conceptual link between indigenous religiosity and disease throughout the wider world of colonial New Spain.[7] Only by fully recognizing European understandings of indigenous religion can the impact of the Virgin of Itzmal's 1648 procession to Mérida be fully appreciated. Given that the peninsula's Creole population deemed *traditional* Amerindian religiosity as both amoral and a corporally contaminating entity, it is surprising that during the yellow fever epidemic they summoned the assistance of the Marian icon they knew to be so closely linked to Maya modes of sacrality. As European Mérideños came to define precontact Maya religion as a contagion, it appears that they reframed Maya Catholicism as the antidote for bodily suffering and thus ideal for the spiritual and physical cleansing of a plague-ridden city.

To draw a substantive link between indigenous religion and disease requires a meandering path. I start with the textual sources that make explicit a relation between illness and idolatry, particularly those that reference indigenous religion as a kind of vomit. Then I turn to early modern ideologies of corporeal disease, paying particular attention to how these medical conceptions were imported by the Spanish colonists of Yucatán. The two reigning theories of disease, that of miasmic factors and that of contagion, can be directly charted against the given rationalizations for the continued idolatries. I then turn to the rhetorical devices employed by writers in early colonial central Mexico, who drew fundamental links between the religious and medical professionals and between disease, morally suspect individuals, and idolatry, frequently using metaphors of the body to discuss unorthodox religious practices. The visual world came to reflect and subsequently reinforce a link between illness and precontact rhetorical practices, which were certainly deemed "idolatrous." Finally, the chapter presents an argument for how this conceptual link affected Amerindian peoples, in both their secular and religious lives. I argue that Spanish colonists employed strategies for combating physical disease at the level of the indigenous pueblo to alleviate the threat of the spread of idolatry among recently converted Maya populations. In this regard, Iberian tactics of epidemic avoidance served to dictate colonial administrative practices. In an ironic twist, this rhetorical conflation served to not exactly replicate but bring Spanish conceptions of material artifacts into line with those of the indigenous community, dramatically affecting understandings of Catholic icons.

Idolatrous Vomit

The conceptual link between physical illness and idolatry has a very long history in the Christian world. In fact, the earliest treatise written on the subject, "De Idololatria," makes this conceptual link explicit. Its author, Quintus Septimius Florens Tertullianus (commonly Anglicized as Tertullian), a native of Roman Carthage, converted to Christianity, becoming one of the earliest Christian authors to write in Latin.[8] Among his better-known texts, "De Idololatria" was a succinct treaty that venomously denounced the improper veneration of images, arguing that the commandment ("thou shall have no other gods before me") was a veiled form of a later one ("thou shall not murder"). Arguably, Tertullian set the stage for the rest of Christian history and the religion's relationship to objects, framing the inappropriate use of images as a simulacrum of many of the other mortal sins outlined in the Decalogue.[9]

In the passage most relevant to my historiographical argument, Tertullian states, "I think we are not free of the contagion of idolatry, we whose (not unwitting) hands are found busied in the attendance, or in the honor and service, of demons." And so begins a conceptual trope that lasts millennia, having particular resonance and repercussions for the cultural context that is the subject of this text, colonial Yucatán. In so many ways and despite the reversal of power relations, the ancient north African world of Tertullian prefigured that of the early modern Americas, where the Spanish introduction of Christianity into the polytheistic world of the precontact indigenes created a similarly dramatic societal upheaval. As was the case in the north African world, in the Americas, Christianity mixed with ancient belief, creating a dynamically integrated third religious system ultimately defined by its own cultural codes. The men who introduced this early modern Christianity expressed similar revulsion at the indigenous use of material objects that echoed the concerns of Tertullian when he claimed that idolatry is "the principal crime of the human race."[10]

Primary among these is a letter written to the Spanish Crown in the early seventeenth century, Pedro Sánchez de Aguilar's *Informe contra idolorum cultores del obispado de Yucatán*. The primary motivating question of the friar's letter was to answer Philip IV's query of "whether the Bishop of Yucatán is allowed to arrest, imprison, dispossess, punish, and whip Indians of this Province, idol worshippers, without the secular arm helping."[11] The upshot of his response was an affirmative yes (he even advocated for capital punishment in some cases), but his conclusion follows only five counterarguments, ten distinct reasons in favor of ecclesiastical jurisdiction, and sixteen recommendations for remedying the idolatry. Although Aguilar's work must be weighed within the context of the region's contemporaneous political context, it provides localized insight into how a Creole, born in the middle of the Yucatán and then ordained as a priest, understood exactly what constituted idolatry.[12] His thoughts reveal the semantic and conceptual field in which the very notion of idolatry operated.[13]

It is buried within a final section titled "Remarks on the Inquisitor's List and Directory" that we find Aguilar's conflation of idolatry and illness, as he uses the singular word *vómito* (without penning the implied "of idolatry") to simultaneously reference precontact religious practices and express his absolute revulsion elicited by their discovery, summarized in the following passage: "And what if the recently converted Indians should revert to the vomit? The said Pope Paul III commands that the [indigenous] neophytes who return to the vomit of idolatry will be punished." Aguilar cannot take credit for coining this turn of phrase, as he directly transcribed it from the very papal bull he was referencing, Pope Paul III's "Cupientes Judaeos" of 1542, in which the pontiff refers to ongoing Jewish practices as the "vomit of Judaism."[14] In this he is not dissimilar from other missionaries in the Spanish colonies, all of whom were similarly confronted with the varied and unorthodox nature of indigenous practices.[15] In his use of terms such *vómito* (vomit) and *rebrote* (outbreak), Aguilar summons the semantic field of illness and disease, framing idolatry as a sickness of the spiritual soul rather than an illness of the physical body.

Pope Paul III and the early generations of Mexican religious were operating within an established rhetorical system; as historian Martin Nesvig has convincingly shown, the "disease metaphor" (or what historians of science have termed the "medical metaphor") had been used to describe idolatrous practices since the late Middle Ages and permeated early modern commentaries on Jewish, Islamic, and Amerindian religious traditions.[16] But Aguilar utilizes this viscerally acute image only two times in the 124 pages of his *Informe*, and, as such, it stands out among the more banal and certainly less damning common occurrences of *el delito* (the offense), *el crimen de la idolatría* (the crime of idolatry), and the like.[17] Taken as a rhetorical construction, the phrase appears uniquely repellent among Aguilar's idiomatic formulations, for what other substance on earth communicates such absolute disgust as vomit?

Within the context of early colonial New Spain, the turn of phrase cannot help but conjure up the nightmarish visions of the actual illnesses ravaging indigenous populations, the various epidemics that claimed thousands of native lives, for many of which profuse vomiting was a known early symptom. From the beginning of the sixteenth century (and thus before European contact in Yucatán) through the end of the seventeenth century, the peninsula was plagued by numerous distinct epidemics, among them smallpox, measles, typhoid, and, lastly, yellow fever; a conservative estimate hypothesizes a loss of 25 percent of the Maya population.[18] Concurrent with these epidemics were fraught attempts at a systematized extirpation campaign, launched primarily by the Franciscan order but frequently overseen by the ecclesiastical authorities and their secular soldiers, such as Pedro Sánchez de Aguilar.[19] It is within this context of concurrent idolatry discovery and mass illness that this rhetoric became particularly apt. What remains to be seen is what effect such ideologies had on orthodox Catholic practices, particularly in the context of disease prevention and its relief.

Early Modern Disease

Modern scholars often describe European medical traditions before the discovery of germ theory in the late nineteenth century as a hodgepodge of competing and conflicting ideologies. Afflicted patients relied on seemingly contradictory theories and treatments practiced by medical professionals whom we would term doctors and surgeons, but they were also attended to by lay healers and midwives. Since the Christian Godhead was deemed ultimately responsible for every human illness, whether caused by a regional pandemic or individual disease, spiritual authorities, such as priests, were also consulted, as they were understood to intervene on the patient's behalf.[20]

Most scholars tend to divide these medical professionals into two distinct and sometimes competing camps: one argued for humoric explanations, and another supported theories of material contagions.[21] Like so many other aspects of early modern intellectual culture, all period medical theories and practices were largely derived from the work of the ancients, in this case, primarily the fourth-century-BCE Hippocrates and his followers, later glossed in the second century CE by Galen of Pergamum. Expressed most succinctly in Hippocrates's "On Air, Water, and Places," an unhealthy human body could be attributed to a variety of external factors, such as weather, winds, and sunlight and land, water, and air quality.[22] More to the point, a population's physical character and behavioral patterns could also be directly linked to its specific environmental niche. Hippocrates famously mapped the physical stature and inherent character of tropical populations thusly: "The inhabitants of hollow regions, that are meadowy, stifling, with more hot than cool winds, and where the water used is hot, will be neither tall nor well-made, but inclined to be broad, fleshy, and dark-haired; they themselves are dark rather than fair, less subject to phlegm than to bile. Similar bravery and endurance are not by nature part of their character, but the imposition of law can produce them artificially."[23]

The earth's divergent environments, and thus differential quantities of "heat," also had the potential to variously affect the resident population's humoral balance. Galen understood heat as directly related to "generation and growth," "digestion, distribution of food to the various parts of the body," and, most important, "the generation of humours."[24] A healthy human body was one in which the four humors, described as black bile, yellow bile, phlegm, and blood, were ideally kept in perpetual balance with one another (*eucrasia*). If one humor was dominant or deficient, the result would be an ill body (*discrasia*), one in need of medical intervention. The practice of medicine was aimed at the restoration of corporeal balance, either the reduction of the dominant humor through practices such as bloodletting or the ingestion of foodstuffs and medicines that counteracted humoral deficiencies.

Galen, following Hippocrates's lead, also advocated for "putrid airs," or what would later be termed *miasmas*, as the cause of epidemic disease.[25] Individual susceptibility to these malodors could be directly related the balance of one's humors. By 1348, the date of the Black Plague's first appearance in western Europe, medical practitioners blamed the crisis on putrid air, in addition to being caused by God's wrath for the population's various unrepented sins.[26] Jacme d'Agramont, writing in Catalonia during this initial outbreak, summarizes this theory as such: "I maintain that pestilence is a contra-natural change of the air in its qualities or in its substance; from which arise in living things corruptions and sudden deaths and various maladies in certain determined regions beyond their ordinary."[27] Thus, in this relatively condensed sentence, d'Agramont successfully reconciles theories of humoric causes with divergent environmental factors.

Despite the Galenic school's attribution of epidemics to "putrid airs," it appears that early modern medical professionals simultaneously recognized most epidemic diseases to be caused by some kind of material contagion.[28] Owing to the practical and technological limitations of scientific inquiry (primarily the absence of microscopes powerful enough to view individual cells) exactly *how* seemingly healthy bodies contracted diseases was the debated topic, not *if* a physical element was responsible for the spread of diseases such as the plague and smallpox; of course, the nature of this element had to remain solely conjecture until Louis Pasteur's discoveries in the late nineteenth century. Most clearly articulated in the 1554 *De contagione*, by the Veronese doctor-poet Girolamo Fracastoro, this theory argues for three distinct modes of disease transmission.[29] Disease was caused by material entities he terms "seeds," which were understood as "corrupt substances" and could be passed along and infect the healthy through three distinct modes: (1) bodily contact, (2) from a great distance, or (3) indirect contact. As pointed out by Vivian Nutton, in his first two explanations, Fracastoro was merely engaging with the theories of his predecessors; in fact, Galen himself had hinted at a simplified form of contagion theory in his own works.[30] Fracastoro's real innovation has been understood as his third cause of epidemic transmission, through indirect contact via material elements he termed *fomes*, or "seedlets of contagion" (*seminaria contagionis*). He posited that these invisibly tiny elements could embed themselves in inanimate objects such as clothing or furniture and infect unsuspecting parties. As summarized by Nutton, "His intention in *De contagione* was not to separate himself from the mainstream Galenic tradition but to carry out more deeply the investigations already begun by others."[31]

That the first generation of Spanish colonists of Yucatán carried with them versions of the medical conceptions outlined here, albeit in a simplified, layperson's form, is obvious in numerous archival sources, but it is perhaps most systematically expressed in the responses to Philip II's "Relaciones geográficas" project. Seeking to acquire an encyclopedic grasp of every province in his empire, the king commanded his chronicler-cosmographer of the Council of the Indies, Juan López de Velasco, to compose a fifty-point questionnaire (the "Instrucción") that addressed a variety of topics including local histories, economies, agricultural potential, and so on.[32] Between 1577 and 1581 this "Instrucción" was disseminated to the farthest reaches of Philip's American territories, and the responses slowly began to trickle back to Seville.[33] Question 17 specifically asked local civic authorities, "If the land or site is healthy or sickly, and, if sickly, what is the cause (if it is understood) and the illnesses that commonly occur and the remedies that are often made for them?"[34] While the typical Yucatecan response was rather succinct, when the fifty-two responses are taken in sum, some conceptual patterns emerge.[35]

The first was that illness in the peninsula was most obviously caused by bad air, specifically the *nortes*, violent winds that sweep off the northern shore, typically between the months of January and September. Joan de Aguilar, the encomendero of the Maya village of Mama, summarized it as such: "The primary cause that had been found [for all the illnesses] is the *nortes*, which come with so much coldness that it is a thing the Indians feel a lot; the worse that they suffer are fevers, pains in their chests and heads." These sicknesses were understood to predate the Spanish conquest, since "in ancient times, there had been the same illnesses and other ones among them." But colonists recognized that "the Indians suffer greatly" and that the diseases of the colonial period afflicted the Indian population more violently than the European one. Clearly positioned as a miasmic reasoning, the land itself was also to blame for the poor health of the peninsula's Spanish population. In relating the early settlement history of Dzonot Aké (Dohot) and Tizimin (Tetzimin), Giraldo Díaz de Alpuche explained that "the land is very sickly because of the lagoons and bogs, and, in the span four months, more or less, we had a great illness that this site gave to us and also to our servants, who were *indios* and *indias*; a great quantity of them died, and all the others of us were sick, and this caused the depopulation of this site."[36]

Following the miasmic cause of the nortes, the Maya bathing traditions are frequently cited, echoing Hippocratic and Galenic ideas surrounding the influence of temperature on physical health. Not only did the indigenous population bathe too often; they washed themselves as a remedy for particular illnesses, which, according to the colonists, results only in death. In particular, the Mayas had a habit of bathing in a hot bath (most likely a sweatbath) to alleviate "hot" symptoms such as the high fevers associated with both smallpox and typhus, the two most deadly diseases of the colonial period before the lethal 1648 yellow fever outbreak. Other Spaniards, clearly not as versant in proper Galenic techniques, blamed the tradition of cold bathing to alleviate the hot symptoms. Early modern medicine advocated the use of bathing as a curative in certain circumstances, but, as a general rule, physicians and laypeople alike tended to follow Hippocrates's dictum that "warm bathing invigorates the system whilst in a vigorous state, but otherwise it tends to weaken it."[37]

One colonist followed up on this indigenous misunderstanding of the importance of temperatures in healing practices. In addition to citing the inappropriate use of cold baths, the encomendero of K'inakma (Quinacama) and Muxup'ip' (Moxopipe), Pedro de Santillana, cited the eating of foods deemed cold in the Galenic tradition, specifically the "corn mush that they drink diluted" (*atole*), as ushering death. Unlike the Spaniards, the Mayas clearly did not understand "atole to be very cold in its quality"; instead, this drink was deemed "hot" up until the 1930s.[38] The improper use of purgative techniques is also mentioned repeatedly. Not only do the Mayas apparently not know how to administer the remedy correctly; they don't know the appropriate protocol either. According to the encomendero from Mama, Aguilar, the Mayas "bleed themselves without rhyme or reason and because of this many of them die."[39]

Interestingly, for some Creoles, a direct link was made between the Mayas' physical health and their new spiritual and cultural enlightenment. Writing from the Indian parish of Tekit, encomendero Hernando de Bracamonte declared that his Indians were unhealthy only following the imposition of Spanish lifeways: "After the religious took the ancient customs that they had away from them, saying that they were bad, I have understood that this was very harmful for their bodily health even though it was good for their souls."[40] The singular example he gives is the new requirement of covered bodies. In the past the Mayas "often walked naked," while in Bracamonte's day they were required to dress. According to his logic, since the Mayas are hot (*calurosa*) people because they live in a hot (*caliente*) land, they were better off going nude because now they had no recourse but to bathe continuously to cool off. Like his fellow settlers, Bracamonte attributes his Indians' "chest aches, tummy aches and head colds" to their constant bathing.[41]

What is lacking in the colonists' assessments is evidence that they ascribed or were even aware of the recent development of contagion theories, which were circulating among intellectual circles of Italy, France, and Spain. Given that a royal administrator from the Protomedicato was not stationed in the province until the beginning of the eighteenth century, it is understandable that these geographically provincialized settlers would not have been up on the most recent trends in academic medicine.[42] Clearly, when Creoles were asked to intellectualize the cause of bodily disease in the new province, they invariably relied exclusively on Galenic theories of humoral balances and environmental effect. But, using evidence from both central Mexico and the Yucatán Peninsula, when called on to explain the root cause and enduring presence of the native population's endemic spiritual diseases of the soul, the primary symptom of which was idolatrous practices, colonists utilized both medical frameworks, but perhaps ultimately favored that of contagion.

The Medical Metaphor

While it is to be expected that the early modern Europeans who colonized the American continents brought with them lay understandings of medical theory, what is more surprising is the degree to which the first generation of religious authorities similarly appropriated these notions to conceptualize their own role in Spain's expanding empire. Time and time again, priests from the three represented mendicant orders write of their role in the Americas in terms we would gloss as "spiritual doctors" whose primary objective was the "remedy" of the "disease of idolatry." Bernardino de Sahagún penned what has become the most famous example of the doctor-cum-priest analogy, using it as his conceptual frame in his prologue to his *Historia general de las cosas de Nueva España*; it is arguably the most recognized use of the medical metaphor in colonial Latin America. To justify the need for his lengthy project (and perhaps to rationalize the fact that his order's provincial, Francisco de Toral, had relieved him of his pastoral duties so he could compose his tome), the Franciscan relied on the metaphor of disease to describe the idolatrous practices of his Amerindian neophytes: "The doctor cannot apply with certainty medicines to the sick without first knowing what humor or cause came before the sickness; in this way, the good doctor should be educated in the knowledge of medicines and in sicknesses in order to suitably apply the contrary medicine to each sickness. Preachers and confessors are doctors of souls; in order to cure the spiritual sicknesses, they should know the spirit of the medicines and of the spiritual illnesses."[43] The Franciscan's allusions to the Hippocratic-Galenic school is inherent in his use of "humors." He was also clearly knowledgeable of that school's theory of curing with opposites: "the contrary medicine." What is more intriguing is Sahagún's idea that precontact traditions should be understood as "spiritual illnesses." The friars working in central Mexico understood their neophytes to be spiritually unwell, and so they framed themselves as doctors, professionals capable of first diagnosing and then curing diseased elements. Sahagún does not explicitly reference the exact nature of his intended spiritual medicine, but in his deployment of "preachers and confessors" to describe the army of healing friars, he clearly alludes to their rhetorical prowess as being integral to the cure.[44]

The art of oratory became a kind of spiritual remedy, throwing into relief the evocative illustration that introduced this chapter, Diego Valadés's schematic representation of indigenous rhetoric, imaged as a regurgitation of despicable animals. This conceptual link between rhetorical practices and disease described earlier is clearly referenced by the friar, but here precontact rhetoric itself is posed as the very disease the friars are trying to cure. This mode of representing speech immediately suggests the eloquently rendered "speech scrolls" of the native painting tradition, whereby orators were imaged with spirals emanating from their mouths to register simple speech or more flowery scrolls to evoke more elaborate oral traditions such as poetry or song. Even in his compositional choice of multiple registers, Valadés appears to be intentionally repositioning the precontact pictorial tradition as a satanic practice, since late postclassic codices and murals frequently rely on this organizational scheme to schematically diagram discrete narrative events.

There is a causal relationship between Valadés's engravings and a folio illustration from the Florentine Codex's pictorial predecessor, the "Primeros memoriales." Composed between 1558 and 1561, this manuscript in similarly encyclopedic in scope, albeit not as lengthy as the later Florentine Codex.[45] Sahagún's indigenous collaborators described in detail and provided a full folio drawing (with color wash) of Atamalqualiztli (fig. 31), "The Eating of the Water Tamales," a ritual performed every eight years to honor the deity of water and agricultural fecundity, Tlaloc.[46] In the accompanying textual description, the rite is recounted as encompassing the expected abstinence and fasting, followed by the dancing of performers elaborately costumed as "hummingbirds, butterflies, bees, flies, birds, beetles, dung beetles," and so on, donning various kinds of tamales worn as ritual necklaces. The native informants then go on to describe a curious ethnographic detail, relevant to Valadés's imagining of indigenous idolatry. The participants placed, before an effigy statue of Tlaloc, a pool of "water which was filled with snakes and frogs. . . . Those called Mazateca each swallowed the snakes, which were alive, and the frogs. They seized the frogs with their mouths, not their hands; they just chewed them up. . . . And they rewarded those who swallowed the snakes."[47] This

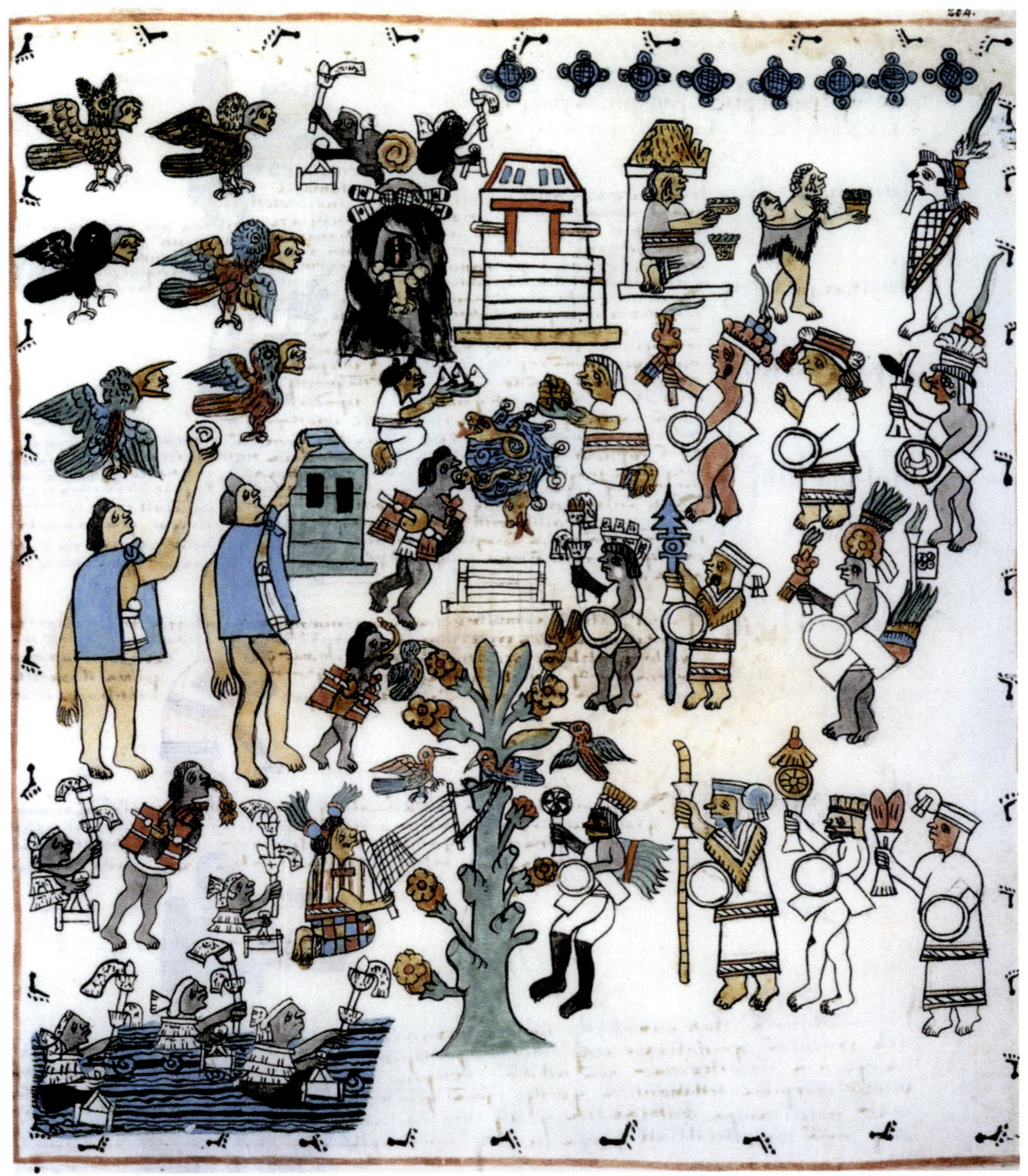

FIG. 31 The Atamalqualiztli rite, in Sahagún, "Primeros memoriales," 254r. MS. 3280, Real Biblioteca del Palacio Real, Madrid. Photo: author.

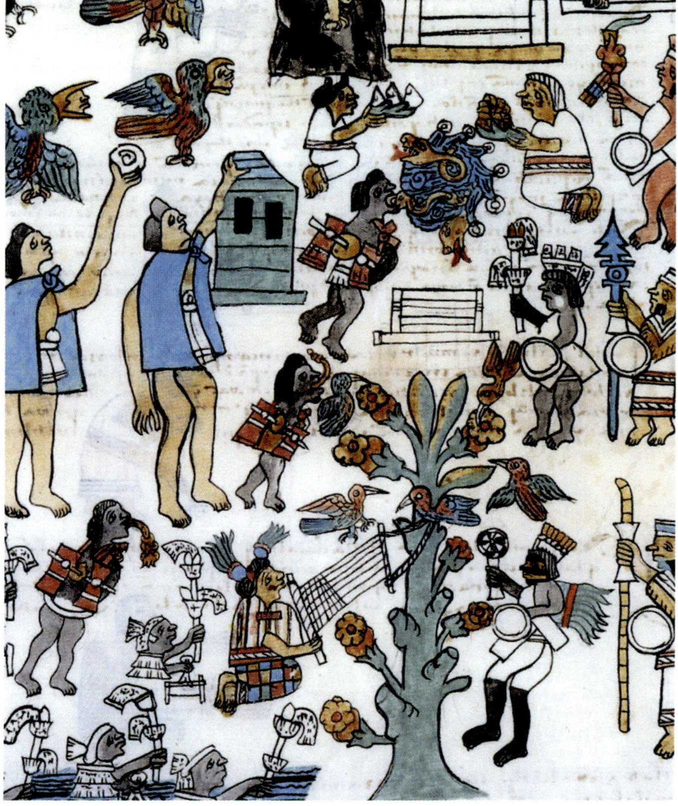

exact ritual moment was portrayed toward the center of the Atamalqualiztli image, where two ritual participants, visually differentiated by their black tinted skin, consume live snakes (fig. 32). Just below and to the left, an additional black individual appears to vomit a liquid substance that was rendered in the same orange hue as the serpents above, presumably representing their regurgitated remains.

It is impossible to definitively argue that Valadés was referencing these kinds of ethnographic details in his own visualization of precontact idolatries, but the similarities between the ritual details of the Atamalqualiztli rite and the engravings included in the *Rhetorica christiana* provide a tempting avenue to argue for direct intellectual and artistic influence.[48] What is certain, however, is that Valadés intended to transmit to his audience the conception of Mexican rhetoric, and by extension idolatry, as a diseased entity, a vile force that he represented in pictorial terms as a kind of vomiting of the earth's most repugnant creatures.[49] He even goes so far as to use the very term *pestilentia* in his description of blasphemy, describing those beings as "pestilential animals."[50] Animals, especially reptilian creatures, in their early modern conception as inherently immoral, easily lent themselves as avatars of dangerous entities such as diseases of the body or soul.[51] Idolatry is here cast as a plague of the mouth, an oral affliction visualized by reptilian vomit, that only the word of God (or a helpful angel sent by God) was capable of curing.[52]

In Mexico City, the link between disease and morally suspect human actors is also evident in a variety of other sources, but in the interest of space I provide only two examples, one penned by a secular source and the other religious.[53] Writing in 1577 to the Spanish Crown, Dr. Don Sancho Sánchez Muñón provided the clearest example of this medical link to negative cultural influences. According to Muñón, one of the greatest challenges to the spiritual integrity of burgeoning Mexico City, and by extension the entire viceroyalty of New Spain, was "the multitude of free mulatos, mestizos, blacks, and criollos that there are in these kingdoms." He saw their very presence and unmediated movement as "something that causes apprehension," because of his inherently racist assumption that people of the various mixed castas were somehow less morally sound than those of pure Spanish blood. He goes on to provide the king with a possible alleviation of this problem, the physical removal of these questionable elements from the social world. While this isn't a provocative suggestion (it is often repeated throughout Spain's territories, and we'll see a Yucatecan example of this later), what is intriguing is the use Muñón makes of a medical analogy: "The remedy that this could have, it seems to me, is to do in this land that which the doctor does for a body too overfilled, which is to diminish the too abundant blood and bad humors that for being a lot cannot be naturally used up."[54] By placing this social problem within the framework of Hippocratic-Galen medical theory, Muñón directly engages with the conceptual field outlined earlier, one in which morally suspect comportment, the outward sign of one's internalized moral fiber, is framed within the ideology of corporeal illness.

This linkage is even more concrete in Franciscan friar Gerónimo de Mendieta's retelling of the waves of epidemics that affected the indigenous population in the early years of the conquest.[55] According to the friar, the first massive smallpox outbreak was introduced by the crew of Pánfilo de Narvaez's 1520 expedition, sent by the Cuban governor, Diego Velázquez de Cuéllar, to bring Hernando Cortés to justice. Not surprisingly, Mendieta targets a morally questionable member of this expedition as spreading the disease, an African slave who was infected when they disembarked on Mexican soil.[56] In due course, the epidemic spread *pueblo a pueblo*, until "there wasn't a single corner left healthy in all of this New Spain."[57]

Like Sahagún, Mendieta framed himself and his fellow clergy as doctors of souls. Just as suspect morality was responsible for the physical disease sweeping the land, spiritual guidance could be used to combat the diseases of those souls. According to the Franciscan, the rampant idolatry was the greatest cause of Spanish concern, "whose remedy and medicine is the Sacred Inquisition."[58] But soon after Mendieta penned these words, the Spanish Crown made it illegal for the Inquisition to prosecute indigenous bodies, prompting the religious debate discussed by Aguilar and necessitating a reimagining of possible solutions to the problem of indigenous idolatry.[59] Interestingly, once their judicial authority had been severely circumscribed, Spanish colonists turned to remedies associated with the outbreak of bodily epidemics to cure the spiritual diseases that continued to similarly ravage native communities.

Diseased Morality and the Precautionary Measures

In addition to deeply seated biases about the intellectual capabilities of the native population, one of the most frequently cited reasons for the continuation of idolatrous practices among supposedly converted peoples in Yucatán (and beyond) was, first, the dire need for friars in the region, specifically friars who spoke the Mayan language. In a 1575 letter from the governor Francisco de Velásquez Gijón to the Spanish Crown, the politician summarizes it as such: "There is a great lack of doctrine because most of the [Franciscan] superiors have ten or twelve thousand souls that come to the benefit of the sacraments . . . and there are few religious who are *lenguas*."[60] A second reason was the excuse of *poco castigo* (too little punishment), repeated again and again; the defense of religiously dictated corporal punishment was the motivating factor in Aguilar's tome.[61] Intriguingly, following a Hippocratic model, the Yucatec landscape itself is also to blame for the numerous idolatries discovered during the first hundred years of missionary efforts; the Mayas were continually returning to their precontact ways because the regional topography afforded them the opportunity.

While Hippocrates was clearly writing centuries before the European American encounters of the fifteenth and sixteenth centuries, his view on populations of tropical climates is clearly echoed in colonial-period discussions of indigenous capabilities, specifically those of the Yucatán Peninsula.[62] Like the locales discussed by Hippocrates, the province was also "low-lying," had an abundance of hot winds, and was replete with warm coastal waters. Its inhabitants were deemed lazy and capable of work only when directed by their overlords. In the words of Bishop Mercado to the king of Spain, the Maya Indians had "little capacity and even less liking to the things of the faith and religion." The nature and character of the local environment had a direct impact on this human temperament and its related behaviors. In a 1605 letter to the Crown, Governor Carlos de Luna y Arellano explained that the heresies were rampant in southern Yucatán because "the mountainous land is terrible and full of caves and very ripe for similar sins."[63] The peninsula's physical topography not only provided a convenient location for clandestine religious activities but also influenced recent neophytes in demonic ways.[64]

Colonists adopted the rhetoric of disease to conceptualize the ongoing idolatries. Beyond the landscape itself, they deemed idolatrous practices an illness in need of specific cures. "Remedy," "sickness," and "affliction" are themes that pervade this discourse. In 1604 Andres Fernández de Castro, provincial of the Maya church in Valladolid, produced a probanza and sent it to the Spanish Crown. A witness who provided testimony of Castro's contributions to God and country described them in medical terms, likening Castro to a spiritual doctor who successfully cured the resident Mayas' disease: "He is vicar and judge of the Indian's idolatries, to which he has come with great zeal, whose cause and by love with which he always came to *remedy* their needs, visiting them and scolding them for their *sicknesses* . . . punishing and *remedying* with all of his ability and charity."[65] In another instance, when discussing idolatrous populations, a secular friar, Antonio de Arroyo, who worked in the Maya village of Peto for more than twenty years, described his parishioners using the medical trope of affliction: "The idolatry of which almost all of the gentiles are afflicted."[66] Perhaps even more evocative are Bishop Mercado's words, composed in 1606, to the Audiencia de México. Among other issues that beleaguered the mission, the bishop lamented the continued idolatries of the Mayas, specifically decrying their use of the fermented honey-based beverage, balché, in ancient rituals, describing it as a "contagious stench."[67] Clearly, in his use of the word "contagious," Mercado understood these practices to be transmittable, like a deadly plague.

Although the rhetorical structures and medical metaphors utilized by this handful of Yucatec colonists evinces the conceptual conflation of disease and idolatry, the simplicity of their words do not reveal how and if this discourse impacted everyday practice. The *Relación geográfica* responses to question 17 reveal that colonists understood the environment and the Mayas' poor understanding of Galenic medicine to be the primary causes of corporeal diseases. Alternatively, when it came to idolatry, the primary disease of the soul, these same colonists applied the complementary model of contagion to prevent its ongoing spread.[68] Both the official ordinances and individualized punishments very frequently have one thing in common: they appear to replicate the same tactics frequently taken by European communities as steps toward ensuring the avoidance of mass epidemics, such as the Black Plague.

Academic literature on the Black Death is vast, and I cannot do it justice within the space limitations of this chapter.[69] For the purposes of my argument, however, I will make a few salient points. The first is that although the majority of the medical professionals blamed the spread of the plague on putrid air, the actions taken at the community level to avoid the spread of the disease clearly stemmed from a recognition that the plague was contagious, that direct bodily contact or secondary contact through clothes and the like (à la Fracastoro) was the primary cause. One only has to remember the medieval tactic of burning a deceased victim's clothing and bed linens to fully appreciate to what degree individuals believed in the notion of invisible "seeds." As early as the fifteenth century, Spanish medical authorities touted physical distance as the most effective measure against avoiding infection. In the now infamous words of Dr. Alonso de Chirino: "The most important thing is to get out of the [infected] land where the disease generates itself or is generating, and as quickly as you can."[70] My second point is that once news of a distant outbreak reached administrative personnel, their primary response was that of quarantine; city gates would be closed (or in some cases erected), thereby making the likelihood of infected individuals entering civic space a near impossibility.[71] In port cities, individuals on recently docked ships would not be allowed to leave to confines of their vessel until the threat of disease had passed[72] Large public gatherings were deemed illegal, as close contact between individuals could result in an outbreak. Above all else, air, winds, and environment aside, physical contact with infected individuals or their effects was understood to keep the march of the disease at a steady pace.

In a similar vein the most common tactic deployed in an attempt to halt the spread of idolatry was the avoidance of contact between indigenous neophytes and nearly every other "kind" of colonial actor, mestizos, mulatos, blacks, and especially un-Christianized or apostate Mayas. Like in the colonial capital, Mexico City, in the provinces mere communication with morally suspect individuals could entice a Christianized Maya to return to their traditional cultural practices. The threat of this contact prompted a series of what could be called spatial ordinances as early as 1552. Sent by the Audiencia de Guatemala in response to the Franciscan accusation of abusive practices wrought by resident encomenderos, royal *oidor* (judge) Tomás López Medel administered the region's first set of official decrees.[73] Today López Medel's decrees are preserved only in transcription, published as a discrete chapter in López de Cogolludo's *Historia de Yucathán*.[74] While it is inarguable that the ordinances certainly carried administrative weight, the title of López de Cogolludo's chapter, "It Was Necessary to Make Laws with Royal Authority, in Order for the Indians to Avoid Some Rites of Their Gentility," suggests that, from the Franciscan perspective, the edicts were simultaneously related to the avoidance of idolatry.[75] López Medel's first ordinance insists that the indigenous leadership, the "Caziques, y Governadores, y Principales, y Alguaziles," reside and stay in the pueblos over which they govern and that they not be absent from them for an extended period (more than forty or fifty days). The unspoken fear was that these indigenous leaders would vanish into the monte to conduct idolatrous rites, initiating other Mayas into their cult. López Medel went on to argue that "one of the things that has impeded and impedes *policía*" (living in a civilized manner) is the manner of the Indians living so far apart from one another in the monte. As a resolution, he proposed that the Mayas be forced to settle in organized towns, defined by a strict traza, in well-made houses. These Mayas were disallowed from moving between pueblos, with the excuse given that "by moving from one pueblo to another, they are made vagabonds, escaping from the doctrine."[76]

Of course, this notion stems directly from the idea that the native population needed to be Hispanicized as well as Christianized to be a worthy subject of the Spanish Crown, but I would argue that these kinds of ordinances also expose a Spanish fear of unmediated contact between Indian neophytes and potential spiritual contaminants. For example, in a letter of 1601, Governor Diego de Velasco describes the following scenario: "The greatest nuisance the Indians make are those that live as in their gentility, hidden in the fragmented mountains, some having secret communication with those who are Christians and living in *doctrinas* (mission towns) with all the caution that could be mustered they are now imprisoned, they don the hairstyles that they used in their gentility, [and are] circumcised, which is something that has never been found in this land."[77] Thus, by coming into direct contact with the uninitiated brothers, Christianized Mayas immediately returned to their heathen ways.

These decrees were reformalized nearly three decades later, in 1583, when the Audiencia de México tasked oidor Dr. Garcia de Palacio with a similar commission.[78] In many senses Garcia de Palacio approached his task with a more dire sense of its urgency; given the ongoing discovery of indigenous idolatry in the intervening thirty years, it was clear that his predecessor's decrees had not fully resulted in "the Indians of these parts being in concert and *policia*." As such, the oidor ruled with a slightly firmer hand, explicitly prohibiting any indigenous movement away from Christian spaces that had previously been legal, for example, to tend to distant milpas. More specifically, Garcia de Palacio targeted indigenous individuals who, to meet tribute demands, left their assigned towns to fish or to procure salt, dyewood, chocolate, or indigo. These tribute obligations unwittingly gave the Mayas ample opportunity to, in Garcia de Palacio's words, "go to the monte to idol worship."[79] To alleviate this threat, he commanded the indigenous officials not to consent to their residents participating in such unassuming activities. All access to the dangerous monte must be closed.[80]

So infectious was this plague of idolatry that even fully confirmed Catholic Spaniards were at risk of affliction.[81] A lengthy case heard by the Inquisition in Mexico City involved the religious crimes of Juan Vela de Aguirre, the Creole encomendero of the Maya village of Homun.[82] Aguirre became romantically involved with a Maya woman, Magdalena Chan, and eventually took up residence with her. Magdalena's father, Andres Chan, was the "great priest of all of these idolatries and a publicly known witch doctor," who had repeatedly had run-ins with religious authorities for engaging in idolatrous activities.[83] According to the witness testimony of six resident Mayas, Aguirre was strongly influenced by his father-in-law and began engaging in ancient Maya rituals, was eventually caught, and then charged with "idolatry and witchcraft." The detail given in the case file is intriguing, prompting one to trust its veracity, despite the fact that the indigenous testimony may have been extracted "under duress." For example, Aguirre is specifically charged in three distinct instances of ingesting food and drink previously offered to Maya deities. The Mayan names for specific objects utilized during the course of the ceremony are given, such as a particular kind of bread and a beverage, *tutul uah* (*tutul wah*) and *huisil haa* (*wisil haa'*), as well as descriptions of the ritual vessels used. From the Spanish perspective, cases such as these stood as cautionary tales for how powerful the disease of idolatry actually was. Not only were indigenous Mayas at risk for backsliding; fully Catholic Spaniards were as well. Aguirre's Catholic status could not protect him from this deadly disease: isolation from Christian Spanish society and continual contact with diseased indigenous elements resulted in his inevitable infection.

The Spanish fear of contact inevitably brings up issues of pragmatics, and it becomes necessary to question exactly how these colonists conceived of the mechanics of idolatry's spread. This is extremely difficult to access in the extant archival sources, but when Spanish acts are analyzed, an answer emerges. For example, Garcia de Palacio's ordinances seem to suggest that "seeds" of idolatrous sins could be carried in the materiality of Maya-made goods and commodities; not only did he replicate his predecessor's decree that forbade Spaniards, mestizos, mulatos, and blacks to live among the Mayas, but he also disallowed these same colonists from selling or buying anything in native homes.[84] Beyond the physical contact between human subjects, the exchange of material objects or foodstuffs was deemed hazardous for the potential spread of this spiritual plague. Punishment for such an infraction was strict: for Spaniards, a fine of twenty pesos; for Mayas, fifty lashings. One could argue that López Medel's own decree that Spaniards should burn Maya villages that were depopulated also spoke to this assumption. Like the burning of plague victims' personal effects, the fiery demolition of abandoned Maya homes assured the destruction of whatever idolatrous essence still inhabited that space.[85]

There was, however, always hope for a cure. Inherent in some of these "cures" is the assumption that living in a purely Spanish environment could potentially heal a diseased soul. In his probanza of 1606, Rodrigo Tinoco describes a case he oversaw that dealt with the physical removal of a spiritual contagion from the Maya village of Telchac: One evening the local cacique held a fiesta at his home and served an alcoholic beverage, in all likelihood balché, but described as a "jug of wine" (*botijuela de vino*).[86] At some point in the evening, two Maya women got into a scuffle; one was unnamed, and the other, Maria Dzul, was an intoxicated widow from the neighboring village of Sinanché. During the fight Maria tore the burlap shirt off her combatant and the next day was brought before the local alcaldes. Tinoco, in concert with the local indigenous leaders, responded to the public outcry by exiling her to the convent of nuns in Mérida, where she presumably served as a domestic servant. While it is impossible to know from the admittedly abbreviated account the subtle intricacies of the social life of Telchac, it is clear that the friar understood physical removal and subsequent quarantine as the only method of saving both the community and the individual.[87] Treated as a diseased and infectious element, Dzul was materially exiled from her home village and placed in the cloistered center of feminized Catholicism, where she could be cured. The purity of this religious space had the potential of absorbing and thus eradicating Dzul's spiritual disease through the sustained contact of orthodox Christianity.

In addition to the technique of spiritual quarantine, the Spaniards employed another strategy to avoid an infestation of idolatry, seemingly taken from the "plague playbook." This was to disallow Maya peoples from gathering in large numbers, in an attempt to avoid the kind of debauchery described in the Maria Dzul case. López Medel understood the necessity for this, having decreed that no Indian of "any condition," Christian or not, should "host such assemblies, and meetings." Moreover, he commanded that at these kinds of events (should they occur), it was forbidden for the indigenous elite to "preach, nor publicly teach, nor secretly [enact] their rituals and past heathenisms, nor things of their gods, nor renew the memory of them," since the fear was that knowledge of these ancient practices would then be "stirred up" (*para alçarse [alzarse]*), and infection would occur.[88] Garcia de Palacio was even more explicit when he stated that "the fiestas and other gatherings that occur far from their houses . . . have resulted in some diseases and other inconveniences in disservice to God our Lord."[89] This kind of decree was necessary, since the Mayas had proven to "remain dissolute and distant from the Christian Doctrine," while "memory of their past rituals had stayed fresh in their minds."[90]

Conclusion

In the historical theater of New Spain, two of the defining characteristics of sixteenth-century colonialism—epidemic disease and ongoing idolatries—appear to have operated in a collapsed conceptual sphere, whereby a conflated relationship existed between the two distinct phenomena. I have argued that this can be seen in period rhetorical devices, simple turns of phrase, and visual culture. To understand the ongoing outbreaks of indigenous idolatry, Spanish colonists turned to a convenient and relevant intellectual model, that of bodily illness, to explain the mechanics of heretical transmission. Given the communal memory in the Iberian world of mass epidemics such as the plague, Spanish colonists rightly understood that widespread civil and religious unrest could be blamed on an unseen enemy: "seeds of contagion," invisible to the naked eye but still threatening to unsuspecting populations. Similarly, in New Spain another invisible contagion, the workings of the devil and his blind minions, could be responsible for infecting otherwise healthy souls.

Given this ideological relationship, the fact that Creole residents called on a Maya icon to assist during the 1648 crisis is all the more powerful. While traditional Maya religion was deemed a disease, its counterpart, orthodox Catholicism as practiced by indigenous peoples, was seen as a bodily antidote. What remains to be seen, however, is how Maya peoples viewed this event and the icon that served as its protagonist.

⁊ℰ 5

Maya Conceptions of Mary's Birth

In mid-October 1768, Marta Mis, a Maya resident of the town of Ixil (map 1), lay dying. In her last hours Marta's family members summoned the town's notary, a Maya man, to take her last will and testament. A comparison between this document and those composed by Marta's neighbors reveals that, in relative terms, she was among the wealthiest residents of Ixil.[1] Having predeceased her husband, Marta divided her worldly goods between him and their four sons, one daughter, and their spouses.[2] Monetarily, her most precious possessions were two house plots with accompanying wells and milpa lands, all of which her parents and in-laws had previously bequeathed to Marta. Before dying, she divvied these lands among her children, while also bestowing to them a wooden chest, her house's central beam, a dress, and a petticoat.

As a final thought, immediately preceding "the end of my statement in my will," Marta included a last request. She determined that her middle son, Nicholas Yam, be given "our sacred lady," a statue of the Virgin Mary. Given the formulaic nature of this notarial genre, and its traditional lack of descriptive elaboration, Marta's ultimate bestowal leaves many unanswered questions. She reveals nothing about her statue's physicality: How large was the icon? Of what was it made? What did it look like? What advocation of Mary did it resemble? She is similarly silent about its production: Who was responsible for its creation? Where was it carved and painted?

Colonial-period domestic statuary from Yucatán has not fared well in the centuries that separate Marta's death from our own time—and the fate of her valued Madonna remains unknown. I imagine that Marta's statue may have resembled the humble icons crafted later in the peninsula, during the nineteenth century. Marta's Mary is likely to have resembled figure 33, an Inmaculada, whose green cape is a rather shoddy overpainting of her originally blue gown. This roughly hewn statue represents the Virgin Mary in her most simplified form, a conically shaped robe that sprouts a human head and arms, hands nearly clasped at her chest. The small rectilinear pedestal (likely added at a later date) completes the form.

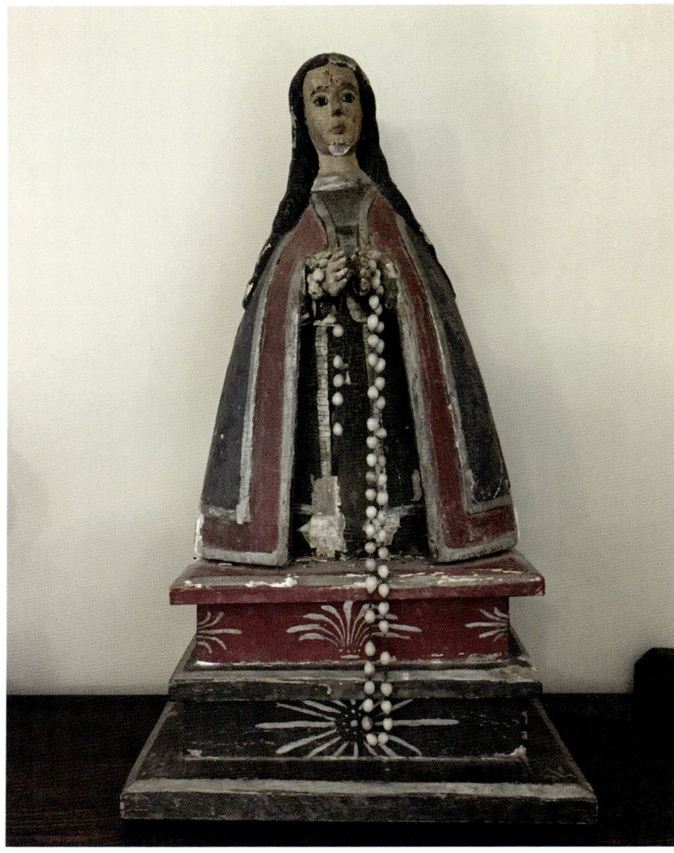

Even more difficult to ascertain from Marta's will is the religious use to which the icon was put. How did family members use this icon? Was she dressed, fed, given offerings? Did the family speak to her? Petition her? For what did they ask? And, finally, what did Marta think of when she looked at her Virgin Mary? In listing it as her final object, was she referencing its elevated worth?[3] What kind of emotive response did she garner? How was she understood to represent the religious system of Marta's family and the Maya population of late-eighteenth-century Ixil?

Marta's will of 1768 exists as one of a very small handful written in Yucatec Mayan that explicitly mentions a specific Catholic image—in this case, a diminutive duplicate of the Virgin of Itzmal. The will's brevity and lack of description stands in stark contrast to Spanish sources that describe Itzmal's Marian icon, such as Lizana's and López de Cogolludo's texts, whose length, depth, and complexity allowed me to reconstruct her early history and analyze the religiosity she inspired. But Maya voices are lacking from these European accounts, silencing indigenous perceptions and receptions of this new Catholic deity's introduction. To fill this historical gap, this chapter brings together all extant native sources of the virgin, either in a specified sculptural form or as the abstracted deity, to try to ascertain how the Mayas of Yucatán came to accept the Christian mother of God.[4]

I begin this final chapter by analyzing the abbreviated account of the Virgin of Itzmal's birth, as recorded in "The Book of Chilam Balam of Chumayel." For the Yucatán's native population, the installation of the Virgin Mary was deemed a cosmogonic event. That is, the Mayas framed the appearance of this new deity within traditional modes of mythical history that viewed the expanse of time as ever-repeating cycles dominated by differing supernatural forces.[5] I argue that Maya devotees were particularly attracted to Marian icons of the Immaculate Conception, as this particular advocation had a clear resonance with multiple methods of precontact ritual engagement. These modes allowed for the Maya population to associate statues of the virgin as particularly capable of serving as healing icons and thus interceding on its behalf during the 1648 epidemic and subsequent regional crises. I end the chapter by briefly turning to a later icon, the Virgin of Tabí, a miraculous Inmaculada who appeared in the first years of the seventeenth century. The icon's origins and the visual culture produced in response to her growing popular following synthesized the peninsular religiosity that had been developing for the previous century and a half.

The Birth of the Maya Mary

During the course of the eighteenth century, Maya elders and intellectuals desperately endeavored to preserve native knowledge systems amid the violence of colonization and forced conversion to Catholicism. One mode of this effort was the transformation of accordion-folded, hieroglyphic codices into European-style books, with the simultaneous transcription of hieroglyphic text into Latinized Mayan. Community leaders created collections of transcribed precontact writings, bound into manuscripts, known collectively today as the "Books of Chilam Balam." In addition to including the precontact subjects such as ritual prognostications and astronomical observations, these native authors often supplemented them with descriptions of historical events that had transpired following the arrival of Europeans, as they strove to continue, albeit clandestinely, their traditional modes of knowledge production, preservation, and dissemination.

The Maya elders of a small village called Chumayel (map 1) included one such section in their community's manuscript; they penned an abbreviated account of the early years of Spanish colonization. Amid the discussion of the "depopulation" (*paxal*; *paxi*) of the peninsula's monumental cities such as Chichén Itzá, Uxmal, Cobá, and Ake in the terminal classic period (circa 1000 CE), the author follows up by inserting a pithy aside that describes the establishment of the virgin's cult at Itzmal. The author then maintains that it was at this point in peninsular history when the Itza dynasty fled the province, eventually establishing a new capital city to the south at Tayasal (Tah Itza), located in today's central Guatemala.[6] In terms of a true chronology, the author's anecdote is decidedly out of place, but this is typical in "Chilam Balam" nonlinear narration:[7]

> Then descended[8] the daughter, the divine flood of the Lord of the Sky, the female lord, the female virgin, the female incorruptible one. And then the lord said, "the netted bag[9] descends; Kinich Kakmo will not be given form[10] as a lord." He shook him off the tree. Today the incorruptible female, the merciful female, will be given form. The thick thing descends; the cord descends, coming from the sky. The word descends, coming from the sky. Like so, blood[11] was tied.[12] And the Lord got rid of him because the towns completed their tribute; they doubled it themselves. It was never again depopulated.[13]

When compared to his Spanish contemporaries' words, this Maya author's account of the virgin's arrival at Itzmal is admittedly condensed. For modern readers its meaning is also elusive, veiled as it is in the typical Maya shield of metaphor and word play. In his choice of a handful of key terms, however, we are granted a privileged insight into how the native scribe incorporated this Catholic deity into his hybridized religious framework. In the next few pages, I argue that, at the most basic level, the appearance of the Virgin at Itzmal mirrors the earlier creation of Maya deities in other extant pictorial and textual sources. As such, the Maya author effectively framed the introduction of the Virgin Mary as a kind of creation narrative, signaling a new era of localized religious history. It will become apparent that he made very little differentiation between old gods and the new; his word choice suggests that the Maya author conceived of the Catholic icon in terms that replicated traditional concepts of materialized divinity.

The scribe makes abundantly clear that where once Kinich Kakmo reigned (Itzmal), the Virgin Mary now effectively dominated the town's religious life. To describe this act, he utilized conjugations of the term *emel*, which can be defined by a variety of English words and phrases but essentially means "to descend," "to lower," "to fall," or "to set" like the sun.[14] Kinich Kakmo was a solar deity, the avian animal familiar of Itzamnaaj, to whose worship Itzmal was previously dedicated. As such, to describe his removal from power as a solar-like "setting" is appropriately evocative. Confusingly, the same verb is also used to describe the virgin's assumption of authority. From the Western mindset, this might seem contradictory, but a short segue into creation narratives can clarify this apparent ambiguity.

Much has been written on Maya creation narratives, so I will limit my discussion to only what appears relevant to the discussion at hand. Most scholars agree, utilizing

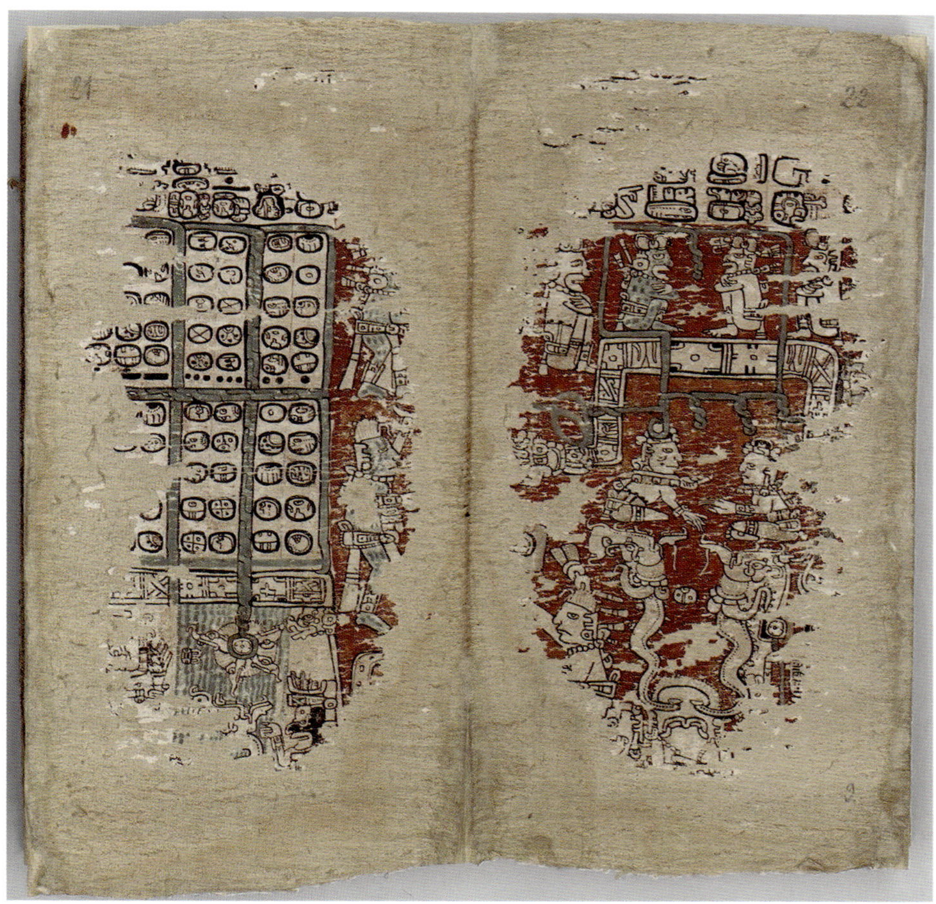

FIG. 34 Artist unknown, Paris Codex, postclassic period, fols. 21, 22. Bibliothèque nationale, Paris. Photo: author.

a variety of visual and textual sources (both precontact and colonial), that the Mayas conceived of a universe that had been created and destroyed numerous times; at the time of contact most Mayas thought of themselves as living in the fourth age, or "sun," of the cosmos's existence. At the dawn of each new era, a suite of primordial gods descended on the earth, frequently described in ink or paint as climbing or falling down entwined ropes that reached to the sky.[15] In visual terms, this is most clearly expressed on folios 21 and 22 of the Paris Codex (fig. 34). Although badly preserved, the images, to be read from right to left, illustrate the destruction and subsequent creation of the cosmos. At the top of the image on folio 22 (shown here on the right), the Maya artist represented the primordial creator couple (Itzamnaaj and Ixchel) seated on a reptilian sky band, facing each other. They are surrounded by a complicatedly entwined blue cord that extends below the sky into the terrestrial realm of the cosmos. The scene continues

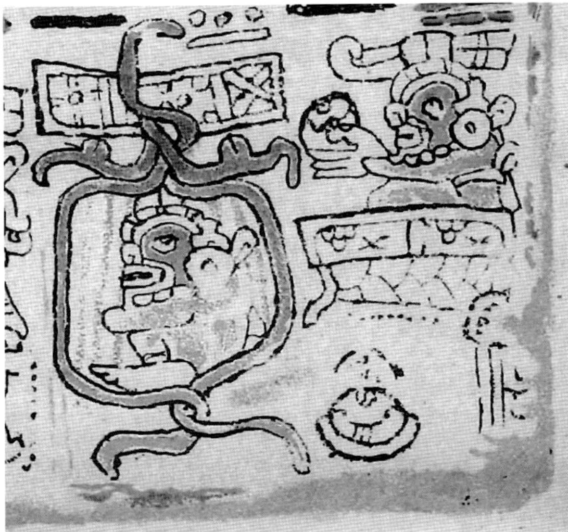

on the next folio (here on the left), where the sun descends from that same blue cord
to emerge "from the Underworld . . . into the sky." As Gabrielle Vail and Christine
Hernández have convincingly argued, to a late postclassic viewer, these kinds of ropes,
be they of cloth, vegetable matter, or even serpents' bodies, would have immediately
registered notions of a new creation.[16] This is evident in images such as the Madrid
Codex, on folio 10, where a deity is born via his descent on entwined cords from the
celestial realm (fig. 35). Since at least the late classic period Maya *ahuahob* (rulers) envi-
sioned themselves—the very materiality of their bodies—to be conceptually linked to
the supernatural world and deified ancestors by a system of connected cords or ropes.[17]

It is within this complex intertextual world of mythical history that the Chumayel
scribe operated. While surely a hybridized colonial artifact (given its repeated transcription over the course of multiple generations), the manuscript embodies a Maya
view of the virgin's birth at Itzmal. That the Chumayel author describes the virgin's
appearance as a descent from the sky via a "thick thing" (*sum*) and "cord" (*tab*) betrays
the fact that he understood this event as something akin to a new world beginning.[18]
In his reference to her as the mother of the martyr, Jesus Christ, the scribe differentiates the virgin from other Maya goddesses, such as the primordial Ixchel. In doing so
he signals that she is accepted as a distinct deity recognized on her own accord, not as
a hybridized colonial religious personage. He also indicates that Christian narratives
have been fully incorporated into indigenous religious belief, and thus the introduction of a Catholic personage could be reframed as a new era of Maya existence.

A final linguistic clue confirms that the installation of the Virgin of Itzmal was
deemed a cosmogonic event: the Chumayel author's use of the phrase "divine flood" as

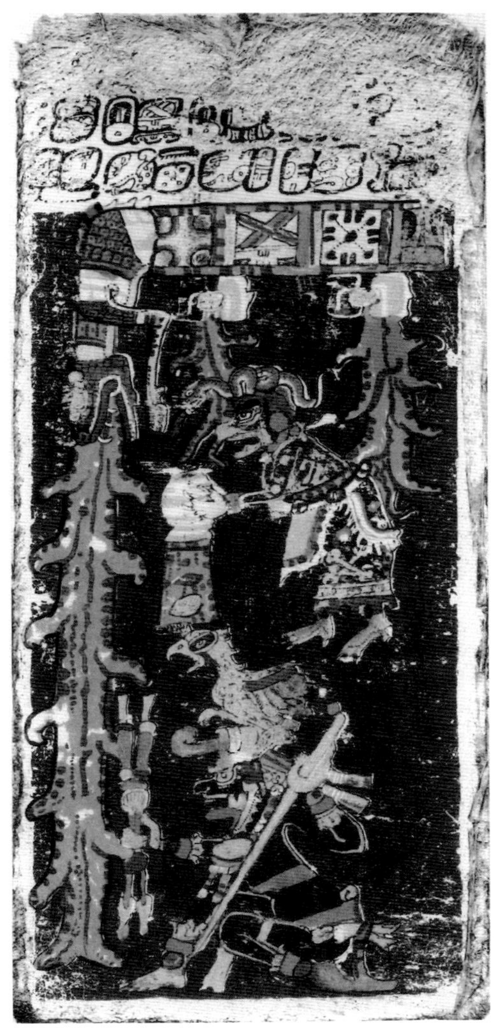

a metaphor for the virgin's descent. He claims that she is the "divine flood" of the Sky God. Catastrophic floods had marked other world-altering events in Maya mythical history; in fact, this seems to be a pan-Mesoamerican literary trope, as it appears in the cosmogenesis of other cultural groups, such as the Mexica. For the Mayas, floods are described in the "Chumayel," and also in the K'iche' Mayan *Popol vuh* from Highland Guatemala, as destroying the world to bring about a new sun.[19] Moreover, the event of a cosmic flood destroying a world age is illustrated in the Dresden Codex, where one can see a sky deity vomiting a deluge of water to wipe out all earthly existence (fig. 36). Beneath this reptilian sky deity, Ixchel, the Maya goddess of fecundity aids in the process by pouring water out of a ceramic vessel, directly onto the head of a black-skinned Chak.

The Maya author's use of the terms *paat* and *pati* is similarly revealing. Most directly, *pat* denotes a kind of declaration or the action used to incite this declaration.[20] But it also had a more nuanced translation, one that does not necessarily negate the more obvious reading. In the last quarter of the sixteenth century, the Franciscan Antonio de Ciudad Real completed the earliest extant Mayan-Spanish dictionary, the "Motul Dictionary."[21] According to Ciudad Real, in addition to "declare," *pat* can also be rendered as "to give form to something" or, more evocatively, "to make idols" (*hacer ídolos*).[22] In fact, the Franciscan relates that the noun for "idol," *patbil*, or something made out of "clay, wax, or corn mush," shares the same *pat* root.[23] By using this term, the Maya author appears to understand the Virgin Mary not as an abstracted historical actor from Christian mythology, but instead as capable of being embodied in the very materiality of the sculpted icon herself. The descent to which the Chumayel author refers is undoubtedly the arrival of the Marian statue; she came to power the day Diego de Landa installed the statue on the Itzmal altar.

After her installation and the spreading of her cult, there is textual and visual evidence in the Chumayel "Chilam Balam" that she was deemed the primary deity of the colonial period. In one section Maya elders included updated explications of a handful of astronomical principles, among these the solstices and solar and lunar eclipses.[24] In their description of a lunar eclipse, the scribes included a highly schematized diagram of the earth and its spatial relationship to the sun and moon (fig. 37). Here, the artist placed an image of the virgin, identifiable by her crown, but, more important, by her conical dress and hands clasped at her chest, at the apex of the earthly realm (labeled *tierra*).[25] Her corporeal body appears to grow from the earth itself, the deity and terrestrial realm registered as a single being. Her crown stretches into the circular form of the heavenly firmament marked by an arc of eleven stars, clearly demarcating her status as the supernatural being who reigns over the cosmos.[26]

This sentiment is repeated again in the manuscript, in the section dedicated to the *k'atun* counts, a twenty-year calendrical system used in the late postclassic and colonial period. Here the Maya author provides a pithy description of the cycle that occurred between 1540 and 1560, the first two decades of Spanish colonization.[27] This period is described as a time of upheaval, when scattered human settlements were brought together under the *congregación* project, and then tribute payments began to the "foreigners." It is also the era when the Mayas learned the Christian faith, when they were baptized and administered the seven sacraments, and when the foundation of the Mérida cathedral was laid. Incredibly, among all this action, these dramatic changes to the social fabric of Maya society, the author ends his account of this twenty-year period by mentioning the virgin, rhetorically positioning her as the primary mover of these dramatic shifts: "She is called the ritually pure woman, the mother of the seven solitary movable stars."[28] Directly beneath this passage the author inscribed seven rudimentary

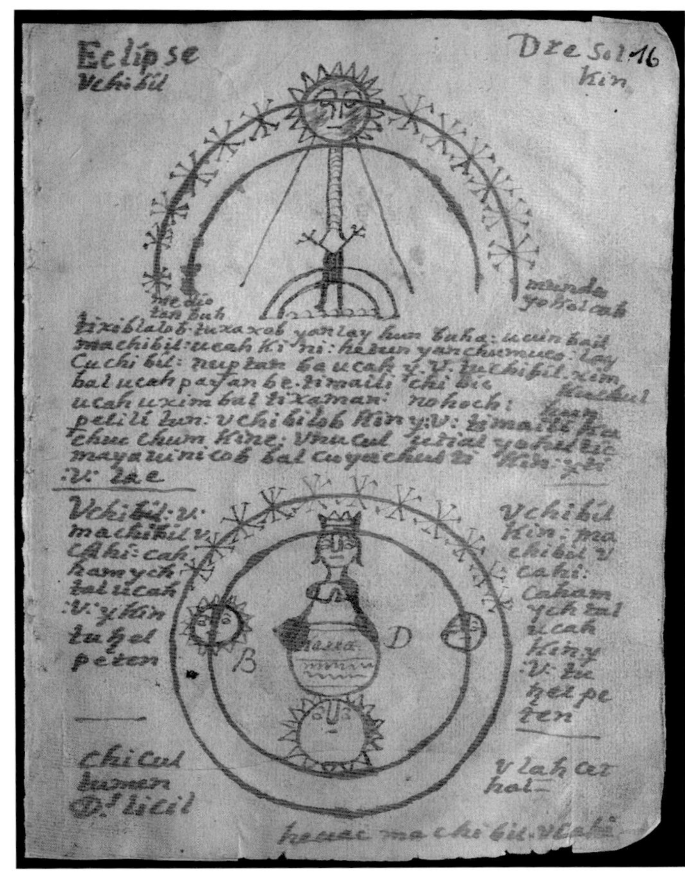

star forms. In terms of a rhetorical device, her mention as the capstone event of this k'atun signals her dominance of colonial-period Maya religiosity—just as the virgin's statue as Marta Mis's ultimate bequeathal signaled her singular preciousness.

The Ritually Pure Woman

Given the fact that the Virgin Mary had become the primary deity of Yucatecan Catholicism, it makes sense that it was to her that residents turned during the health crisis of 1648. For the Creole population Mary had long been associated with the easing of human suffering; her role as a benevolent, caring mother who intercedes on her son's behalf had been a trope in European Christianity for centuries. What is less clear is how and why the Mayas appear to have so seamlessly appropriated this aspect of the virgin. Why did this indigenous population come to see the mother of God, and in

particular physical statues of her, such as the Virgin of Itzmal, as an appropriate supernatural to be summoned during moments of bodily suffering? I argue, rather than just
assume, that a simple native appropriation of traditional Spanish modes of iconic healing, the Maya veneration of Mary, can be more rightly attributed to the ways in which
her biography and mode of production resonated with traditional Maya understandings of ritual purity. This fact, coupled with the Virgin of Itzmal's peripatetic movement
during the summer of 1648, poised her to perfectly coalesce the Spanish and indigenous understandings of the numinous to create a uniquely Yucatecan Marian tradition.

Unlike the Spanish accounts of that epidemic, the Maya sources are extremely
thin. The most effusive of them is an annals-like summary of peninsular sixteenth- and
seventeenth-century history, included in "The Book of Chilam Balam of Chumayel":
"We entered into Christianity in the year 1519. The Tiho [Mérida] church was founded
in the year 1540. Then the Tiho church was completed in the year 1599. The death from
the plague of bloody vomit began in the year 1648. The death from hunger began in
the year 1650, the year 1651, the year 1652, the year 1653, the year 1654. Then the hunger
was completed."[29] This short paragraph covers 135 years of meaningful historical events,
siphoned down to only the most significant, among these indigenous conversion, the
building of the Mérida cathedral (during which residents from Chumayel served as
labor), and the 1648 epidemic. The Maya scribe coined a neologism for the new disease,
xekik, which translates into "bloody vomit," prefiguring the gruesome effect the disease
has on the suffering human body. The fact that none of the region's earlier pandemics
are mentioned suggests the social severity and cultural impact that this particular virus
had on the Maya population.

Beyond this scant reference, extant Mayan sources are relatively silent on the
unprecedented social devastation. As such, to determine the Maya relationship with
Mary I am forced to look elsewhere, to textual references that chronologically book-
end the 1648 epidemic. My first line of evidence is an investigation into the linguistic
idioms developed by the Mayas to describe Mary. In table 2, I have gathered an assort-
ment of Mayan-language sources that speak to and of the Virgin Mary in general, and
in some cases the Itzmal icon in particular. These terms come from a variety of genres,
ranging from the clandestinely composed "The Books of Chilam Balam" to the more
mundane world of wills, testaments, and land documents. Providing a developmental sequence of these terms' usages is exceedingly difficult, given the undated nature of
many of the documents. Table 2 is an attempt to place these terms in a loose chronological framework; I discuss the Mayan terminology from the earliest to latest, insofar
as such a trajectory is possible.

Although lacking in firm provenience, a collection of documents known as the
Morley Manuscript includes an inscribed date of 1576, making it the earliest known
Mayan inscription of a Marian appellation.[30] The text's seminar translator, Gretchen

TABLE 2 A chronological sampling of Mayan phrases for the abstracted Mary and Marian icons

Date	Document title	Provenience	Mayan appellation	English translation	Current location
1576	Morley Manuscript (confessional manual)	unknown	Ca colel ti suhuy santa maria	Our lady, the ritually prepared Santa Maria	Museum of Indian Arts and Culture, Santa Fe, New Mexico
1616	Documentos de Tekanto (land title)	Tekanto	Ca cilich colel tu suhuy santa maria	Our sacred lady, her ritually prepared Santa Maria	Archivo Notarial del Estado de Yucatán, Mérida, Documentos de Tekanto, i. 27
1620	Discursos predicables, by Juan Coronel	Tekax	Çuhuy Santa Maria	Ritually prepared Santa Maria	Published text
1621	Teabo Manuscript (Maya Catholic copybook[a])	Teabo	Ca cilich colel suhuy SSt Sta M.	Our sacred lady, ritually prepared Saint Mary	Brigham Young University Library, MSS 279, fol. 3r
1621	Teabo Manuscript (Maya Catholic copybook)	Teabo	Cilich Santis Ma	Sacred Santa Maria	Brigham Young University Library, MSS 279, fol. 5r
1647	Will of Bonaventura Canche	Cacalchen	Ix bolon u pixan ca cilich c[tear] ti çuhuy Santa Maria	She of the nine-souls, our holy lady, the ritually prepared Saint Mary	Tulane University Library, Libro de Cacalchen, 7
1654	Will of Andres Uitz	Cacalchen	Ix bolon u pixan calich colol ti çuhuy Santa Maria	The nine-souls, our holy lady, the ritually prepared Saint Mary	Tulane University Library, Libro de Cacalchen, 27
1678	Will of Don Franca Uitz	Cacalchen	[Tear] pixan ca cilich colel ti çuhuy Santa [tear] calich colel[b]	[Tear] soul, our holy lady, the ritually prepared Saint [tear holy lady]	Tulane University Library, Libro de Cacalchen, 31
Eighteenth century[c]	"The Book of Chilam Balam of Chumayel"	Chumayel	Yx ahau: yx suhuy. Yx mactzil	Female lord, ritually prepared female. Incorruptible female	Princeton University Library, Garrett-Gates, Mesoamerican Manuscripts, no. 4, fol. 10v
Eighteenth century	"The Book of Chilam Balam of Chumayel"	Chumayel	Ca cilich colebil y ahau candelas hacha cibe	Our sacred lady and lord of the candles, true wax	Princeton University Library, Garrett-Gates, Mesoamerican Manuscripts, no. 4, fol. 18r

Date	Document title	Provenience	Mayan appellation	English translation	Current location
Eighteenth century	"The Book of Chilam Balam of Chumayel"	Chumayel	Suhui chuplale	Ritually prepared woman	Princeton University Library, Garrett-Gates, Mesoamerican Manuscripts, no. 4, fol. 36v
Eighteenth century	"The Book of Chilam Balam of Chumayel"	Chumayel	Ix Kalem	She of the two times	Princeton University Library, Garrett-Gates, Mesoamerican Manuscripts, no. 4, fol. 36v
Eighteenth century	"The Book of Chilam Balam of Chumayel"	Chumayel	Çuhuy chuplal	Ritually prepared woman	Princeton University Library, Garrett-Gates, Mesoamerican Manuscripts, no. 4, fol. 48r
Eighteenth century	"The Book of Chilam Balam of Chumayel"	Chumayel	U colel caan	The mistress of the sky	Princeton University Library, Garrett-Gates, Mesoamerican Manuscripts, no. 4, fol. 52r
n.d.	Codice Pérez	Mani	Suhuy kulbil na	Ritually prepared divine mother	Unknown,[d] 142
n.d.	Codice Pérez	Mani	Zuhuy ahualil	Ritually prepared female ruler	Unknown, 144
n.d.	Codice Pérez	Mani	Zuhuy chuplal	Ritually prepared woman	Unknown, 92
n.d.	Codice Pérez	Mani	Cilich Nabil	Sacred Mother	Unknown, 178
n.d.	"The Book of Chilam Balam of Tizimin"	Tizimin	Consepsion[e]	Our Lady of the Immaculate Conception	Museo Nacional de Antropología e Historia, Mexico City[f]
1709	Will of Lucas Euan	Sicpach	Ca cilich colebil consepcion	Our sacred lady of the Immaculate Conception	Centro de Apoyo a la Investigación Histórica de Yucatán, Colección Carrillo y Ancona-Chichí, 3, fol. 107v
1739	Will of Juan Ake	Tekanto	Colebil	Lady	Christensen cites P. Thompson, *Tekanto*, 128
1748	Will of Phelipe Tec	Peten (?)[g]	Mesa y ca cilich colebil	Table and our sacred lady[h]	Archivo Histórico de la Arquidiócesis de Yucatán, Mérida

Date	Document title	Provenience	Mayan appellation	English translation	Current location
1766	Will of Bernardino Coot	Ixil	Ca cilich colebil - y u tabernacula Ca cilich colebil ti xan y u messayl	Our sacred lady and her altar[i] Our sacred lady and also with her table	Centro de Apoyo a la Investigación Histórica de Yucatán, Colección Carrillo y Ancona, Testamentos de Ixil, fol. 24
1766	Will of Juan de la Cruz Coba	Ixil	Ca cilich colebil y u tabernacula	Our sacred lady and her altar[j]	Centro de Apoyo a la Investigación Histórica de Yucatán, Colección Carrillo y Ancona, Testamentos de Ixil, fol. 37
1768	Land title	Near Tahcabo and Kaua	Cah cili[c]h Colebil Santa maria	Our sacred lady, Santa Maria	Princeton University Library, Garrett-Gates, Mesoamerican Manuscripts, no. 18, fol. 1r
1769	Will of Marta Mis	Ixil	Ca cilich colebil	Our sacred lady[k]	Archivo Notarial del Estado de Yucatán, Mérida, 1819iv, fol. 37r

Note: This table was created by collating my findings with those of Restall, *Maya World*; Christensen, *Nahua and Maya Catholicisms*; and Christensen and Restall, *Return to Ixil*.

[a] I am indebted to Mark Christensen for bringing the Teabo examples to my attention. The Maya scribes used variations of this appellation throughout the manuscript, relying heavily on *suhuy* as a qualifying term. Christensen has insightfully called manuscripts such as the Teabo "Maya Catholic copybooks," because they don't easily lend themselves to categorization as "Chilam Balams" (*Teabo Manuscript*, 12–18).

[b] *Calich colel* was used three times in reference to donated alms, likely in reference to a particular Marian icon, the nearby Virgin of Itzmal.

[c] Scholars have dated the extant manuscript's creation to this century, but it was clearly transcribed from much earlier textual and pictorial sources.

[d] As the original manuscript has been lost, I reference the location of Marian phrases as listed in Solís Acalá, *Códice Pérez*. Photographs of the now lost original are held in Harvard University's Peabody Museum.

[e] This term was added as a marginal gloss.

[f] I have been unable to consult this document in person and instead relied on the transcription provided in Edmonson, *Ancient Future of the Itza*, 128.

[g] Matthew Restall and Mark Christensen note that this will was contained within a folder that had recently had "Peten Itza" scrawled across the top, so it is possible that it comes from a Maya village in this region.

[h] This quote references a bequeathed Marian icon.

[i] Both references to "our sacred lady" in Bernardino Coot's will refer to Marian icons that he bequeathed to his family members.

[j] As in the will of Bernardino Coot, this mention of the virgin refers to an icon left to an heir.

[k] This "sacred lady" is also a reference to a Marian icon.

Whalen, convincingly argues that the manuscript is a copybook of a native *maestro*, one of the many Maya men Franciscan friars trained in the early colonial period to assist with the academic and religious education of elite Maya children. Unlike the European versions of similar books, the indigenous author chose "genres and themes likely to entertain and engage his audience," thus suggesting that he was cognizant of the fact that, for the new religion to be easily incorporated, he needed to graft its stories and concepts onto the familiar stalk of traditional Maya religion. My translation differs slightly from Whalen's, having dramatic repercussions for our interpretation of a Maya Mary.

Significantly, the native author of the Morley Manuscript refers to the Virgin Mary in three distinct instances, each time prefacing her referential noun with the adjective *suhuy*: "our lady, the ritually prepared Santa Maria" (*ca colel ti suhuy santa maria*); "the sacred mother, the ritually prepared Santa Maria" (*U cilich na. ti suhuy santa maria*); and "the sacred person, our sacred lady, ritually prepared Santa Maria" (*U cilich Uini-cil- ca cilich colel—suhuy santa maria*).[31] A few decades later, in 1616, a similar phrase appears again, this time in a more mundane document, a land title from Tekanto (see map 1), revealingly located only 6.2 miles from Itzmal. Here the Maya notary preceded the Morely Manuscript's initial formulation with a single Mayan term, *cilich* (sacred), thus referring to the abstracted Mary as "our sacred lady, her ritually prepared Santa Maria" (*ca cilich colel tu suhuy santa maria*).[32]

Every translator of this term, from the colonial period until the modern era, has translated *suhuy* as "virgin," using it interchangeably as an adjective and a noun. The crux of my following analysis is based on a reexamination of this term as it is used in the previous and additional linguistic formulations. Rather than utilizing this word as a commentary on the unsexualized nature of Mary—although with the passage of time, this may have been implied—I argue that Maya authors, scribes, redactors, and transcribers strove to reference a long-standing concept of "ritual purity." The prior academic focus on the mother of God's sexual virtue has effectively glossed over the larger sacred connotations that the Mayas would have associated with the newly introduced female divinity, impeding our understanding of the apparent ease with which the indigenous population accepted her.

Revealingly, the sixteenth-century "Motul Dictionary" includes five entries that incorporate the root *suhuy*:

çuhuy cab: virgin honey, the first that is taken from the hive
çuhuyil: virginity and a virgin thing
çuhuy kax: forest or monte that was never worked
çuhuy kin: exactly midday
çuhuy luum: virgin land and they also use this to refer to land of the church, cemetery, land which is blessed or sacred, and which they haven't sinned upon[33]

It is to Ciudad Real's second entry that scholars have turned for their own translations of period terms for the Virgin Mary, *suhuy* directly translated as the English noun "virgin." Rather than evidencing a direct conversion of the Mayan term into Spanish—implied by the friar's simplistic entry—the use of this expression as a referent to Mary is rather a Franciscan appropriation of a conceptually related, but not semantically identical, word.[34] Ciudad Real (and likely other friars before him) applied the fortuitously similar *suhuy* to the newly introduced Catholic personage, whose early modern period sacrality was defined by her "untouched" state.[35] By 1620, when Juan Coronel composed the earliest surviving *Doctrina* in Mayan, *suhuy* had been fully transformed into a formalized appellation for Mary; he uses *çuhuy* in every instance where Mary is mentioned.[36] In the seventeenth century the trend continues, as is evident in a fortuitously preserved collections of wills from the Maya village of Cacalchén (located only 13.7 miles due west of Itzmal on the road that ran from Mérida to Itzmal).[37] In three wills dating from 1647, 1654, and 1678, Mary is referenced in their testators' formulaic preambles. In all three instances, the term *çuhuy* (*suhuy*) was appended to "Santa Maria," prefaced by a reference to her soul (*pixan*).[38]

Prior to the introduction of the virginal female divinity during the evangelical campaigns of the sixteenth century, *suhuy* would have been reserved to describe the untouched state of defined entity: land (*suhuy monte*), honey (*suhuy kab*), or new fire (*suhuy k'ak*).[39] In these linguistic contexts, *suhuy* conveyed the concept of unworked, undiluted, uncontacted, or simply pure. As late as the 1930s, Redfield and Villa Rojas noted that Maya religious practitioners in the village of Chan Kom utilized this term to describe the appropriate nature of objects given as offerings to their various deities; the water and animals sacrificed to supernaturals could not be tainted by human intervention.[40] Objects that originated or resided outside of the human realm, such as in the unpopulated monte, were also frequently termed *suhuy*.

The adjective could also be applied to humans, albeit in precise and circumscribed ritual moments. Not all humans were perpetually deemed suhuy; it was a state of being that could be engendered amid correct ceremonial protocol. As is well documented, primarily by Landa and a variety of twentieth-century ethnographers, there appears to be a pan-Maya notion that ritual practitioners must endure a period of cleansing before they were worthy of participating in a ceremonial event. Most frequently, these proscriptions took the form of fasting, bathing in a sweat bath, bloodletting, or most important for the purposes of my argument, abstaining from sexual relations. Taken in total, these proscriptions all involved the avoidance or physical evacuation of material substances deemed impure from a ritual standpoint. Flora and fauna became contaminated the moment they were modified by human hands to be foodstuffs and therefore could not be ingested. Similarly, sweat baths ensured perspiring and thus the removal of unwanted corporeal entities, and sexual abstinence guaranteed that foreign bodily

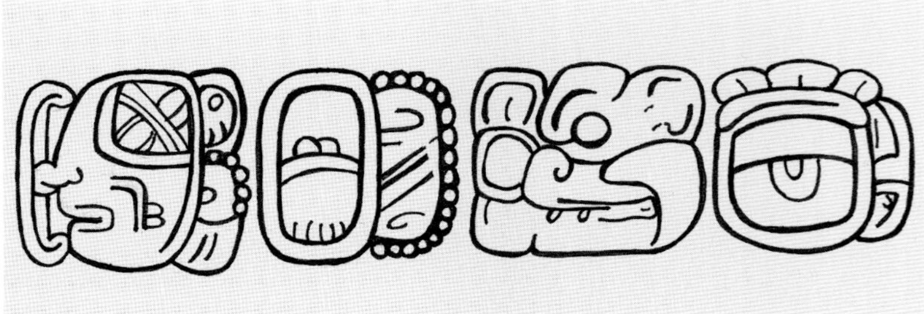

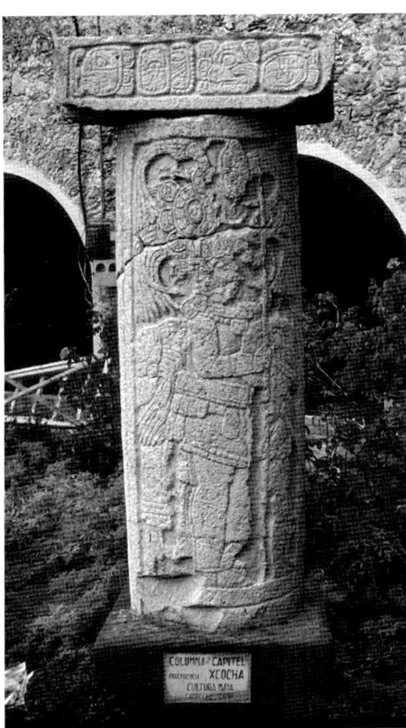

FIG. 38
Inscription from the "Building of the Glyphic Band," Xcocha, Yucatán. Drawing by Catherine Popovici, after original in Pollock, *Puuc*, fig. 856b.

FIG. 39
Column from the "Building of the Glyphic Band," Xcocha, Yucatán. Photo: The Mesoweb-PARI Photo Database, file D40461 (Irmgard Groth).

fluids would not be exchanged. Only in this dematerialized condition could a religious practitioner be capable of contacting deities or deified ancestors and thereafter absorbing the sacrality offered by the supernatural world. At the termination of a rite, when normal human activities had recommenced, a human's suhuy state was understood to evaporate; it was a temporary state of being.

Despite the term's ubiquitous use in the colonial period, only a single precontact stone inscription that includes it has been found to date. Perhaps not coincidentally, the carving comes from the classic period site of Xcocha, located northeast of Campeche. In the city's ceremonial center, the eastern wing of the building, known as the Building of the Glyphic Band, contains a double colonnaded doorway. Originally, each column featured an incised image of a standing ruler grasping a diminutive prisoner by the hair. A rectilinear capital, carved with hieroglyphic inscription on the front and sides, surmounted the columns. Today only the western column and the eastern capital have been restored, now displayed in the Museo de la Arquitectura Maya, Baluarte de Nuestra Señora de la Soledad, in Campeche, Yucatán (figs. 38 and 39). The text demonstrates the depicted ruler's ownership of the building, declaring it to be owned by "he of the name Balam, the ritually prepared artist/sage/craftsman" (*suhuy* is the second glyph block from the left).[41] In this singular precontact usage, *suhuy* is part of the ruler's royal title, a linguistic qualifier that deftly articulates his temporary ceremonious preparedness for the rite in which he is shown engaging, likely ritual execution.

This classic period notion of ritual purity's temporality in human actors appears to have been transformed in the colonial period, particularly in reference to Mary. The Catholic catechetical education offered to Maya neophytes imparted a vision of Mary that defined her as in a perpetual state of suhuy. She was conceived, born, lived, and died in this ritualized condition. Time and time again the mendicants who oversaw the evangelical mission in New Spain stressed the biography of the Mary, specifically with a mind to impress on the indigenous community the miraculous nature of Mary's own Immaculate Conception and the virgin birth of Jesus. This was particularly true of the Franciscan order, which had taken the verification of the Immaculate Conception as a kind of pet cause in the early sixteenth century. To further emphasize Mary's sexual purity, the order also stressed the mode of Jesus's conception. For example, the Franciscan Pedro de Córdoba's *Doctrina christiana*, published in central Mexico in 1544, describes Mary's conception as such: "The Sacred Virgin didn't conceive in her womb like other women; she conceived without the coupling of a man. Miraculously, but by the power of God, without corruption she remained a virgin like she was before. In this way, they are engendered, the bones inside the skin, without corrupting nor opening the flesh. And like the cherry engenders the pit without opening the cherry, in this way the son of God was conceived and engendered in the womb of his mother, the Sacred Mary, without opening or any corruption."[42]

That this biography of Mary was instrumental to a Maya vision of her perpetual suhuy is evident in a rather obscure passage from the "The Book of Chilam Balam of Chumayel." In a single instance the Maya scribe refers to Mary as "Ix Kalem." This does not have a simple translation into English but can be loosely glossed as "she [*ix*] of the two times."[43] Although vague, this is an instance of a Christianized Maya placing Mary's biography within a meaningful cultural system. The "two times" refers to Mary's two distinct lives, an aspect of her personal history that differentiated her from most other human beings, save her son. Recall that in early modern Christian theology, believers understood Mary to have been born uncorrupted, owing to the magical impregnation of her mother, Saint Anne. Mary's divinely sanctioned birth thus made her an ideal receptacle for the living incarnate of God. This same purified state made it possible for her body to transcend physical decay, as tales of her Assumption make clear. From a Maya perspective, this Assumption would have been understood as her second existence, thus the appellation "she of the two times."

As a final consideration of the Maya use of *suhuy*, I want to point out the perhaps overlooked but obvious fact that Spanish appellations for Mary appear only in a handful of the documents noted here, primarily in notarial genres of legal import.[44] Only in the 1576 Morley Manuscript, the 1616 Tekanto land title, the 1620 Discursos, the 1621 Teabo Manuscript, and the mid-eighteenth-century Tahcabo land title do the name "Santa Maria" or a direct translation of the Spanish "Nuestra Señora" appear. Incredibly, both Hispanicized names are flagrantly absent from the interceding nearly two centuries of Mayan referents to their female deity. From this we can surmise that in the earliest moments of the evangelical campaign, Mayas adopted the Catholic Church's accepted title—but of course adding the native term *suhuy* to ensure a proper resonance with preexisting sacred modes. As the decades progressed, however, it seems that this indigenous population made Mary their own, reframing her within Maya understandings of sacred bodies and idealized ritual purity, completely disconnecting her from European linguistic referents. Only within the context of legal documentations, last wills, and testaments do the Hispanicized formulations reappear, from the author's desire to ensure the legal status of the prepared will. Clearly, Mary had been remade as a distinctly Maya deity, a kind of "Mayanization" of the mother of God. The further in time communities got from original evangelism, the more localized she became.

Thus far I have reserved my discussion to Maya references to Mary the historical actor, but it appears that, by the middle of the eighteenth century, the Mayas had developed a terminology to refer to her physical representations as well. Wills are extant from the Maya village of Ixil (located in proximity to Itzmal, map 1) that include the bequest of iconic statues of the Virgin Mary. In his translations of these wills, Matthew Restall identified two testators in addition to Marta Mis who owned home altars with tabernacles (*hunpel ca cilich colebil—y u tabernacula*), those of Bernardino Cot and Juan de la Cruz Coba.[45] It is an unlikely coincidence, however, that the three towns that display a marked interest in Mary during the first 150 years of evangelism, Tekanto, Cacalchén, and Ixil, are all located in proximity to Itzmal. I would argue, in fact, that rather than referencing the abstracted Mary, the bequeathed images of Ixil may actually have been small-scale representations of the Itzmal Marian icon.

In their status as functional similitudes of the Itzmal icon, these household statues clearly derived some of their power as copies of a numinous prototype. Additionally, given what is known about the Maya relationship with sacred matter, we must attend to how the physicality of these virgins, both the large-scale icon and her representatives, may have been conceived. The Mayas traditionally deemed the manufacture of a religious statue a sacred act, and a proscribed series of ceremonial steps had to be taken to ensure an effigy's ultimate power. First, a religious specialist had to commission a recognized artist. Next, the raw material of the object had to be gathered, and subsequent production always took place far from the public's view, in a locale made for this purpose. Until they were introduced to the community, the icons were held in particular kinds of boxes. All the while the participants maintained a ritually pure body, ensured by fasting, sexual abstinence, and autosacrifice.

From the perspective of the resident Mayas who remained in Itzmal while Landa made his journey to Guatemala, Landa would have appeared to follow this exact same procedure. The friar, a religious specialist, journeyed to a distant site to engage the assistance of a renowned sculptor. This artist created the Marian icon out of elite raw materials, introducing an artistic technique, *estofado*, and a resulting visual experience heretofore never witnessed in Itzmal. She was then transported back to Itzmal in a specially crafted crate, only to be revealed to the community at her installment in the church's altarpiece. In all ways, her mode of production would have perfectly resonated with Maya understandings of the appropriate sacred protocols. Her early and profoundly felt acceptance by the Itzmal indigenous community suggests that she was recognized as miraculous not only because of her physical link to the local landscape but also because of Landa's great efforts of production and procurement. In this way her crafting ensured that she was a sacred effigy perfectly positioned to engage with precontact notions of sacred materiality. Although we do not have access to how the household copies would have been produced, it is safe to assume that they derived their power from replicating in microcosm the material sacrality of their larger prototype.

The question remains, however, as to how the colonial Mayas came to deem these representations of the Virgin Mary as capable of healing a physically or spiritually unwell community. I've argued that the historical Mary's biography ensured her perpetual state of suhuy, as did the production techniques of her physical representations. These biographical and creative aspects coalesced to result in a female deity whose very materiality, the corporeal matter of the Marian icon, was capable of physically absorbing bodily contagion. Seen in this light, the Itzmal icon was primed to be a community intercessor equivalent to the foodstuffs and figurines created and utilized during the course of k'ex healing rites.

That a Marian icon would have been deemed an appropriate tool of communal healing is evident when one considers how this particular epidemic resonated with indigenous Maya understandings of contagious disease. Recall that this plague seemed portentously caused by a kind of "bad air," as described by López de Cogolludo, and that it clearly originated from a body of water, spreading as it did from the Caribbean Sea. K'ex rites were specifically performed under these circumstances, albeit in Redfield's observations, at a more humble, domestic level, aimed at the suffering of an individual. In the twentieth-century examples, the k'ex was performed only when disease could specifically be linked to a contagion carried by evil winds. The 1648 yellow fever epidemic fulfilled this requirement. For Maya believers, the Marian icon's journey orchestrated a newly created healing rite that effectively combined aspects of precontact traditions for healing: the k'ex and the long-distance pilgrimage. Her involvement was possible only because, in her state of perpetual suhuy, she was recognized as primed to absorb the infectious elements emanating from Mérida.

The Cleansed Virgin of Tabí

It is this exact aspect of the virgin's being and biography that is emphasized in the origin story and artworks associated with one of Yucatán's later miraculous icons, the Virgin of Tabí. The small Maya village of Tabí is located in the middle of the peninsula, halfway between Mérida and Valladolid (map 1). Although founded as a Franciscan mission, it was secularized in 1581, and the religious education of its Maya inhabitants were overseen by secular priests. Like so many other religious statues in the region, the Tabí icon disappeared during the Caste War of the late nineteenth century. But her loss is made up for by the ample archival accounts of this icon's appearance and the extant decoration of her home chapel.

Her story was recorded in 1639 in a lengthy manuscript penned by the *bacchiler* Francisco de Cárdenas Valencia.[46] Four years prior, in 1635, King Philip IV had requested by royal cédula that the Franciscans in Yucatán provide him with an ecclesiastical history of the province. In 1638 Cárdenas Valencia accepted this commission, submitting his final manuscript to the Mérida cabildo a year later.[47] According to the friar, the Virgin of Tabí had miraculous origins. His predecessor, Diego Velásquez de Arceo, relayed this tale, which bears repeating, as it suggests that by 1700 this icon's popularity—even among Creole devotees—stemmed from her engagement with the local topography and embodiment of suhuy.

As the story goes, one evening early in the first years of the seventeenth century, the church bells of Tabí's church began to ring spontaneously. Awakened by the racket, the town's encomendero, Rodrigo Alonso García, and a handful of other Spanish residents jumped out of bed and made haste toward the church. Once they arrived it was not clear from where the sound emanated. They began to return home, passing by the double cenote that marked Tabí's central zone, abutted to the town's plaza and church. There on the edge of the cenote appeared a statue of the Virgin Mary, perched on the side of the sinkhole. After repeated attempts, the icon was installed in Tabí's church. Thereafter she began to work miracles.

The original church of her installation underwent a massive project of reconstruction in the last years of the seventeenth century and was finalized in 1700. By this point the icon had amassed an impressive public following, rivaled only by that of the Virgin

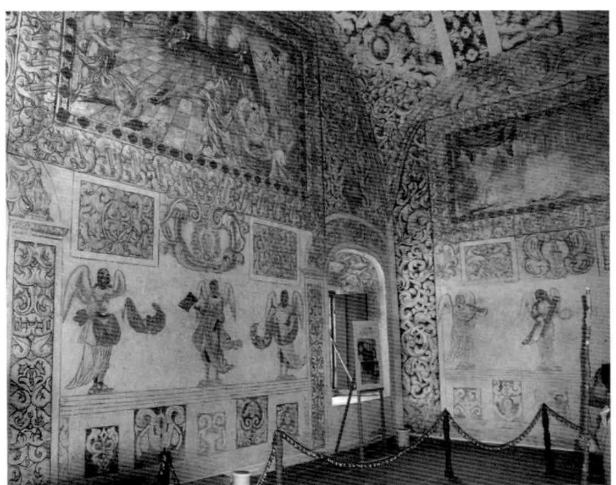

of Itzmal. The reconstruction included the addition of a camarín; while originating in Spain, the camarín became wildly popular in Yucatán after the 1648 epidemic, an architectural history that deserves much closer scholarly attention. Tabí's camarín hosts Yucatán's most impressively preserved series of architectural murals, offering particular insight into period visual culture and associated religious devotion.[48]

As can be seen in figure 40, every available surface of the small room's walls has been shrouded in painted detail. Beyond the impressively baroque decoration of gold volutes, the most revealing pictorial moments for my argument are three delineated panels located high on the chamber's walls. The rectilinear forms are differentiated from the rest of the walls' adornment by the use of thick fictive frames. All represent scenes from the life of the virgin, with multiple narrative moments compressed into the compositional space of a single frame. Each of the chosen biographical events highlight the pristine nature of Mary's corporeal body.

Linda K. Williams's insightful analysis of this mural cycle has revealed the nuanced modes of Inmaculada imagery in seventeenth-century Yucatán. She writes that "the flexibility of Maya religion allowed for the incorporation of new ideas in ritual practice.... Some elements of doctrine and representation at Tabí likely dovetailed with Maya belief, resulting in a Christianity [that appeared] more or less orthodox." By Williams's account, the "Maya belief" that so neatly and serendipitously coalesced with the Tabí origin story is her miraculous appearance from the local cenote. Recall that, for the Mayas, such topographical features were deemed convenient portals to other realms of the universe and thus ripe for supernatural events. I would expand on this perceptive realization and add that all icons dedicated to the Immaculate Conception, such as that of Tabí and Itzmal, were appealing to a Maya audience because of Mary's perpetual embodiment of suhuy.

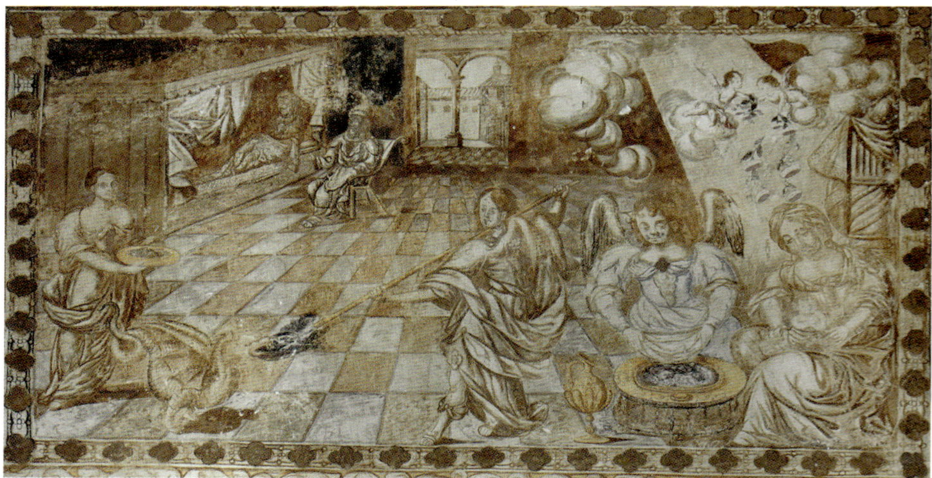

FIG. 41 Mural of the *Birth of the Virgin Mary and Michael Slaying the Dragon*, camarín of the Church of the Immaculate Conception, late seventeenth century, Tabí, Yucatán. Photo: Linda K. Williams.

Specifically, these scenes image moments taken directly from the early life of Mary as recorded the apocryphal Protogospel of James, composed by 150 CE, which influenced Jacobus da Voragine's circa 1260 *The Golden Legend*, reprinted under various titles during the course of the early modern period.[49] The artist's choice of depicted narrative details and avoidance of others in particularly revealing. Interestingly, Jesus Christ, the supposed primary deity of Christianity, is completely absent. The primary event for which Mary was known and revered, the birth of her son, has been wholly erased from the original decoration of the Tabí camarín. Instead, viewers are granted a privileged and detailed vision of Mary's conception, birth, and childhood. This Mary-centric vision of Catholicism echoed that being espoused across the Atlantic, where contemporaneous clerics similarly promoted the Immaculate Conception as a tactic against "heretical" Protestants during the Counter-Reformation. According to Miri Rubin, "The Immaculate Conception was the symbol of world Catholicism."[50]

The painting that represents the earliest narrative moment of this mural cycle—Anne and Joachim's embrace at Jerusalem's Golden Gate, which results in Anne's immaculate conception of Mary—inhabits the chamber's northern wall, but it is severely damaged and therefore evades interpretation. But the other two images of the cycle, Mary's birth (east wall) and her presentation at the temple (south wall) are wonderfully intact, if over-restored in places. I'll begin with a discussion of the earlier of the two narrative moments.

In the painting *Birth of the Virgin Mary and Michael Slaying the Dragon*, the native artist forgoes visually highlighting the supposed central topic of the scene and instead emphasizes a relatively minor detail to foreground Mary's inherent purity (fig. 41).

Following the scene's traditional iconography, the artist imaged Anne's bedroom, a deep, tunnel-like space, made optically more profound, given the composition's high vanishing point defined by the floor's prominent checkerboard tiles. Anne lies in bed, a diminutive moment compressed to the back left of the image. Joseph is seated beside her. In the foreground a series of six figures are imaged. At the far left a woman carries a tray, likely holding sustenance to revive Anne. In the center the archangel Michael spears a winged dragon. Finally, at the far right a midwife holds the infant Mary, while an angel washes her birth clothes in a circular water basin. Billowing clouds, rays of light, and flower-throwing cherubs visually highlight this moment.

I would argue that this composite scene is united around the theme of cleansing, of both a physical and spiritual nature. In colonial New Spain these concepts appear to have been conflated: a cleansed body was mirrored in a cleansed soul. According to Williams, Saint Michael is included in this scene because the physical destruction of the dragon signaled to a seventeenth-century audience a metaphoric reference to the slaying of other kinds of evils. In the context of Yucatán, this other evil was certainly the ongoing idolatry repeatedly discovered during the course of the past century and a half. Like the reptilian creatures vomited out of the mouths of idolaters in Valadés's image, here native heresy is embodied by the serpentine form of the slithering dragon. Only divine intervention, in this case Saint Michael, ensures the successful eradication of such wickedness, resulting in a spiritually pure world.

In a similar vein, the bathing of the infant Mary serves to erase any form of contamination from her physical body. She has just been bathed; the right-most seated woman is holding a naked, swaddled baby. Even though she had been conceived free of sin, the physical experience of birth certainly resulted in an unclean body. Recall that, for the Mayas, ritualized bathing was a dominant part of pre-rite practices that ensured the suhuy state of a ritual participant. By highlighting this portion of Mary's personal narrative, which is never mentioned in the Protogospel, Maya viewers would have been assured of her cleansed state, from the earliest moments of her life she was appropriately prepared for ceremonial intervention.

The room's directional associations impact this connection to cleansing as well. Recall that the *Birth of the Virgin Mary and Michael Slaying the Dragon* is located on the room's eastern wall. For the precontact Mayas, the eastern horizon was associated with birth and various other aspects of renewal, making this the ideal site for a mural of the virgin's birth. In fact, in the middle of this wall, exactly at average eye level, the artist imaged a iconographically pristine rendering of the Virgin Mary (fig. 42) Williams has noted that "both the natural light and symbolic message of dawn would frame the paintings, an association understood by the Mayas as imbricated within the renewal of life through the daily return of the sun."[51] For Mesoamericans renewal was possible only when ritual protocol had assured appropriate levels of spiritual and bodily cleansing.

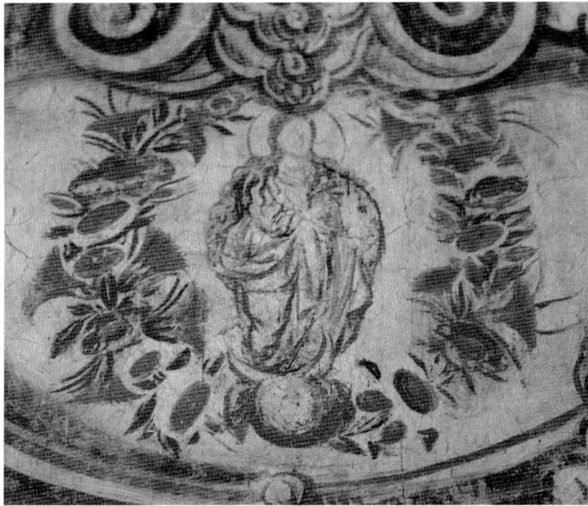

Similarly, Mary was prepped for a life of spiritual leadership through an additional anecdote from her personal biography, her acceptance into the Temple of Jerusalem. This is the topic of the series' final mural (fig. 43). In this scene the native artist imagined another complex architectural context, the tiled forecourt of the temple; statue-laden niches decorate the background of the scene. Joachim and Anna are placed in the center of the composition, as they watch their daughter mount the steps toward a waiting priest, arms outstretched. Though the image is faded, one can still make out the pained expression on the parents' faces as they watch their daughter walk away. A group of two women, babes in arms, and a small toddler are placed at the extreme left of the composition. They are visually prominent from the inclusion of a dark, billowing cloth above their heads. These figures are likely onlookers who traditionally crowd presentation scenes. The woman on the left is imaged as looking directly outside of the picture plane to meet the gaze of living onlookers.

Like Mary's birth scene, her presentation at the temple similarly spoke to her ritual preparedness. This visual anecdote served to highlight a biographical moment, in which Mary was deemed as spiritually other, when she was formally received in the temple. Moreover, this image serves as a mnemonic for the additional narrative details left out of the image, most significantly the passage that prefigures Mary's physical body as the ideal receptacle for God incarnate: "The Lord hath magnified thy name among all generations: in thee in the latter days shall the Lord make manifest his redemption unto the children of Israel."[52]

Charlene Villaseñor Black has argued that, despite the intentional suppression of Saint Anne's cult in post-Tridentine Spain, her popularity surged in New Spain during the seventeenth century. She attributes this difference to missionaries' self-conscious

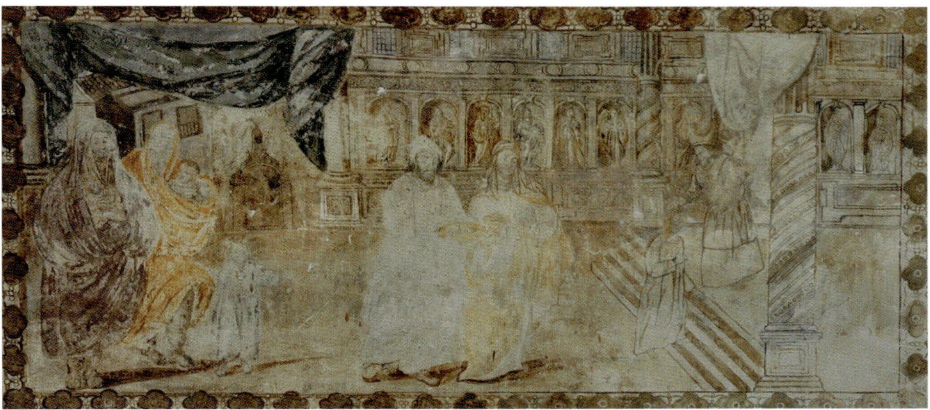

FIG. 43 Mural of the *Presentation of the Virgin*, camarín of the Church of the Immaculate Conception, late seventeenth century, Tabí, Yucatán. Photo: Linda K. Williams.

conflation of Saint Anne with central Mexican goddesses such as Toci, particularly in their role as the patron saints of midwives, a role Saint Anne had embodied since the medieval period.[53] To this reading I would add that Saint Anne's biography served as a kind of preface for the story of Mary's pristine state. The Tabí murals' theme suggest that, for the Mayas (and perhaps all seventeenth-century Yucatecos), Mary's incorruptible state was not directly linked to her own sexual virginity but rather that she (and her son afterward) had been made by a human who was ritually prepared, who had abstained from sexual relations and thus was not materially corrupted. As such, Mary, much like a properly crafted effigy deity, had been ritually activated in such a way that unwarranted material elements were absent from her corporeal body; she was properly suhuy. She was thus capable of "absorbing" the Holy Spirit, as it was sent from Saint Gabriel (just as her son's eventual virgin birth would prime him for the physical absorption of human sin). This biblical account of bodily absorption positioned her material representations as ideal objects for use in healing ceremonies, thus justifying her deployment during the 1648 plague.

Conclusion

By the end of the sixteenth century, the Virgin of Itzmal was fully incorporated into the community fabric of her home village, standing in as the prevailing supernatural force that created the new colonial world order. Because of Landa's perhaps unintentional engagement with Maya modes of effigy production, her status was assured; her form was imbued with numinous qualities because the materiality of her body had been ritually activated in meaningful and expected ways. Mayan-language documents evidence the role of the virgin in textual accounts of her appearance and visual representations of her placement at the apex of the earthly realm, posited as an intercessor between terrestrial humans and celestial beings.

Epilogue

Modern Materiality

On October 8, 2012, thousands of Maya Yucatecans gathered in the sleepy village of Sitilpech (map 1) to engage in a communal ritual that stretches back at least two centuries. Rising at dawn, residents and those from surrounding villages gathered in the small Church of San Jerónimo (fig. 44) to hear mass before their resident sacred icon, the Santísimo Cristo de la Exaltación (Most Holy Christ of the Exaltation) or, more commonly, the Cristo Negro (Black Christ). After the service male members of a local workers' guild carefully removed the Black Christ from his installation in the altar, placed him on a lavishly gilded litter decorated with white lilies, and hoisted the hefty weight onto their shoulders. Exiting the chapel, they proceeded to walk three miles westward along a dusty country road toward the much larger town of Itzmal.[1] En route, Mayas paid homage to the icon, following slowly behind, carrying lit candles. Upon reaching Itzmal, the icon was processed through the town's streets, eventually winding up the ceremonial ramp that leads to the monastic complex of San Antonio de Padua, raised sixteen feet above plaza level on the remains of a precontact pyramid (fig. 5). The Black Christ crossed the monastery's vast open atrium to enter the church's nave, where his journey reached its destination, an in-person conversation with the resident Virgin of Itzmal.[2]

In figure 45 the Black Christ is shown installed at the foot of the Itzmal altar, framed by a flowered arch and surrounded by other vibrant blooms and candles. In the image's upper left corner, poised directly above and behind the icon's right shoulder, the virgin peeks out from her crystalline niche embedded in the middle of the church's lavish nineteenth-century retablo. Following an annual ceremonial protocol that dates to at least the late nineteenth century, the Black Christ will converse with his mother for the better part of the next month.

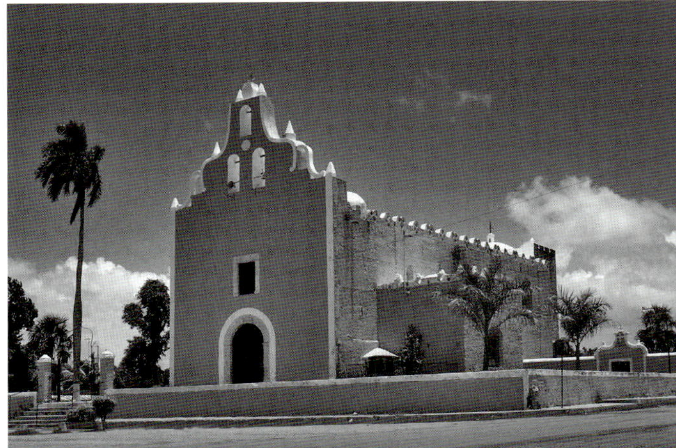

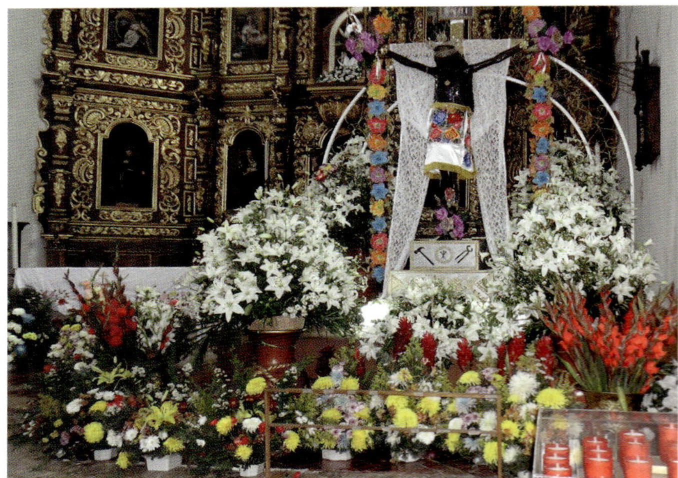

Despite his relatively late birthdate, the exact details of the Black Christ's appearance remain the stuff of legends. According to the orally circulating tale, which I have been unable to verify with archival evidence, in the distant colonial past two unknown brothers, perhaps twins, appeared in Itzmal. Over the course of two years, they hired themselves as handymen to local Izamaleños, becoming extremely devoted to the Virgin of Itzmal. They eventually took up residence in two of Itzmal's visita towns; the older brother built a choza in Sitilpech, located due east of Itzmal, and the younger chose the village located due west, Citilcum, as his home. The older brother continued to attend weekly mass at the Itzmal church, while the younger ventured to Tekanto, located 4.7 miles north. According to the tale, the older brother was much disturbed by the virgin's absences, when she was taken to Mérida to intercede on the population's behalf during times of communal crisis. During these brief absences, this older brother would take up residence in the Itzmal monastery, anxiously awaiting her return, reasoning that her spot on the altar shouldn't be left empty. After one such stay, he proclaimed that "the house in which she lives shouldn't be open until the third day of her absence. . . . They shouldn't leave unprotected the Itzmal church when the virgin isn't there."[3]

The next day the older brother disappeared from Itzmal. On the third day of the virgin's absence, the townspeople gathered in front of his choza in Sitilpech. Opening the doors, they immediately fell to their knees, because placed before them was a statue of the crucified Christ. The icon was delicately carved, life-sized, and of a deeply brown hue—this is the Black Christ still venerated today. The townspeople immediately carried their new icon to the Sitilpech chapel. Thereafter, every time the Virgin of Itzmal had to be carried to the provincial capital, the Black Christ of Sitilpech would be transferred to her home sanctuary to ensure that it would not be abandoned.[4]

Since the story began to circulate, the Black Christ's local responsibilities have shifted slightly. He is no longer required to replace the virgin but instead asked to take up residence with her. Each day of this festival is sponsored by one of the area's active guilds, ranging from the secular Gremio de Herreros, Mecánicos, y Carpinteros (Iron Workers, Mechanics, and Carpenters Guild); Gremio de Taxistas (Taxi Drivers Guild); and Gremio de Meseros (Waiters Guild) to the religiously oriented Gremio de la Unión Católica (Catholic Union Guild). Men are primarily represented, but the Gremio de Señoras y Señoritas (Married and Unmarried Women Guild) and the Gremio de Señoras Obreras and Campesinas (Female Workers and Farmers Guild) also help to defray the cost of such an expensive event. Taken in total, nearly every common Yucatecan profession is represented, effectively making the Black Christ the patron saint of Yucatán's laboring classes.

The theme of physical suffering permeates this ritual, perhaps made most evident by the icon itself, a representation of the crucified Christ. One cannot escape ruminating on his final moments of physical and emotion pain, despite the placid facial expression with which he is rendered. He is imaged just moments after death, head hung and limbs relaxed after the abating of his physical agonies, but the history of his tortures are ever evident, given that icons from the *arma christi*, the "arms" used during Christ's Passion, decorate his small pedestal, reminding petitioners of his suffering in the days leading up to his eventual crucifixion.

It is fitting, therefore, that the cult of the Black Christ appears to have gained popularity in the years of the most intense physical suffering the Maya population of Yucatán had ever endured, the era of intense henequen (or sisal) production. Known colloquially among Yucatecos as the time of *esclavitud* (slavery), the late eighteenth and nineteenth centuries bore witness to the only agricultural boom the peninsula had ever experienced, the implantation of a distinct plantation society for the cultivation of henequen. The production of ropes made of henequen's tough fibers, used to make shipping cordage and components of wheat harvesters, provided an immediate influx of egregious wealth for the region's Creole population, garnered by the implementation of a forced labor system, peopled by the large Maya populace.[5]

It is possible to understand this shift from the popular veneration of advocations of the Virgin Mary to that of her son as one that perfectly replicates a shift from a sympathetic to an empathetic response on the part of the believer.[6] In the earlier colonial history of the peninsula, the sixteenth and seventeenth centuries, community struggles with dramatic population decline, poverty, and famine could be understood as perhaps likely to evoke a mother's sympathy, thus making the Virgin Mary an appropriate iconic personality. Conversely, by the nineteenth century, when the Mayas' physical suffering reached its apex, a new kind of icon was needed, one that not simply sympathized but emulated the physical pain and oppression with which the Mayas were faced. In the tortured and suffering body of Christ, Maya petitioners found an empathetic icon.

Yet, despite this new religious interest in the suffering body of Christ, there remained vestiges of the old religiosity. In fact, the very power that the Black Christ derives comes from the perseverance of these religious practices. I've ended with this short contemporary account of Yucatán popular religion because it perfectly coalesces many of the themes that have run through the text's preceding chapters. It brings the historical arguments into the present day, solidifying my earlier assertions that the development of colonial-period religiosity laid a firm foundation for the religious practices that define the peninsula in the twenty-first century.

The previous chapters have argued that religion in colonial Yucatán was a complex web of mutually informing associations. Religious practices that on the surface appear orthodox and directly imported, adopted, and appropriated from their Iberian precursors were in fact nexuses for the meeting of dramatically divergent understandings of "holy matter." The Maya population approached physical objects with a nuanced sense of that object's potentiality. Given the appropriate modes of production, ritual activation, and continued upkeep, sacred icons could manifest the divine. Once embodied, that sacred essence had the potential to substantially absorb unwanted elements or corporeal ailments, as my discussion of the k'ex ceremony maintained. This exemplified a form of ritual exchange, whereby the materiality of an activated icon had the power to heal a single body or an entire community by physically absorbing undesirable components into the matrix of its form. These aspects of Maya religiosity become associated with icons of the Virgin Mary, especially in regard to her embodiment of a permanent form of ritual purity.

Coeval with the transference of these religious ideologies onto newly introduced Catholic statuary was a growing Creole fear of Maya religiosity, primarily in its precontact forms. People of Spanish descent came to conflate native idolatry with somatic disease, collapsing the divide between the spiritual and physical worlds. Indigenous belief was deemed materially contagious and quarantine, avoidance, and isolation were thought to circumvent the rampant spread of Maya religion. But seemingly orthodox Maya practices, such as officially sanctioned ritual processions, were understood as testaments to God's divine intercession, making indigenous participation in communal penance particularly effective; it was the spiritual antidote to communal ailments of the body.

By requiring the Black Christ of Sitilpech to annually process to and then converse with his Itzmal mother, petitioners actively recognize that their revered icons still embody these long-standing ideologies. During the course of their twenty-seven-day visitation, the Virgin of Itzmal, conceived of a sacred contagion, literally "infects" her son with divine power, effectively transferring the potency of her own material agency into the physicality of his suffering body. He is thereby reimbued with a recharged ritual potency that ensures his own divine efficacy. What we are witnessing in this annual rite is a modern-day k'ex ceremony, a ritualized exchange of supernatural abilities. Once re-upped, the Black Christ is reprocessed back to his chapel in Sitilpech, which local petitioners refer to as a *santuario temporal* (a temporary or provisional sanctuary), and continues to successfully intercede on the behalf of his parishioners.[7] In the words of a reporter who witnessed the processional event in 2014, "The religious fervor was contagious."[8]

Appendix A: Petition of the Mayas of Itzmal, Summer 1648

Don Juan Ek, governor of the town of Itzmal; don Bartolomè Cauich of Pomolche, Alonso Canche, Gaspar Pech, alcaldes of Santa Maria; don Matias Canche, governor of the town of Citilpech; don Pedro Chim of Pixila; don Bartolomè Uitz of that of Xanaba; don Francisco Ke of Kantunil; don Francisco Ve, governor of Zuzal; don Sebastian Men, governor of Chalmte; don Bonifacio Zul of those of Uizi; and tocbaz [*sic*] with all the mayors, councilors, and elders of this guardianship and town of Itzmal, together in this Hospital of the Mother of God the almighty, we determine, being together of one opinion, to give our petition before you, our revered Father, and spiritual Friar Bernardo de Sosa, Provincial of this Province of Yucatan, and that you are in this Convent of Itzmal, and we bow at your feet, and at the habit of San Francisco in order to kiss them, asking you that you help us by the mercy of God, because we have no other recourse except you, that our Sacred Mother of God should be moved from this Convent of Itzmal, as the lieutenant, cabildo, and royal officials of the city ask us, in order to bring her to the city and pray to her blessed Son to help them, and for health in such grave illnesses, and also you have asked us for her to go to give mercy. To that we say, that we arrive [at this decision] voluntarily, with pleasure, and on our knees, prostrated before our *padre*, guardian friar Antonio Ramirez of this Convent of Itzmal, we ask you that you stay in the said convent, so that you wait for our Lady to return, and you should deliver her over to us, like you are delivering her to the lord lieutenant within seventeen days, four days for the trip there, nine days that she is in Merida, four days for her trip back, that is the count totaling seventeen days. And for this we present to you this petition, and we ask that you sign it with your signatures that are here below, that she has to be returned within the said time. And because it is forever on record we put our signatures, etc.

Text included in López de Cogolludo, *Historia de Yucathán*, 716–17.

*Appendix B: Decree Issued by the Cabildo of Mérida,
August 19, 1648*

Because the Most Holy Virgin of Itzmal has brought so much to this City, so that with her assistance she asks and supplicates God our Lord to calm his fury, and take the hand of so many dead people in this City, now that there are hardly any people in this city today, and each day more and more are going to die: by means of her prayers, and by protecting sinners and the heartbroken, and there are so many in this City it seems it will be destroyed. Because the fervor of our hearts is never missing and is constant, as we should be, they count together and rendered thanks, we have proposed to elect the said Most Holy Virgin of Itzmal our patron and advocate against plagues and illnesses, like that which is present in our town right now, like those that have come before. We beg the Most Holy Virgin, allow us and be our protector, patron, and advocate, now and forever more endlessly. And in the name of this city, town council, and its regiment that at present we are, and forever more, we will be here; we will protect you. We commit ourselves to celebrate the feast of the Most Holy Virgin of Itzmal on the day of her glorious Assumption, the fifteenth of August, each year perpetually forever. For this two knightly regiments from this said city will go to the village of Itzmal, where the Most Holy Virgin will be attended to, so that they will be present as the vespers celebration that have been said. They will be elected by votes or take turns. In order that at the same time the lordship of this city's ecclesiastical council will supplicate, which today governs her bishopric, so that the primary authority of the said festivity will be served by one of the lord prebendaries, going each year to say the said mass and vespers, in that the lordship will do his part so, as one who has so much desire for the health of this City, and is righteous, as we trust in his Christian conduct. And we promise by us and those who will come after us, and will happen in our offices and duties, that we will protect and see this vow through, with a perpetual promise forevermore, through which with all submissiveness we supplicate to what the Most Holy Virgin asks and supplicates to her precious Son our Creator and redeemer Jesus Christ, that no more deaths of such a severe plague come to pass in this city, that it runs its course. And we want and consent that one, two, or more witnesses take down this vow, which will be in the Archive of the Most Holy Virgin of Itzmal and is recorded for all time. In this way, we agree on it for the greater honor, glory, and service to God Our Lord and the blessed Mother, and we sign it, etc.

Text included in López de Cogolludo, *Historia de Yucathán*, 718–19.

We will not keep order in reference to the miracles of this most sacred Virgin of Itzmal, owing to the little knowledge of so many that there are. It is necessary to investigate the truth of each one. I confirmed the causes that easily offered themselves, having at hand a true account and eyewitnesses that could testify to what happened. But all the dates and causes couldn't be fixed all the time because so much time had passed or for not having an entire memory of it, so in this way it isn't as certain as it could be. Each case will be recounted because at least the traditional devotion that the Indians and Spaniards have for the miracles of this Queen of Heaven will be certain.

The first that it seems to me I should include, because it is so true and known, and no less delightful for those devoted to this Queen of the Sky, was when some Indians, husband and wife, who some said were natives of the pueblo of Iixo Iuk, they had had the fruit of benediction. They had a son, who was born shrunken, crippled, and lame and had grown up like this until the age of twelve years. Since the parents loved their son so much, they tried to cure him with all the care that was within possible reach, but no human remedy was enough to enable him to be healthy. It was so much work that the parents had with their son, loaded down, carrying him from one area to another, that they became very resentful and pained. What happened was that some other Indians heard talk of the miracles and wonders that the most sacred Virgin of the Convent of Itzmal made every day to those who came with devotion to visit her at her sacred temple, already, [they were] having a vision of some [of the miracles] and already returning with talk of other [miracles] and many other such wonders. The parents of the crippled child asked others who returned from having novenas said for this sacred image if they had brought some offering, or they asked them for some payment for the healing of their illnesses. They responded, "No one asks for anything, nor forces us to bring anything, but everyone who goes to visit the Virgin of Itzmal brings many candles, cloths, fruits, and each what they can in the end." After the parents of the crippled boy heard these reasons, they said, "It will be good for us to go to Itzmal, and we will take our son, and with any luck we will bring him health, so that he can make a milpa for us and bring us firewood, so that he doesn't trouble us anymore. It will be good if we

Text found in Lizana's *Historia de Yucatán*, pt. 2, fols. 22v–31v.

bring three *reales*, and when we return we will give two *reales* to our Lady and we will save the other *real*. And if he is healed we will give it to our son, and if not, no." They came thus and offered the two *reales* on the altar, and they saved the other one. They stayed in a vigil for that day and during all of it their son wasn't healed; they remained inconsolable. They returned another day, and they stayed until the afternoon. Seeing that he hadn't been healed, they said, "Let's go and bring the *real* that we haven't given to our Lady, since she hasn't healed our son." They brought it up, now so distrustful of remedy, and they exited the church, now saying good-bye, going toward the road to the back of the convent. The crippled boy said to his father that had been carrying him, "Father, put me on the ground so you can make this difficult for me." The father replied, "Well, how are you going to go on foot, when you haven't in your whole life?" The son insisted and sobbed so much that he forced his father to angrily lower him to the ground. Oh wonder of God, the boy stayed on his feet, free from his paralysis, healthy and good, graceful, and on his feet, which had been his hardship. He returned to [the arms of] his parents, amazed, and bewildered they said, "Let's go again to Our Lady and give her thanks, and we'll give her this *real* in payment because she has cured us and our son." And so they did it, remaining so focused on the Faith, and certain of the omnipotence of God our Lord and the wonders that he works through this sacred Image. This miracle was divulged to all of the natives and the Spaniards, that all of them who were there came to see the miracle, giving thanks for Our Lord, and his blessed Mother.

CHAPTER 6: IN WHICH IT IS REFERRED HOW THIS VIRGIN OF ITZMAL GAVE
A TONGUE TO A SPANIARD, WHICH WAS CUT OUT BY HERETICS

The ancient [Mayas] offered excised tongues to their gods, as a symbol of the silence that was a much-desired plate on the divine table, and they adored the crocodile, which is an animal without a tongue, signifying that he has no language to offend anyone, deserving to be feared like God. More than all, the tongue is esteemed in nature, so that a man who lacks one remains with a lack of reason, and he is almost despaired for seeing in himself the impossibility of expressing his heart to others: moreover, if he is in God's glory and His Sacred Catholic Faith, and in particular against heretics, enemies of the Church, and blind Gentiles of the Faith of Christ, who with insolence and without respect refuse the articles of the Faith, and even the faithful want to refuse them with threats and punishments, where the Lord wants us to lack language in order to contradict their blasphemies. Moreover, he promises you to give them the words that they would speak.

What happened in this regard was that English heretics took a Spanish ship off the coast of Yucatan, and after some insults that such tyrants usually make to the poor kidnapped ones, they told them that they were Papists, liars, and other blasphemies and disgraces, wanting to force them to disavow their obedience to the Pope and other articles of the Faith. The good Spanish Christians, and true sons of the Catholic Church, they abominated them of their errors, defending the Roman Apostolic See, to such a degree that the heretics became angry with the Catholics. So they cut out the tongue of the most knowledgeable one who had spoken for them all, so he couldn't talk about God, or defend His cause and repute His errors. After beating them they threw them onto the mainland of Yucatan. With this affliction, they walked to the city of Mérida. On the way the story became known to the residents of the land. A devotee of the Queen of Heaven of Itzmal said to him who had the cut tongue "Go, brother, to the pueblo of Itzmal, where there is an image of the most holy Virgin who does many miracles, and trust in God that she will return your tongue to you like you had before." After this good man had been given news of this sacred image, he came here directly, to her sacred temple. He got onto his knees and put his mouth on the floor, asking how the most sacred Virgin could return his tongue, and he spoke; it was a wondrous thing. And knowing that it was one of the rarest miracles that there is, well, his tongue started growing, little by little, like a plant, strongly, so that after the nine days he attended in the Church, he had an entire tongue, and his speech was restored like before, and like that he said, speaking to the Creator of heaven and earth, and lapping up his omnipotence, giving him thanks for the blessing he had received and to his most holy mother, all glorious, promised to be very devoted to her, and forever publicly proclaiming her wonders and miracles, that each day she does, and that she has done. With that he bid good-bye very happily, leaving those who had seen it and knew, such admirers, as devotees, of this Queen of Heaven.

CHAPTER 7: HOW THE VIRGIN OF ITZMAL HEALED A CRIPPLED INDIAN IN FULL VIEW OF A LOT OF PEOPLE

Nearly in this way what happened in this sacred temple of Itzmal, there was a case of a very old crippled Indian, who came to this most holy image. He placed himself at the gate of her temple, and there asked for alms to those who entered and exited. One time, being very sad to see him like that, obstructed, he took his crutches, and as he could he went to the altar of the Virgin. At the first step he fell to his knees. Propped up on his crutches, he raised his eyes to the most holy image of the mother of piety, and with great yearning he asked her for the charity of health. From there, a little bit later, he ascended another step, and he found himself more fluid, so that he left one of his two crutches at the foot of the stairs. Saying another prayer with much devotion and tears, he wanted to go up more stairs. He moved so smoothly that he could put down the other crutch and with the help of his hands was strongly ascending; kneeling next to the same altar, [he] turned to supplicate the celestial Queen to grant him health. After a little while he went to rise, and he found himself so agile that in his whole life he had never been so nimble and strong, that he lowered himself on his feet and left his crutches. And saying mercy and most welcome to the priests, he asked them if they could keep his crutches there so they could be memorials of those miracles. I was a witness to this miracle, as was an inhabitant of this Convent, and many other priests, and many people who had found themselves present.

CHAPTER 8: ABOUT AN INDIAN GIRL CHILD WHO THIS SACRED IMAGE RESUSCITATED

Some Indians, a husband and wife, residents of Itzmal, came to this convent of Itzmal, to say novenas to this image. They brought with them a daughter who was five years old. For the past two days she had been sick, and as they entered the town of Itzmal, the child died. Her parents loved her a lot and felt her death like parents do. In order to soften the blow that had been placed in their heart, it would be good to carry her in front of the sacred image of our lady. And so, they said, full of faith, "We bring our dead daughter to the Virgin, who had given to us her life, and now she has died; you will resurrect her for us?" And so they carried her and placed her in the middle of the main chapel, in front of the sacred image, who was present in the middle of the chapel on a throne, because it was during the time of her festival of the Immaculate Conception. There, on their knees they asked with great tears for the Queen of Heaven to resuscitate their daughter. And it was a miraculous thing, the dead child started to sweat and to moan. Recognizing that, the parents, seeing that their child had moved, they spoke together, giving thanks to God our Lord. There were more than a hundred people present, including the governor of these provinces, don Antonio de Figueroa, with his wife and family, and many other noble people were there, and they saw the dead child and her resuscitation. The same governor dropped to his knees before the image, and at the same time his wife took the child in her hands. The child, standing up, they asked her who has resuscitated her. And being five years old, she responded with these following words in her language: "My Lady the Virgin Mary, who is there above, placed on high, she resuscitated me." And another miraculous thing happened on this occasion to this child, who not having learned the Christian doctrine, said the Ave Maria, very well pronounced, in front of all of the referred to people, for the governor and the Spanish people. Even though the miracle was such, she didn't cause them much admiration, for to be certain that God and Lord is Lord of life, and that other such miracles God has been known to do, as omnipotent as he is. And they, as such likely Catholics, they gave thanks to the Lord, and his sacred mother, for having made such a great miracle, on the occasion when so many people attended the celebration of the festivities of the Immaculate Conception.

What happened was that an Indian woman, mute from birth, native of the pueblo of Homun, came to this church to visit the most holy image. She asked God our Lord with such insistence that he restore her speech though the intercession of his most holy Mother. God of the mercies, showing pity toward this poor mute, he restored her speech. And it happened like this: being in her lodgings in the house of a resident of Itzmal, at night they heard talking clearly from she who was so soon before a mute, and they heard that she knew very well without having it known in all of her life, for having been a mute, and like that the landlords entered the room and they asked her how she spoke being mute. She responded that the most holy Virgin had brought her the speech and that she had put it in her mouth, and they said, "Thanks be to God our Lord and to his most holy Mother." Later they made this story public and everyone recounts this miracle that God had worked in this mute through the merits of his most holy Mother.

Another Indian, deaf for a long time, also came to ask for hearing from this most holy image, and they were known to her, staying healthy and safe and very devoted to this sacred image.

Likewise, an Indian, blind since birth, obtained sight through the intercession of this Queen of Heaven.

Also, a black man, slave of the Canon Alonso Rodriguez of the city of Mérida, came to this sacred image, so sick that he had exhausted the doctors, and very big maggots erupted on all parts of his body. The most holy Virgin gave him health in the sight of all of the priests of this convent, and of his same love, of many Spaniards and Indian residents of the pueblo of Itzmal, giving their whole life thanks for God our Lord and his sacrosanct mother for such miracles as she has worked and works each day for her devotees.

Also, what happened during the feast of the Immaculate Conception, last year, 1625, a very old crippled Indian, it had been ten years since he had come to the Mother of God's festivities to ask for health. As he saw her, others had already reached her, and the faith that the cripple had, being seated at the door of the church very sadly; his companions asked him why he was sad. He responded that he was laughing with the Virgin and that he hadn't come more to visit her, but he didn't want her to grant him health. In the interim, a donor of the convent managed to enter, and he understood the complaint that the Indian gave. And he said to him, "Why did he have such little trust in God, and his sacred Mother, that he had come again and many other times if he came to minister and asked the Virgin to heal him." In this way the crippled Indian did it; he dropped to his knees, even with a lot of trouble, in front of the image and asked for health with many tears. After a short while the Virgin told the Indian to pass below her litter. He started off, going on the floor and healthy to the above-mentioned donor. And this same Indian publicized his health, with the moving of his legs and hands smoothly and with agility, with that the miracle remained evident, giving everyone many thanks to God our Lord, he who in this way comforts the afflicted ones, granting speech to the mute, sight to the blind, hearing to the deaf. What is more is that with these miracles these Indians are affirmed in the faith of Jesus Christ and their devotion to his sacred Mother.

CHAPTER 10: OF OTHER MIRACLES THAT THIS SACRED VIRGIN
HAS DONE WITH SPANIARDS WHO HAVE ENTRUSTED HER

Each day they see many miracles worked by the omnipotent God, by the merits of his sacred Mother, since the needs of man are so many and so extraordinary. In this same way his creator shows to them, like a father, helping them to get through whatever happens to them. I ask this, why a Spaniard from Seville came to this sacred image to ask for help with an illness? Since I wasn't an eyewitness, nor were many other religious and Spaniards, many have doubted the truth of the case. It happened like this: this man for many months wasn't himself. He ate more than two people with a good appetite and had the appearance of health, of good color. He had said that he felt the affliction a lot inside, that it seemed to embrace him. He had stopped sleeping for some time. In this way he turned to the source of his suffering, dismissing human remedies that many doctors had done. When he entered this sacred temple, he said that masses were said for him, filled with devotion, and that he had promised the sacred Virgin not to leave her sacred temple, without leaving healthy or in it meeting death with her comfort. Like this he stayed for almost two months, trusting in God and his sacred mother, making general confession. God was served, and he improved and stayed healthy and free of the illness so particular that he had. He remained so devoted to this sacred image that he said that he wouldn't be married in Seville; he would stay in the service of this church for the entire passage of his life. Moreover, he promised to come and visit her during all of the journeys he would make to the Indies and, being possible, bring her offerings and be a permanent town crier of this sacred image's miracles, preaching that all who make their devotions, winning her favor for their hardships.

It also happened in the city of Mérida of this Province; some Spanish children were playing on some tall roof or terrace. One boy fell from the height to the ground, the son of Francisco de Espinosa and of doña María de Matos, his wife. Taking the child for dead and frail, his mother offered to take him to this Virgin of Itzmal, asking with great insistence and tears that she heal him. God was served. In twenty-four hours the child returned to himself, remaining healthy and safe as he was before; attributing this miracle to the sacred Virgin, they said a novena for her as they promised. Today the boy is alive and free of a lesion, with which the miracle is revealed to us all.

Also, the wife of the encomendero of this same village of Itzmal, called Rodrigo
Alvarez de Gamboa, came to ask for health from this sacred image of Itzmal. His wife,
doña María de Sosa had an illness of fire in her hand; the waning of the moon afflicted
her to a great extreme. With the waxing it lessened, but with time the pain returned in
waxing and waning so that she couldn't sleep or eat. She tried many remedies, but she
was not healed. More than before they increased, the burning and pain. Her husband
saw this and said to her that she should leave behind the human remedies and should go
to the Virgin of Itzmal. And she should bring her an ornament for her altar. She waited
for our Lord to bring her health through intercession of his sacred mother. They came
thus to say novenas, and they said nine masses, and on the day of Our Lady, which was
the Expectation, listening to mass this devoted woman with much devotion, feeling that
as they were saying mass, her hand became better, and it was lucky that the mass ended
and so ended her illness. Her hand remained healthy, without lesion, without signal or
face of that which had been ill. It was, in view of the religious and of her same husband,
a clear miracle. Admired by all, they remained more devoted to this sacred image.

CHAPTER 11: OF OTHER MIRACLES OF THIS SACRED VIRGIN

The [seamen] went by sea in a ship of Capitán Domingo Galvan. A great storm was
given to them, and it wanted to sink them together on a crag and an enormous rock,
between very dangerous sandbanks. Now without hope of rescue, the sailors lost their
strength. With great bravery, the Capitán said to everyone, "Brothers, God wants to
punish us for going against his divine orders, taking offence by the minute, and with [this
storm] our sins drown us. Only God can help us; we promise to be very great servants
to you, writing a new book every day of our lives, and we all make a promise to go visit
the temple of the Virgin of Itzmal, to whom we are devoted to being worthy of on this
occasion. We all ask you with much humility, free us from such a dangerous manifest."
And like that all of them dropped to their knees, and then the storm calmed. Finding
themselves in deeper water, and in a known spot, and a thriving, northwesterly wind
followed their course, which was very brief and successful. And everyone was amazed
to see themselves free of a danger that they had never seen before, with the impossibility of human salvation. They said thank you to God our Lord, and they promised again
to come to visit the Itzmal temple and the image of his sacred mother, who had with
certainty freed them of danger [and] to whom they had entrusted. And so they went
on pilgrimage, and they were there nine days, listening to nine masses, and publicly to
be saved and free of the danger related by this Queen of Heaven.

It also happened to some Indians of the port of Campeche, that they left to fish
with some canoes, as they often do. A storm came upon them that carried them away
with such violence that the ocean took them out of their canoes and the canoes were

capsized, so they nearly drowned. Seeing themselves like this in such the most dangerous situation possible, one said to his companion, "We are lost; our sins led us to go fishing today. All is impossible without the demons, to whom we give credit and adore, who want us to be lost. We place our trust in the Virgin of Itzmal, Mother of the true God, releasing our hearts from this bad inclination that we have to practice idolatry, and you will see how Our Lady frees us from this danger." And the companion said, "Good, we will go to Itzmal, and we will bring our alms, and from that point on we entrust this Virgin." The storm carried them to the port of Alvarado, close to Veracruz. The inhabitants were impressed to see that they hadn't been drowned by the storm, in such a small canoe, asking them how they had happened to escape, and having arrived at that port, so far from their land. They said that having gone out to fish, the storm grabbed them, and seeing themselves so lost, they turned to be worthy of God and his sacred Mother, promising to come to the town of Itzmal. And like that they were miraculously freed. It seemed that they didn't feel the storm from the point that they had entrusted the Virgin of Itzmal. They had so much trust that she had freed them, like she had taken them. From there for some days they went along the coast to the port of Campeche, without fear of danger on the voyage. Later they arrived; they told of the miracle that the Virgin had done for them. Then, they set off to fulfill their promise and vow that they had made. Arriving at this sacred church of Itzmal, they offered their alms, and they said their divine thanks, publicizing the received mercy, and saying that only God should be trusted. When deceived they lived as idolaters, and they put in doubt the things of the sacred Catholic faith, and they had put some trust sometimes in some idols, deceived by some liars, and that they had seen all to be false that it does not serve the true God, believing in the faith of Christ and the article of it. Likewise, there was a fool who didn't value the help and protection of the sacred Virgin with his troubles, and [those troubles] being so serious, and having been resolved, he seemed free of the great danger these troubles had on his life. They talked to those who asked him what had happened, in particular their other Indian companions; they advised them to be truly faithful, casting their heart away from idolatry, if perhaps they did it, and that they be very devoted to the sacred Virgin. We see that this and other incidents have been part of the increasing devotion to this sacred Image in their hearts. Clearly see yourself, so each day we see more and more devotion in them, and that they continue to come all the passing of the year to ask for help in all of their trials from the Mother of Mercy, who always helps, when she is invoked, as has been seen, and will be seen, by her miracles and wonders.

Appendix D: Additional Miracles Enacted by the Virgin of Itzmal

CHAPTER 2: OF THE VERY CELEBRATED AND DEVOTED
IMAGE OF THE SACRED VIRGIN OF ITZMAL

When they carried [the virgin to Mérida after her original production in Santiago de Guatemala], they put many papers in her crate, so that she wouldn't be disturbed with the movement of the road. With those papers her devotion began. A lady resident of the city of Mérida hung on to those papers out of veneration. An Indian servant of that lady fell from a tall roof terrace of her house, where they had been working. The fall was such that they took him for dead, even though with some medicines he came around to his senses, but they left him with a broken arm and leg. They went to find someone to cure him, and in the interim the good lady took out the papers and wrapped the damaged arm and leg in them. When the surgeon arrived, looking for the damage that needed to be repaired, he asked why he had been called, that the Indian was good and healthy, and so was contented, attributing the health to a miracle of the sacred Virgin of Itzmal, God giving supernatural virtue to those papers that had been touched by the image of his sacred mother.

CHAPTER 3: OF OTHER MIRACLES OF OUR LADY OF ITZMAL

In September of 1634 Capitán Alonso Carrió de Valdés was en route from Spain, when his ship was on this coast in view of the land, an afternoon we all heard about, the ship touched the ocean floor with its keel twice, in very short succession. Recognizing that the ship risked running aground, and at least losing the ship, he said aloud, "Sacred Virgin of Itzmal, help us so I offer you the worth of a silver cable." When he said this, the ocean wind, which approached us on the land, instantly returned to the part of the land, so the ocean removed them and freed the ship from that danger. After, the Captain gave the silver cable to the sacred Virgin, as he had promised.

Governing this land, wife of the Marqués de Santo Floro, Doña Jerónima de Laso y Castilla, fell sick. She reached her end, and for moments they understood her to have expired. She entrusted with great effect the Virgin of Itzmal, and, when hopeless, she regained her health, which she had for certain because she beseeched the Virgin. So as

Text included in López de Cogolludo, *Historia de Yucathán*, 310–16.

a memory, she had made a painting on a cloth that is placed in her chapel, which she sent with other gifts in thanksgiving for the health she had received.

During the month of October of last year, 1654, I found myself with an attack, not deadly, but very terrible, it went through me, extending through all of my body very quickly. I tried remedies that were said to be effective, but very noticeable, so that they caused considerable pain and didn't work or stop it. Seeing myself afflicted with this, I entrusted myself to this sacred image, and made a promise to her. Ever since I started to improve, and even though it's true that I applied the other less noticeable medicine first (so as to not recklessly wait for God to work an obvious miracle through me, being able to apply natural causes), the attack healed, as I understood it, attributable to the mercy of the Sacred Virgin; she had made the medicine effective since I became healthy so quickly. God bless your mercy, and your sacred mother. Amen.

Notes

1. In this book all the foreign-language translations are my own, unless otherwise noted. For sources written in Spanish, Italian, French, German, or Latin, I have not included the original quotation in the notes. But for indigenous-language sources, such as Mayan and Nahuatl, I have transcribed the original orthography, as these languages are more open to scholarly interpretation. For the first epigraph an alternative English translation of the entire episode can be found in Whitehead, *Of Cannibals and Kings*, 110.

2. Although originally composed in Ramón Pané's native Catalan, only the report's Latin translation and transcription have survived, titled "Antiguidades" by Fernando Colón and included as chapter 61 of the *Historie del S. D. Fernando Colombo* (also known as *Life of the Admiral*).

3. The description of this event, which was directly taken from Pané's account, can be found in Herrera y Tordesillas, *Historia general de los hechos*, 1:88.

4. For an overview of the *Piss Christ* controversy, see Steiner, *Scandal of Pleasure*, 10–14. As recently as 2012, this image was still causing social havoc when a New York City gallery sought to include it in an exhibition (Amanda Holpuch, "Andres Serrano's Controversial Piss Christ Goes on View in New York," *Guardian*, September 28, 2012, Art and Design).

5. José R. Oliver has provided an overview of how other scholars have interpreted this event, ranging from a traditional agricultural rite to the desecration as understood by Pané ("Tiempos difíciles," in Museo Barbier Mueller de Arte Precolombino, *Caribe precolumbino*, 90). In an earlier section Pané relates how cemíni could be utilized to influence positive outcomes, primarily in regard to personal health, but could also inflict pain.

6. Gerónimo de Porras y Montalvo and Bernardino de Lizana to the Crown, Archivo General de Indias (hereafter cited as AGI), México 301 (unpaginated ramo).

7. I have argued that the veneration of the Virgin of Itzmal as a healing icon is not so much owing to her functional similarity to Itzamnaaj but rather to the Maya conception of the local landscape as imbued with specific powers of healing (Solari, *Maya Ideologies of the Sacred*, 153; this book expands on that initial analysis, specifically in chapters 4 and 6).

8. For decades the Franciscan mission had been plagued by the frequent discovery of Maya Indians performing hybridized religious ceremonies, usually in the uncolonized zone of the southeast but sometimes (much to the friars' chagrin) among previously converted populations living in Christianized mission towns. The most famous of these discoveries resulted in the 1562 auto-da-fé, held in Maní, during the course of which hundreds of Mayas were tortured or executed, or committed suicide. For a documentary overview of the episode, see Clendinnen, *Ambivalent Conquests*, 193–207.

9. Ricard, *"Conquête spirituelle" du Mexique*. While Robert Ricard's text remains invaluable as a historical source, its model for conversion is highly problematic, as many scholars have shown.

10. Anita Brenner coined this phrase in her book by the same name, in which she argued for the veiled likeness of precontact deities and Catholic personages (*Idols Behind Altars*, 128, 142–50).

11. Giffords, *Mexican Folk Retablos*, 1.

12. For an overview of this scholarly turn, see Restall, "History of the New Philology."

13. Given that the Mesoamerican cosmos was defined and directed by dozens of sacred forces, it is mistaken to assume that native people would have not recognized and venerated the Catholic pantheon as discrete spiritual beings. The very nature of a polytheistic religion makes such a replacement or substitution absolutely unnecessary.

14. The Virgin of Guadalupe is the most studied of all American religious icons; her scholarship is vast and comes from a wide variety of academic disciplines. Among the most engaging are Brading, *Mexican Phoenix*; Poole, *Our Lady of Guadalupe*; Peterson, "Creating the Virgin of Guadalupe"; and, most recently, Peterson *Visualizing Guadalupe*. For an insightful analysis of indigenous Marian devotion

before the emergence of the Guadalupe cult, see Burkhart, *Before Guadalupe*.

15. Solari, *Maya Ideologies of the Sacred*.

16. By no means do I wish to suggest that this was an apolitical process, unmediated by various colonial agendas at every level of the social hierarchy and cultural landscape. The quick emergence of native confraternities dedicated to these cults speaks immediately to the relationship between the indigenous political hierarchy and public spirituality. For Yucatán, Nancy Farriss's research remains the most enlightened on this topic, but access to the confraternity records in many parishes remains forbidden by local church authorities (*Maya Society Under Colonial Rule*, 232–37). As such, this is a topic much in need of sustained scholarly attention. Susan Verdi Webster has also completed research on this topic for colonial Ecuador: see "Native Brotherhoods and Visual Culture," in Terpstra, Prosperi, and Pastore, *Faith's Boundaries*, 277–99.

17. Scholars have begun to articulate this lacuna. James Elkins has even gone so far as to refer to art history's "fear" of the material world, an ironic stance given the field's dependence on physical artifacts. As he understands it, within the discipline there has been an assumption that "the 'purely' or 'merely' physical or material is conceived as a domain that is somehow outside of historical interpretation, or even outside of rational and critical attention" ("On Some Limits of Materiality," 29). Michael Yonan has argued for this discipline's embrace of materiality, suggesting that art history has the possibility of impact well beyond its traditional disciplinary confines ("Toward a Fusion," 233–34).

18. Arjun Appadurai's 1986 *Social Life of Things* is now recognized as the seminal text of this new movement. His contributors variously argued for a biographical model that could be applied to objects of the material world. As contributor Igor Kopytoff suggests, "Biographies of things can make salient what might otherwise remain obscure. . . . In situations of culture contact, they can show what anthropologists have so often stressed: that what is significant about the adoption of alien objects—as of alien ideas—is not the fact that they are adopted, but the way they are culturally defined and put to use" ("Cultural Biography of Things," 67). More recently, Rosemary A. Joyce and Susan D. Gillespie (building from the work of Hans Peter Hahn and Hadas Weiss, *Mobility, Meaning, and Transformations*) have criticized this model's applicability to the excavated archaeological record, opting instead for that of the itinerary, because of the inherent "difficulty of singling out such 'benchmark' events as 'birth' or 'death,' which are both obvious and critical to delimiting human biographies" ("Making Things

Out of Objects," in Joyce and Gillespie, *Things in Motion*, 11). Such a model allows scholars to "highlight the non-linear character of an object's mobility and the subsequent changes in its contexts and roles" (Hahn and Weiss, introd. to *Mobility, Meaning, and Transformations*, 8).

19. Of course, in the medieval period and later in the post-Tridentine context of Europe and the viceroyalties, living aspects of sacred sculpture were very much emphasized. Sculpted icons and holy relics were understood to cry, lactate, bleed, and directly produce miraculous changes in the human world, a shift in religiosity that Caroline Walker Bynum has dated to the late medieval period (*Christian Materiality*, 21–22).

20. Houston, *Life Within*, 4, 81.

21. Throughout this book I use "Mary" or "the Mother of God" to refer to the biblical personage and abstracted spiritual deity. Conversely, when discussing a particular statue of this deity, I employ "the Virgin of" each named town from where she is housed or the more commonly accepted appellation that refers to a specific icon's particular advocation.

22. Gruzinski, *Images at War*.

23. Hanks, *Converting Words*.

24. Inga Clendinnen has drawn a convincing parallel between this Franciscan notion of paternalism and the ensuing violence during the 1562 auto-da-fé ("Disciplining the Indians," 41–42).

25. Early, *Maya and Catholicism*; Christensen, *Nahua and Maya Catholicisms*.

26. For an insightful analysis of the survivability of Catholicism among apostate Maya communities, see Graham, *Maya Christians and Their Churches*.

27. The phrase "power of images" refers to Freedberg's *Power of Images*.

28. Amy Remensnyder has recently illuminated the role of Mary in the military campaigns of Spain and New Spain; see *Conquistadora*.

29. The seminal text for this interchange remains Crosby, *Columbian Exchange*.

30. The literature on the relationship between *mestizaje* and the emergence of the modern nation-state is vast, but for a concise overview, see Doremus, "Indigenism, Mestizaje, and National Identity."

31. "Diligencias practicadas a consecuencia del insendio acaesido en la iglesia parroquial de Yzamal el 17 de Abril," Archivo General de la Nación (hereafter cited as AGN), Bienes Nacionales, exp. 7, leg. 157.

32. During the course of this book's research, which has stretched over a decade, I have accessed the Archivo General de Indias (Seville, Spain), the Archivo General de la Nación (Mexico City), the Archivo General y Notaría Eclesiástica de

la Arquidiócesis de Yucatán (Mérida, Mexico), the
Archivo General del Estado de Yucatán (Mérida),
the Archivo Histórico de la Arquidiócesis de
Yucatán (Mérida), the Centro de Apoyo a la Investi-
gación Histórica de Yucatán (Mérida), the Archivo
Histórico Nacional (Madrid), the British Library
(London), the John Carter Brown Library (Provi-
dence, R.I.), the Tozzer Library (Harvard University,
Cambridge, Mass.), the Princeton University
Library (Princeton, N.J.), the Bancroft Library
(Berkeley, Calif.), and the Sutro Library (San Fran-
cisco State University).

33. For an overview of the ways in which colonial
notarial genres functioned, see Adorno, *Polemics of
Possession*, 4–11.

34. John Chuchiak has argued that the level of
anthropological detail included in some probanzas de méritos attest to their veracity ("Toward a
Regional Definition of Idolatry," 146).

35. Landa, "Relación de las cosas de Yucatán."

36. For an overview of this debate, see Hanks,
Converting Words, 319–26.

37. Bricker, "Last Gasp of Maya Hieroglyphic
Writing," in Hanks and Rice, *Word and Image*,
39–50.

38. Restall, *Black Middle*, 268–77.

CHAPTER 1

1. In addition to the processional events
commemorated in figure 4, the Virgin of Itzmal also
traveled to Mérida in 1730 and 1744 to combat other
epidemics and in 1769 to intercede during a plague
of locusts.

2. Diego López de Cogolludo provided the
grim details of the disease's corporeal development,
describing in a day-by-day progression the external symptoms and physical ailments that appeared
(*Historia de Yucathán*, 721). For an overview of the
disease's transmission, progression, and symptoms,
see Knaut, "Yellow Fever," 621–27.

3. In actuality, the dearth of sources may speak to
the level of upheaval in the wake of this epidemic;
social structures were so completely uprooted that
the usual activities of correspondence ceased to
occur for the following five years.

4. These pamphlets had a threefold function: to
describe the causes of the plague, to suggest medical interventions for those inflicted, and to suggest
future preventative measures (Olson, *Literature as
Recreation*, 166). This modeling is most obvious in
the beginning of López de Cogolludo's recollec-
tion, when he outlines the series of portents that
predicted the coming of the calamity.

5. Canedo, "Fray Lorenzo de Bienvenida," 498.

6. Numerous scholars have contributed to
the growing historiography on this topic. By far
the most significant contributions come in the
form of a handful of historical and anthropological monographs, researched and composed using
Spanish-language source material and traditional
historical methodologies. These include Chamberlain, *Conquest and Colonization of Yucatan*; Blom,
Conquest of Yucatan; and Farriss, *Maya Society
Under Colonial Rule*. More recently, scholars have
examined Mayan-language sources to more fully
appreciate the nuanced nature of this encounter

story. These include, among many others, Jones,
Maya Resistance to Spanish Rule; and Restall, *Maya
World*.

7. The exceptions were survivors Jerónimo de
Aguilar and Gonzalo Guerrero, both of whom figure
prominently in future conquest events (Chamberlain, *Conquest and Colonization of Yucatan*, 15).

8. Most of our information on the first two
voyages come from the detailed account left by
Bernal Díaz del Castillo, whose "firsthand" relation
was recorded only at the end of the conquistador's
life in 1568 and not published until 1632; as such its
veracity has come under recent scholarly scrutiny.
For an overview of this debate, see Restall, *When
Montezuma Met Cortés*, xxiii–xxvi. While this was
the first instance in which Spaniards came into
sustained contact with Maya populations, Díaz's
account does not provide a sense of cultural traditions, as this conquistador was clearly concerned
with the procurement of indigenous bodies to be
used as forced labor.

9. While Díaz was also a member of Cortés's
expedition and thus wrote about it in detail, he
composed his tome as a rebuttal to the version of
conquest events published by Hernando Cortés's
personal secretary, Francisco López de Gómara.
Both accounts must therefore be taken as politicized
narratives.

10. Significantly, both of these original colonial
settlements were built on the ruins of impressive
Maya towns, Campech (or Cenpech) and Tiho,
whose sophisticated urban fabric facilitated the
construction of the colonial settlements. Pertinent to this eventual "success" was the impact
of European diseases on the Maya population;
with increased contact to European bodies came
increased exposure to unprecedented contagion. It
is likely that by the late 1530s and early 1540s Maya

communities had become so devastated by a series of epidemics and their resulting famines they could no longer hold off the Spanish encroachments.

11. For a detailed analysis of the Spanish struggles to control this region, see Jones, *Maya Resistance to Spanish Rule*.

12. Charles Gibson first acknowledged the Spanish use of precontact administrative organization in colonial undertakings, a technique that would be used in the rest of Spain's American territories (*Aztecs Under Spanish Rule*).

13. For an overview of late postclassic sociopolitical organization, see Restall, *Maya World*, 15–40; and Quezada, *Maya Lords and Lordship*, 14–32.

14. Chamberlain, *Conquest and Colonization of Yucatan*, 311; Canedo, "Fray Lorenzo de Bienvenida," 497.

15. Lino Canedo, mining the accounts of the Franciscans in Yucatán recorded by Fray Bishop Diego de Landa and later Fray Diego López de Cogolludo, lists Luis de Villalpando, Lorenzo de Bienvenida, Melchor de Benavente, and Juan de Herrera as arriving from Guatemala and Juan de la Puerta, Angel de Maldonado, Nicolás de Albalate, and Miguel de Vera as being sent from Mexico City ("Fray Lorenzo de Bienvenida," 497). As an interesting aside, the importance of the visual in the evangelical campaign can be assumed, given that Testera personally recruited Bienvenida from Spain and so the latter was likely intimately familiar with Testera's innovative use of graphic systems for conversion strategies.

16. Franciscan friars of Yucatán to the Crown, Archivo Histórico Nacional (hereafter AHN), Diversos-Colecciones 23, núm. 7, fol. 1r. This particular letter is signed by "all the religious present in this province" and, in addition to Juan de la Puerta, included Lorenzo de Bienvenida, Luis de Villalpando, Nicolás de Albalate, Miguel de Vera, and Juan de Herrera.

17. In *Maya Ideologies of the Sacred*, I provide a detailed study of this process in reference to Itzmal (127–44).

18. Valadés, *Rhetorica christiana*. The engraving is included on page 224 and the lettered explanations on pages 224–25.

19. López de Cogolludo, *Historia de Yucathán*, 714. No one understood what was happening until a Spanish ship docked off the northern coast, bringing news of a massive offshore fish extermination that resulted in a pile of carcasses so large it nearly scuttled the ship.

20. This disease exists as one of the last mortal blows of the "Columbian Exchange," arriving late in transatlantic contact history (Curtin, "Disease Exchange Across the Tropical Atlantic," 348). James Ward cites its earliest appearance on the island of Guadeloupe in 1635, but he maintains the first "major epidemic" of it in Latin America occurred in 1648 (*Yellow Fever in Latin America*, 6). It appears to have originated in Central Africa, where European slave trade expanded in the early years of the seventeenth century. Infected individuals must have carried the disease across the ocean with them prior to this date, but a true epidemic did not occur until the first outbreaks in the English colony of Barbados in the summer of 1647. To date, the most enlightening book on the relationship between disease and imperial history can be found in McNeill, *Mosquito Empires*.

21. As has been ably explained by J. R. McNeill, a yellow fever outbreak necessitates a "perfect storm" of environmental and contextual factors, including a humid tropical climate to support its vector, the *Aedes aegypti* mosquito; a large and urban population of nonimmunes; and populations of forest monkeys to ensure the virus's survivability after its initial infection of the human population. Owing to the fact that the virus leaves survivors completely immune, the disease has a kind of episodic rate of occurrence, "making yellow jack the Caribbean's most feared disease" (*Mosquito Empires*, 64–66).

22. López de Cogolludo, *Historia de Yucathán*, 715.

23. Ibid., 721. This direct relationship between personal sin and communal punishment had been made clear from the earliest days of the American evangelical endeavor. As early as 1544 Peter Gerson articulated this when he stated in regard to the seventh commandment (Thou shall not commit adultery), "For this sin God asks for vengeance: many times famines, wars, epidemics, deaths, floods, treacheries, the loss of kingdoms, and many more types of death, according to what the scriptures tell us" (*Tripartito de christianissimo*, 12v).

24. Jonah 3:4–9 (King James Version). "And Jonah . . . said, Yet forty days, and Nineveh shall be overthrown. . . . So the people of Nineveh . . . proclaimed a fast, and put on sackcloth, from the greatest of them even to the least of them. . . . The king of Nineveh . . . caused *it* to be proclaimed and published through Nineveh . . . saying, Let neither man nor beast, herd nor flock, taste any thing: let them not feed, nor drink water. . . . Yea, let them turn every one from his evil way, and from the violence that *is* in their hands. Who can tell *if* God will turn and repent, and turn away from his fierce anger, that we perish not?"

25. During the early moments of the crisis, when the disease appeared to be striking only the peninsula's urban and thus Spanish areas (Campeche, Mérida, and finally Valladolid), the Maya population thought they were finally witnessing the retribution

of abuse they had endured at the hands of the Spanish encomenderos. López de Cogolludo, *Historia de
Yucathán*, 723.

26. Ibid., 715.

27. Ibid., 715–16.

28. William Taylor has argued that Spanish elites
intentionally maintained ties to rural shrine images
as a means to ensure "legitimacy and divine protection" and to guarantee that their city was "more
than a center of population, production, commerce,
administration, and patronage" (*Theater of a Thousand Wonders*, 553).

29. Ibid.

30. Matthew Restall has argued that, given the
precontact tradition of writing among the Mayas,
colonial period Yucatecans were particularly adept at
appropriating Spanish notarial genres for their own
community needs (*Maya World*, 230).

31. López de Cogolludo, *Historia de Yucathán*,
716.

32. Owing to their distrust of the Spanish population, Maya residents of Itzmal took turns acting as
spies on the roads leading out of the pueblo, lest the
provincial try to escape during the virgin's absence.

33. López de Cogolludo, *Historia de Yucathán*, 717.

34. While López de Cogolludo describes these
structures in other sections of his *Historia de
Yucathán*, they do not play prominent roles nor
garner a single mention within the 1648 plague
story. The central organization of a centralized
Spanish core surrounded by a handful of indigenous parishes exactly mirrors that of Mexico City,
which has been discussed at length in Mundy, *Death
of Aztec Tenochtitlan*, 73–75. Matthew Restall has
maintained that the African church, Santa Lucia,
was reappropriated by Spanish residents in the late
sixteenth century when the population of Mérida
outgrew the limits of the original traza (*Black
Middle*, 216).

35. Lindsay, "Spanish Merida Overlaying the Maya
City," 65. Lindsay marks Calle 65 as the termination point of the colonial road that led to Itzmal.
Diego de Landa also mentions the presence of an
ancient road that led from Tiho/Mérida directly to
Itzmal, but he does not list the towns located along
it ("Relación de las cosas de Yucatán," fol. 47r).

36. López de Cogolludo, *Historia de Yucathán*,
717–18.

37. For a discussion of the symbolic import
of triumphal entries in central Mexico, see
Curcio-Nagy, *Great Festival of Colonial Mexico City*,
15–40.

38. Barbara Mundy has proposed that the visualization of social hierarchy was a primary social
motivator for Mexico City's public processions
(*Death of Aztec Tenochtitlan*, 173–78).

39. López de Cogolludo, *Historia de Yucathán*,
717.

40. Ibid., 718. In an earlier chapter, López de
Cogolludo recounts that the convent had been
established on June 22, 1596, when sisters of the
Mexico City house of the Immaculate Conception founded the convent, a block to the west of
Mérida's plaza mayor (214). Their church was not
inaugurated until 1633, shortly before the events
recalled here (Carrillo y Ancona and Rendón,
Repertorio pintoresco, 406). As is well known from
better-documented colonial nunneries, the total
population greatly exceeded the professed nuns and
their charges, as these members of the Spanish elite
class certainly entered the convent with their own
domestic staff members.

41. López de Cogolludo, *Historia de Yucathán*, 718.

42. Ibid.

43. Landa, "Relación de las cosas de Yucatán," 48r.

44. López de Cogolludo, *Historia de Yucathán*,
718.

45. Ibid., 719.

46. This outward movement of the contagion into
the Maya villages had certainly began earlier in the
month when the Spanish families of encomenderos
retreated to their rural land holdings to escape the
sickness in Mérida.

47. Kashanipour, "World of Cures," 43.

48. Lindsay, "Spanish Merida Overlaying the Maya
City," 65, 68.

49. For a detailed account of the regional development of this cult, see Williams, "*Birth of the Virgin*,"
721–23.

50. Turner, *Ritual Process*, 96.

CHAPTER 2

1. In "Thomas Gann in the Maya Ruins," the
Maya scholar J. Eric S. Thompson detailed Gann's
biography.

2. John Lloyd Stephens and Désiré Char-
nay can be credited with introducing the marvels
of the ancient Maya to the nineteenth-century
English- and French-speaking worlds (Stephens,
Incidents of Travel in Yucatan; Charnay and
Viollet-Le-Duc, *Cités et ruines américaines*).

3. Sabas Ojeda had been a member of President
Porfirio Díaz's troops sent to the peninsula to quell

the indigenous uprising now known as the Caste War of Yucatán.

4. Gann, *Maya Cities*, 125, 129, 131.

5. Ibid., 132.

6. Upon his return to London in 1923, Gann presumably sold the remarkably preserved object to the British Museum in 1924, where it still resides in the museum's storage rooms. I use the term *presumably* in the previous sentence, as it is unclear if the object imaged in figure 9 was part of Gann's initial sale to the museum; their registration records are unclear on this point. Regardless, Gann's last will and testament (dated July 23, 1924) maintains that his collection of "jades, flints, pottery, and other archaeological effects" be given to the British Museum. A digital copy of this legal document can be found at "Will and Testament."

7. John Chuchiak's contributions to this line of inquiry began with his dissertation and have subsequently appeared as journal articles and various essays. In researching this book, I have accessed many of the same archival documents cited by Chuchiak in "Indian Inquisition."

8. Ibid., 4.

9. "Méritos de Baltasar de Herrera, clerigo prespitero," AGI, México 292 (unpaginated ramo). Herrera spent most of his career in the Indio village of Petu, located in the center of the peninsula, and thus was positioned on the border between the fully conquered Spanish territory and the monte space of the unpacified zone. Thus, this priest came into continual contact with Maya apostates who had fled to the monte for a variety of reasons, but typically to avoid harsh treatments at the hands of secular Spanish settlers, such as their assigned encomenderos.

10. "Auto of Bachiller Andres Fernández de Castro," AGI, México 294 (unpaginated ramo).

11. Landa, "Relación de las cosas de Yucatán," 22r–22v.

12. To date, the most cohesive overview of this corpus of artifacts is Coggins, *Artifacts from the Cenote of Sacrifice*.

13. The excavated artifacts and field notes from this project are housed in Harvard University's Peabody Museum of Archaeology and Ethnology, where I was able to examine the extant examples. Given the limitations of this study, I have not analyzed the vast quantity of effigy vessels that have been scientifically excavated in Yucatán since the Chichén Itzá cenote project provided an ample and diverse sample.

14. Landa, "Relación de las cosas de Yucatán," 22v.

15. The Peabody houses dozens of these wooden limbs that were separated from their bodies in the depths of the Chichén Itzá cenote. The Gann Collection in the British Museum contains dozens of ceramic equivalents.

16. Diego de Landa later identified this bluish hue as the explicit color most closely linked to sacrificial practices ("Relación de las cosas de Yucatán," 23r).

17. Chuchiak, "Indian Inquisition," 329–31.

18. J. Thompson, "Deities Portrayed on Censers at Mayapan"; Taube, *Major Gods of Ancient Yucatan*, 88.

19. The clearest example is waxen effigy 07-7-20/C4654, where a square-shaped element is prominent on the effigy's back.

20. Landa, "Relación de las cosas de Yucatán," 22v.

21. According to the Peabody Museum of Archaeology and Ethnology's collection data, this vessel was excavated from Burial 1 at Chichén Itzá, but I was unable to verify this with supplementary secondary information.

22. This object was similarly collected by Thomas Gann, specifically from the Belizean site of Santa Rita Corozal.

23. Milbrath and Lope, "Mayapán's Chen Mul Modeled Effigy Censers," in Aimers, *Ancient Maya Pottery*, 209.

24. For the classic period, Prudence Rice has differentiated between figurative and nonfigurative incensarios, arguing that the former are associated with the royal funerary cult and the latter are used in the context of renewal rituals ("Rethinking Classic Lowland Maya Pottery Censers," 45).

25. For example, Landa maintains that the postclassic pilgrimage sites of Cozumel and Chichén Itzá had an oracular function (ibid., 22r).

26. Annabeth Headrick has convincingly argued that this aspect of enlivening allowed for the masks to better serve a convincing oracular function as they were mounted on funerary bundles that lined Teotihuacan's "Avenue of the Dead" ("Street of the Dead," 75).

27. Vail, "Pre-Hispanic Maya Religion," 128.

28. Houston, *Life Within*, 83.

29. McGee, *Life, Ritual, and Religion*, 15. This emigration hypothesis is verified by the fact that the modern Lacandones speak a dialect of Yucatec Mayan; other Maya peoples in this region speak Chol or Tzotzil. This population's isolation in the dense forests of Chiapas undoubtedly assisted them in their desire to maintain traditional modes of Maya life. But, as Joel W. Palka's research has proven, it is misguided for scholars to assume that "Lacandon society . . . was not transformed by outside contact or internal culture process" (*Unconquered Lacandon Maya*, 4).

30. McGee, *Life, Ritual, and Religion*, 44; Palka, *Maya Pilgrimage to Ritual Landscapes*.

31. Ibid., 44, 51.

32. Although scholars have tended to treat Landa's "Relación de las cosas de Yucatán" as a stand-alone text, Restall and Chuchiak have shown that it is actually a scattered collection of documents ("Reevaluation of the Authenticity"). Undoubtedly, these discrete sections were written at various points of the friar's life, and it is likely that some were not even written by him at all. For this reason I depart from the method of most scholars and use the extant manuscript for all of my translations, as opposed to the more common editions by Alfred Tozzer and William Gates (Tozzer, *Landa's Relación de Las Cosas de Yucatán*; Gates, *Yucatán Before and After the Conquest*). A close analysis of these editions against the manuscript has revealed a plethora of translation errors and the complete absence of certain key clauses, based on faulty transcription. In the case of Tozzer's edition, these errors can easily be attributed to the fact that he translated from the French edition of 1864 (Brasseur de Bourbourg, *Relation des choses de Yucatán*). These various editions also reordered the manuscript into discrete sections, apparently to improve the narrative flow. In many ways the life and afterlife of Landa's corpus are plagued by intertextual conundrums. This complex issue is the topic of an upcoming book: Restall et al., *Friar and the Maya*.

33. Of all Yucatec colonial history, Landa's quasi-inquisitorial investigation of 1562 has received the most scholarly attention; see, for example, Clendinnen, *Ambivalent Conquests*; and Clendinnen, "Disciplining the Indians." Landa stands in the unique position of both causing the massive destruction of Maya cultural heritage (he demolished thousands of Maya effigies and burned dozens of hieroglyphic codices) and compiling the most comprehensive account of Maya lifeways to survive to the modern era. The level of ethnographic detail contained in his extant writings leave little doubt that Landa engaged in some kind of early modern participant observation. Although he left us no clue if he was intentionally gathering "anthropological" data to later be used to root out idolatry, his future actions in the region make this a distinct possibility. Like his brother mendicants in central Mexico (I'm thinking specifically of Bernardino de Sahagún), he may have been self-consciously gathering his abundant ethnographic data to correctly identify sacrilegious behavior when he later returned to established mission towns to continue the evangelical effort in a more official capacity. The multifaceted functions of Sahagún's final textual product have been explored in the numerous essays in J. Schwaller, *Sahagún at 500*.

34. Since the surviving text is a copy transcribed in the nineteenth century, it is impossible to discern authorial authenticity based on handwriting or other supposedly diagnostic methods such as watermarks. There are, however, profound rhetorical differences between this section and those preceding and following it. The most likely candidate for Landa's "ghostwriter" would of course be Gaspar Antonio Chi. As a member of the Xiu lineage, Chi would have likely provided information centric to his family. In fact, this bias can be gleaned in various moments of the manuscript and in complete contradistinction to the opinions expressed elsewhere in the document, specifically sections that seem to provide a view more likely held by the Xiu's archrivals, the Cocom family. For biographical details of Chi's life, see Restall, "Gaspar Antonio Chi," in Andrien, *Human Tradition Around the World Series*, 13–31.

35. It is increasingly apparent that the first half of the manuscript does not reproduce a cohesive text but instead is heavily redacted. This discrepancy is evident in particular rhetorical structures (i.e., beginning each paragraph with *Que* as though the transcriber is answering a lengthy questionnaire) that are used only in this section of the manuscript and the continual use of the second person when referring to Landa and his *libro*. Moreover, long sections appear to be heavily based on both Anghiera's *De Orbe Novo* and Oviedo y Valdés's *Historia general de las Indias*.

36. Landa, "Relación de las cosas de Yucatán," 31r.

37. Landa is particularly confusing on this point. While he repeatedly used "called" (*llamado*) in his discussions of particular statues, he states elsewhere in the manuscript, "They well knew that the idols were made by their own hands, and were dead things without divinity. Moreover, they held them in reverence because of what they represented, having been made with such ceremony, especially those of wood" (ibid., 22v).

38. This same passage was analyzed in Chuchiak, "Indian Inquisition," 331–33.

39. Strangely, both Gates and Tozzer translate Landa's *official de los ídolos* as "artist" or "artisan," a semantic leap I am unwilling to make.

40. Landa, "Relación de las cosas de Yucatán," 43r–43v. Numerous scholars have turned to this passage to analyze the anthropological details of Maya carving methods. Most obvious is Ciaramella, *Idol-Makers in the Madrid Codex*.

41. For the social and religious role of Maya religious specialists postcontact, see Chuchiak, "Pre-conquest Ah Kinob."

42. Contemporary Maya sculptors from the Puuc town of Santa Elena (Nohcacab in the precontact era) still prefer to use cedar, but cite its "natural golden color" and "pleasant aroma" as their reasons for selecting it. Moreover, since it is a hardwood, it is

particularly useful for "intricate high and low relief carvings" (Scott and Kowalski, "Imaging the Maya," in Kowalski, *Crafting Maya Identity*, 37).

43. Solari, *Maya Ideologies of the Sacred*, 46–55.

44. Gates translates *tereja* as "urn" (*Yucatán Before and After the Conquest*, 76).

45. Ciaramella, *Idol-Makers in the Madrid Codex*, 7.

46. Bassett, *Fate of Earthly Things*, 141.

47. Ibid., 150.

48. "Carta de Fray Diego de Mexia," AGN, Inquisición 125 (unpaginated ramo).

49. More frequently, the fermented honey beer, balché, is referenced as a food offering, but it is also credited with causing indigenous indignities.

50. The Maya details of this case survive only because of the supposed participation of an African slave, who fell under the Inquisition's jurisdiction; the Maya participants did not because by 1571 it had been ruled that indios would be exclusively tried by the episcopal courts of bishops, not the tribunal of the Inquisition (Chuchiak, *Inquisition in New Spain*, 8).

51. "Auto de Fray Antonio de Arroyo, clerigo presbitero," AGI, México 292 (unpaginated ramo).

52. "Contra Juan Vela de Aguirre de Homun y dos indios por idolatrias y hechizarias," AGN, Inquisición 455, fols. 303r–307v.

53. Included in this petition Herrera inserted the transcription of multiple extirpation campaigns that he personally oversaw during his tenure in the remote towns of Petu (Peto), Poole, and the island of Cozumel, located on the southern and eastern peripheries of the Spanish-occupied territory. The very fact that this secular priest was resident in this difficult peripheral zone speaks to the conflict between the Franciscan order and the seculars that plagued the peninsula for decades.

54. *Boloncolob* (*bolonk'olob*) directly translates into "nine serpents," but I have been unable to identify exactly to what species of plant this refers. In Herrera's own description of the indigenous idolatry (located at the beginning of his probanza), he hyperbolically claims that "the Indians idolize with great ritual and ceremonies, sacrificing animal hearts, fish entrails, ground chocolate and other things."

55. "Méritos de Baltasar de Herrera, clerigo prespitero," AGI, México 292 (unpaginated ramo).

56. Landa, "Relación de las cosas de Yucatán," fols. 40r, 42r.

57. Evidence for colonial-period Yucatecan medicine reveals the practice to be wonderfully hybridized, a syncretic mixture of European, African, and indigenous beliefs, which practitioners accepted as a singularly cohesive system of medical knowledge. As scholars, we are fortunate that several colonial-period medicinal manuscripts have survived, some of which are derived primarily from precontact sources, and others from European texts. As such, it is impossible to use these sources to reconstruct a substantive ideology of the body, illness, medicine, healing, and so forth. But contained within the folio pages are suggestions of some crucial aspects of this traditional system, healing practices maintained through the colonial period, whose vestiges appear in modern anthropological studies from the mid-twentieth century. To date Ryan Kashanipour has conducted the most thorough analysis of colonial Yucatecan medical practices, including a table that lists all extant colonial texts ("World of Cures, 244–45), table 5.2.

58. Today the manuscript is located in "Expediente sobre la visita Yucatán por el Obispo," AGI, México 3168, fols. 28r–36r. A transcription of the manuscript has been revised by Erik Boot (Baeza, "Informe del cura de Yaxcabá"). The "Informe" has also been translated in its entirety into English in Rugeley, *Maya Wars*, 19–30.

59. "Informe del cura de Yaxcabá," AGI, México 3168, fol. 29r. Because of this, my account intentionally omits his pervasive editorializing commentary and focuses solely on the rite's various steps.

60. Ibid.

61. Baeza maintains that when the household members had drifted off to sleep, the diviner would secrete this figure on the house grounds, producing it only after the participants had awakened.

62. I would be remiss if I did not point out the obvious similarities between Baeza's description and rites documented for vodun practitioners in West Africa, the Caribbean, and Brazil. Scholars have long lamented the seeming invisibility in the archival and material record of the undoubtedly profound influence African culture had on the development of early modern religion and healing practices in Latin America. Perhaps this ethnographic description is a rare insight into one of these influences?

63. "Informe del cura de Yaxcabá," AGI, México, 3168, fol. 29v.

64. Ibid. This may be a localized, nineteenth-century version of the Maya Death God, described in Schellas typology as "God A." Karl Andreas Taube notes that the postclassic and colonial name for this deity was likely "Cizin" (*Major Gods of Ancient Yucatan*, 13–14).

65. Vogt, *Zinacantan*, 430.

66. Redfield and Redfield, *Disease and Its Treatment in Dzitas*, 69–71. The various definitions of *k'ex* can be found in Bastarrachea Manzano and Brito Sansores, *Diccionario Maya Cordemex*, 396–97.

67. Some residents even considered it counter to orthodox Catholic leanings and thus deemed it heretical. Structurally, this vision of it as specifically counter to the teaching of Catholicism leads

me to believe that it has deep precontact or perhaps early colonial roots, when Maya healing practices were being mixed with those introduced by free and enslaved Africans resident in Yucatán. Regardless, the controversial nature of the rite certainly raises questions about its modern appearance in the region.

68. Redfield, *Folk Culture of Yucatan*, 305.

69. The manuscript is cataloged as Garrett-Gates Mesoamerican Manuscripts, no. 6, in Princeton University Library, New Jersey. An annotated English translation is Bricker and Miram, *Encounter of Two Worlds*.

70. Scholars have noted the similarity between this system and that of early modern Europe, primarily agreeing that it can be attributed to an appropriation of European medical ideologies by the Maya people. For an overview of the European influence on Yucatecan medicine, see the introduction to Bricker and Miram, *Encounter of Two Worlds*. The "Ritual of the Bacabs" mentions evil winds only in one healing incantation, that for "erotic seizures" (Roys, *Ritual of the Bacabs*, xxii, 32).

71. Redfield, *Folk Culture of Yucatan*, 306.

72. The entry for *çaca* (zaca, sakha) in the sixteenth-century "Motul Dictionary" reads, "atole, in the Mexican language, made of water and corn, drunk cold without cooking or heating (Ciudad Real, 92r).

73. Traditionally, all three of these Catholic personages had been associated with communal and personal healing in European Catholicism.

74. Redfield and Villa Rojas, *Chan Kom*, 174. Redfield's description of the k'ex includes additional anecdotal details, which I did not include in this summary.

75. Redfield and Redfield, *Disease and Its Treatment in Dzitas*, 70.

76. This manuscript is cataloged as Garrett-Gates Mesoamerican Manuscripts, no. 1, in Princeton University Library. To date, the only translation available in the English language is Roys, *Ritual of the Bacabs*.

77. The incantations that use material icons can be found on manuscript pages 31, 43, 61, 75, 81, 88, 90, 92, 97, 132, 144, 149, 150, 151, and 157.

78. Roys, *Ritual of the Bacabs*, 43. In a single incantation, the alternative coupling of the "red modeled female effigy" and the "white female human effigy" is used (31).

CHAPTER 3

1. While Francisco de Florencia wrote his text before his death in 1698, it wasn't published until 1755, after being edited by another Jesuit, Juan Antonio de Oviedo. The text's history is significant. As Jason Dyck has argued, for the authors it provided a means to display a "creole political agenda" ("Sacred Historian's Craft," 92).

2. Florenica's text includes sections borrowed from López de Cogolludo's *Historia de Yucathán*, which was published in 1688. Thus, the Yucatán section of the *Zodiaco mariano* must have been composed after this date.

3. Florencia had earlier devoted a text to this singular icon (*Estrella del norte de México*).

4. Florencia and Oviedo, *Zodiaco mariano*, 1. With this statement Florencia referenced an incident described by Hernando Cortés in 1519 and later by Bernal Díaz del Castillo toward the end of the sixteenth century, in which these early conquistadors convinced Mayas living off the east coast of Yucatán to install an image of the virgin in their indigenous temple. For an academic overview of this event, see Remensnyder, *Conquistadora*, 240–43.

5. Florencia and Oviedo, *Zodiaco mariano*, 2.

6. Amy Remensnyder has discussed the ability of the Virgin Mary to cleanse pagan spaces; see "Colonization of Sacred Architecture," in *Monks and Nuns, Saints and Outcasts*, 189–219.

7. Scheper Hughes, *Biography of a Mexican Crucifix*.

8. "Confirmación de encomienda de Yzamal, etc.," AGI, México 242A, núm. 18; "Méritos de Juan de Salazar Montejo," AGI, Indiferente General 214, núm. 18.

9. Both Juan de la Cueva Santillán's and Joan de Paredes's responses can be found in AGI, Indiferente General 1530, núm. 5, fols. 160–67, 170–77.

10. Bernardo de Lizana specifically mentions using the now missing works of Fray Alonso de Solana, who worked in the province between 1565 and circa 1600.

11. William Taylor has noted that Lizana's miracles "reiterated the Gospel parables" and thus "follow miracles worked by Christ" (*Theater of a Thousand Wonders*, 311, 315).

12. Ibid., 11.

13. It is unlikely that documents from this period don't exist; I simply haven't been able to locate them.

14. It is for this reason that, for chapter 1, I am able to almost exclusively rely on López de Cogolludo's account of the 1648 yellow fever epidemic, as he devoted seven entire chapters to the episode,

describing in detail the spread of the disease and the cultural devastation left in its wake. Most significant, he left us an impressive account of the virgin's procession from Itzmal to Mérida and back, hinting at the social complexities that swirled around this event.

15. Solari, *Maya Ideologies of the Sacred*, 129–44. For a summary of "Maya Catholicism," see Early, *Maya and Catholicism*; and Christensen, *Nahua and Maya Catholicisms*.

16. Quiñones Cetina, "Preclásico medio al clásico temprano," 53–55, 70. For an overview of the site's precontact history, see Solari, *Maya Ideologies of the Sacred*, 29–39.

17. "Relación de Cizil y Sitilpech," AGI, Indiferente General 1530, núm. 5, fols. 160–67. The local encomendero relates that he interviewed *algunos yndios viejos naturales* (some old Indian natives) and *el casique y prencipales* (the cacique and elders) to compose his response. Lizana used similar appellations, attesting to the fact that these names were in popular circulation during the course of the colonial period. See *Historia de Yucatán*, 4v. Strangely, Diego de Landa, who was more intimately aware of these structures than either Parades or Lizana, does not specifically name any of Itzmal precontact buildings.

18. This structure seems to have been stylistically related to one of the largest mounds of Mérida-Tiho; Landa described it in detail and provided an illustration ("Relación de las cosas de Yucatán," 46v–47r). Lorenzo de Bienvenida also left a textual account of the Tiho structure as well (Lorenzo de Bienvenida to the Crown, AHN, Diversos-Colecciones 23, núm. 16, fol. 1v) and was likely a resident during its remaking into Mérida's Franciscan monastery.

19. Lizana, *Historia de Yucatán*, 6v–7r. But it is unlikely that Lizana accurately describes Maya practices, as his account too closely smacks of stereotypical early modern understandings of "pagan" religious acts.

20. Very recent excavations from the metropolis of Chichén Itzá have verified that this is a Yucatecan tradition, as archaeologists have discovered a cenote directly beneath the bulk of the site's largest temple structure, the Castillo ("Descubren universitarios un cenote debajo").

21. For an overview of the scant evidence of Juan de Mérida's life, see Bretos, *Arquitectura y arte sacro en Yucatán*, 25–27.

22. The construction was completed in 1561 under the guidance of the then guardian Francisco de la Torre, as Landa had been elected the order's regional provincial earlier that year and had been recalled to their convent in Mérida. Regardless, Landa supposedly resided in the Itzmal convent whenever his responsibilities in Mérida allowed.

23. Perhaps this absence further evidences the fact that Landa's "Relación de las cosas de Yucatán" was augmented by additional authors.

24. Like many of his fellow Yucatecans, Cueva Santillán had access to information dating to the tenure of his predecessor, Pedro Muñoz, who had originally been granted the encomienda.

25. Bienvendia had been instructed by his superior, Toribio de Benavente Motolinia (1482–1568) of this route (Chamberlain, *Conquest and Colonization of Yucatan*, 313). Bienvenida's letter to the Spanish Crown describing this journey can be found in (AHN, Diversos-Colecciones 23, núm. 16). Elizabeth Graham has used this same documentation to argue for the very early presence of Franciscans in the rural areas of contemporary Belize (*Maya Christians and Their Churches*, 111, 158–61). Graham also suggests that this route was still being used as late as 1638, when López de Cogolludo apparently traveled to Guatemala from Mérida via Pacha, a settlement located north of Bacalar (160).

26. The difficulty of this overland route was articulated decades later, in 1621, by Francisco de Mirones in his textual justification for why the southern portion of the peninsula needed to be pacified: "It would be very useful and necessary to communicate by land with the province of Guatemala, thereby avoiding great risks by sea and enemies that ordinarily infest these coasts" (qtd. in Scholes and Adams, *Documents Relating to the Mirones Expedition*, 8). The authors of this text relate that the original documents can be found in "Cartas y expedientes de personas seculares," AGI, México 141 (unpaginated ramo).

27. López de Cogolludo, *Historia de Yucathán*, 310. Some scholars have attributed the icon's creation to a Spanish sculptor named Juan de Aguirre, who later joined the Franciscan order and was renamed Juan de San Francisco. According to this line of argument, Aguirre was also responsible for carving the Guatemalan Virgin of the Choir, which functioned as a model for the Virgin of Itzmal (Fernández Repetto and Negroe Sierra, *Izamal festivo*, 22–24). I have been unable to locate archival evidence that would substantiate such a claim.

28. Florencia and Oviedo, *Zodiaco mariano*, 2. In the face of Florencia's accolades, Bertha Pascacio Guillén has described the Guatemalan school in this historical moment as "fledgling" ("Tras las huellas de una tradición, 119).

29. Florencia and Oviedo, *Zodiaco mariano*, 2.

30. Chamberlain, *Conquest and Colonization of Yucatan*, 313.

31. "Cartas y expedientes del cabildo secular," AGI, México 364, núm 1, fol. 12v.

32. Lizana, *Historia de Yucatán*, 16r. This Marian icon has been lost in the intervening centuries, although some claim that it is this second Mary that replaced the Virgin of Itzmal after the original was destroyed in the monastery's fire of 1829. In fact, a few decades after Lizana penned his account, López de Cogolludo remarked that the Mérida convent owned only a statue of an Immaculate Virgin Mary (*Historia de Yucathán*, 214). He does, however, note (citing Sanchez de Aguilar) that the cathedral housed a Virgin of the Nativity, apparently sent to Mexico in 1592 to be revarnished (208). It is tempting to surmise that the cathedral Marian icon of which López de Cogolludo speaks is the Virgin of Itzmal's "sister Mary," but from the lack of contextual information, it is impossible to determine. Given the difference of advocation, it is unlikely that the statue venerated today in Itzmal is actually the sixteenth-century Nuestra Señora de la Natividad of the Franciscan convent. Guillén has argued, conducting a visual analysis of the extant presentations of the virgin, that, during the course of her history, there have actually been three different statues of her ("Tras las huellas de una tradición," 125).

33. Lizana, *Historia de Yucatán*, 17v–18r.

34. López de Cogolludo, *Historia de Yucathán*, 310.

35. Lizana, *Historia de Yucatán*, 18r.

36. Florencia and Oviedo, *Zodiaco mariano*, 2.

37. Of course, it is always my hope that further archival research will bring earlier documentation of this cult to light. Because this lapse approximates a generational gap, it is tempting to surmise that we are seeing an example of processual Christianization and therefore a kind of intermediate stage of conversion, what one scholar has termed "nepantlism" (Klor de Alva, "Spiritual Conflict and Accommodation," in Collier, Rosaldo, and Wirth, *Inca and Aztec States*, 353–55).

38. Ciudad Real, *Tratado curioso y docto*, 333.

39. Ibid.

40. Kashanipour, "World of Cures," 60. For these same years, Kashanipour cites eleven additional outbreaks in central Mexico.

41. Tellingly, the Virgin of Itzmal is the only miraculous icon that Ciudad Real mentions; he describes other images, but none that are specifically petitioned to enact change in the lives of their devotees.

42. The text of *Informe contra idolorum cultores* wasn't completed until 1617, when Sánchez de Aguilar was summoned to Madrid to serve as his order's procurator of the province of Yucatán.

43. Pedro Sánchez de Aguilar spent the bulk of his career in the eastern side of the province, having been elected vicar of Valladolid, Chancenote, and Sotuta in 1597. As this eastern boundary of colonial control had for decades been wrought with accounts of idolatrous apostate Mayas, Aguilar was specifically charged with "imparting ecclesiastical justice" (Bracamonte y Sosa, *Conquista inconclusa de Yucatán*, 157.) Shortly thereafter he was named the comisario of the Santa Cruzda Bull, the proceeds of which Pope Clement had recently extended to help fight the "infidels" of the Americas. In this role Aguilar had ample opportunity to intimately know the details of clandestine Maya rites, since, once caught, the accused would surely have been forced to confess sins. Aguilar's biography can be found in AGI, Charcas 89, núm. 9.

44. Sánchez de Aguilar, *Informe contra idolorum cultores*, 95v. In addition, this friar also mentions the Virgin of Calotmul as being particularly meaningful to Maya devotees.

45. Ibid., 109r.

46. Porras y Montalvo and Lizana to the Crown, AGI, México 301 (unpaginated ramo). Porras remains one of the most intriguing characters of the Yucatecan evangelical project; he survived the infamous Jamaican shipwreck of 1602 en route to the peninsula. An account of his experiences can be found in his lengthy probanza de mérito. "Méritos de Gerónimo de Porras y Montalvo," AGI, México 301 (unpaginated ramo).

47. Despite Porras and Lizana's hyperbolic account, there does appear to be a substantive difference between central Mexican domestic Catholicism and that of the Yucatán. As analyzed by Mark Christensen, who relied exclusively on inventories included in testaments, the Yucatec Maya were less likely than Nahuas to own Catholic images such as prints or statues of the saints. Interestingly, the town from which Christensen's most affirmative evidence for Yucatec religious visual culture comes, Cacalchén, is located a mere 14.3 miles from Itzmal, suggesting to me the localized influence of the Virgin of Itzmal's cult (*Nahua and Maya Catholicisms*, 246–57).

48. "Petición de Fray Gerónimo de Porras y Montalvo," AGI, México 301 (unpaginated ramo). As bishop, Salazar had completed three formal tours of the province to instill "sound and orthodox doctrine" among the indigenous population. In the course of these visitas, he claimed to have procured more than twenty thousand Maya effigy sculptures.

49. Porras y Montalvo and Lizana to the Crown, AGI.

50. Lizana, *Historia de Yucatán*, 35v, 36r. This declaration of Amerindian colonial towns as the "New Jerusalem" was a common evangelical trope in the sixteenth century (Lara, *City, Temple, Stage*, 93–98). Intriguingly, Landa had similarly

re-Christened one of Itzmal's precontact mounds, the Kinich Kakmo, as Mount Tabor, in an effort to reinscribe poignant spots of the Holy Land in this new mission (Solari, *Maya Ideologies of the Sacred*, 129–30).

51. "Fray Gerónimo de Porras y Montalvo," AGI México 301 (unpaginated ramo). In the better-documented case of the Maní cofradía dedicated to the Immaculate Conception, it was recorded as early as 1588 that the brothers not only oversaw the cult's basic functioning but also assisted their fellow members in other ways as well (Ciudad Real, *Tratado curioso y docto*, 367).

52. Farriss, *Maya Society Under Colonial Rule*, 342; Restall, *Maya World*, 151–52. Christensen has also found evidence for seventeenth- and eighteenth-century Maya confraternities in the neighboring villages of Tekanto and Cacalchén (*Nahua and Maya Catholicisms*, 246–49), but it is likely that these brotherhoods came into existence much earlier. The nineteenth-century Bishop Carrillo y Ancona, using documents from Merida's Franciscan archive, recounts that the province's first cofradía was, not surprisingly, founded by Francisco Montejo (the son) on November 18, 1542, and dedicated to the Nuestra Señora de la Encarnacion (Carrillo y Ancona and Rendón, *Repertorio pintoresco*, 544).

53. "Sobre la cofradía de Ysamal," AGI, México 3066, fol. 203. Also of interest in this regard is an inventory of the virgin's material holdings, drawn up in 1774 in response to a similar complaint, the mishandling of her funding revenue by the local confraternity. British Library, Ms Add 42568, fols. 135r–144r. A much later statute of the Itzmal confraternity for the Holy Sacrament can be found in *Estatutos de la venerable cofradía*.

54. The relatively few extant copies of Lizana's *Historia de Yucatán* suggest its limited print run.

55. Lizana, *Historia de Yucatán*, 28r–28v, 33v.

56. The friar's detailed descriptions of all the following events can be found in Lizana, *Historia de Yucatán*, 38v–53v.

57. For my argument I take an alternative approach and instead follow the lead of anthropologists and specifically folklorists, such as Alan Dundes, who have argued that an analysis of a culture's popular tales reveals what he calls "folk ideas," the "building blocks of worldview" ("Folk Ideas as Units of Worldview," 96). Dundes also warns, "This image may be distorted but at least the distortion comes from the people, not from some outside observer armed with a range of a priori premises" (*Interpreting Folklore*, viii). Of course, this becomes a complex issue when the tales under analysis were produced in a colonial context, by one of the

"victors," in this case a Franciscan friar tasked with the conversion of a subjugated people. However problematic this context may be, given the paucity of material relevant to the Yucatán's spiritual conquest, it is worth the risk to carefully glean what one can from the rich ethnographic source.

58. In Lizana's day the most popularly read account of miracle legends in the Spanish-speaking world was certainly Gabriel de Talavera's account of the miracles worked by the Extremaduran Virgin of Guadalupe (*Historia de Nuestra Señora de Guadalupe*). As Jeanette Peterson has noted, Diego de Ocaña carried three hundred copies of this text with him during his early seventeenth-century sojourn through New Spain, testifying to this document's cultural influence and its dissemination throughout the Spanish Americas (*Visualizing Guadalupe*, 44). While it is outside the scope of this project to conduct a literary comparison of Lizana's legends and those provided by Talavera, a cursory comparison reveals a great deal of thematic overlap, making it feasible that Lizana had a copy of the Spanish *Historia de Nuestra Señora de Guadalupe* to use as a guide. For example, the structure is similar between Lizana's passage, "medianera y avogada, hallando, como hallan vida para sus muertos, salud para sus enfermos, alivio en sus trabajos, consuelo en sus aflicciones" (28r), and one from Talavera's description of the Spanish Virgin of Guadalupe: "El que avia venido ciego a su casa, bolvia a la suya con vista, el sordo con despiertos oydos, el coxo con ligereza, el miserable tullido con venturosa fuerça, el endemoniado libre, el triste con gozo, finalmente, todo linage de enfermedad, con milagroso remedio" (17r). While this certainly does not evince that Lizana was directly using Talavera as a model, it suggests the ubiquity of these attributions by the seventeenth century.

59. Taylor has noted the relative absence of miracle reports in New Spain when compared to the registers of shrine miracles European contemporaries meticulously recorded. He argues that in the colonial context of New Spain, church authorities wished to keep religious devotion "within bounds" (*Theater of a Thousand Wonders*, 314).

60. López de Cogolludo, *Historia de Yucathán*, 310–16.

61. The remaining three tales involve the virgin interceding in a nautical context, and so physical contact with the virgin or her effects would have been impossible at the moment of the crises. In one case, she saved a Spanish ship from a violent storm, and in another she did the same for some Maya fishermen in a canoe. She also assisted another Spanish ship when it ran aground off the peninsula's north coast. By 1688 the ship of Gaspar de

Pimienta Palacios was named for the Nuestra Señora de Ysamal (and also for El Santísimo Cristo de San Román), further verifying her special assistance to seamen. Mention of this vessel can be found in two separate archival documents, both of which are petitions for the royal approval of their pilots (see AGI, Contración 5782, núm. 33; and AGI, Contración 5782, núm. 62). López de Cogolludo recounts that El Santísimo Cristo de San Román was a black Christ housed in the Campeche church of San Roman Martyr. He was originally deemed miraculous owing to his intervention during a locust infestation but thereafter was renowned for his assistance to mariners (López de Cogolludo, *Historia de Yucathán*, 221–22).

62. Florencia, *Estrella del norte de México*, 12–21.

63. Cárdenas Valencia, "Relación historical eclesiastica," fol. 58r.

64. López de Cogolludo, *Historia de Yucathán*, 314.

65. Peterson, *Visualizing Guadalupe*, 46.

66. A record of the destroyed church ornaments, a description of the structural damage, and an inquiry into the fire's cause can be found in, AGN, Bienes Nacionales, exp. 7, leg. 157.

67. Given this novena's publication date of 1854, it was likely printed as a response to Pope Pio IX's declaration of the Immaculate Conception as official church dogma. I have also located later novenas dedicated to the Virgin of Itzmal: Marín, *Novena de la sacratísima Virgen*; Seguí, *Novena de la sacratísima Virgen*; Christoval and Zúñiga y Ontiveros, *Novena de la santissima Virgen*; and *Novena en honor*. All are currently housed in the Centro de Apoyo a la Investigación Histórica de Yucatán, Mérida.

68. For overviews of these catastrophic events, see Hoggarth et al., "Drought and Its Demographic Effects," 87–88; and Bricker and Hill, "Climatic Signatures in Yucatecan Wills."

69. To date, the best scholarly work on these kinds of devotional images has focused on Andean traditions. See Damian, *Virgin of the Andes*; Stanfield-Mazzi, *Object and Apparition*; and Engel, "Visualizing a Colonial Peruvian Community."

70. Patch, *Maya and Spaniard in Yucatan*, 218–19.

71. Curiously, a copy of this painting was made at some point in the late colonial period and ended up in the collection of Mexico City's Museo del Carmen, a museum refashioned from the remains of a Carmelite convent, the Convento de El Carmen, founded in 1613. Perhaps this speaks to the virgin's growing popularity in the years following the publication of Florencia's *Zodiaco mariano*?

72. López de Cogolludo, *Historia de Yucathán*, 317.

73. In the intervening decades between the seventeenth-century production of the prints and the later paintings, these devotees had given their patron saint a sizable wardrobe that eventually necessitated the construction of a separate room to house the outfits in her home sanctuary. Incredibly, some of these gifts were purchased for the virgin in Spain; López de Cogolludo mentions two garments procured in Spain, brought back to the virgin by the reverend provincial, Antonio Ramirez. One must assume that these imported items held special significance in this isolated town that saw few elite Spanish goods. López de Cogolludo spends multiple paragraphs describing the virgin's riches, most of which were donated following her procession to Mérida in 1648. The grateful Mérideños showered the virgin with jewels, which were appraised and then sold, paying for the construction of an elaborate litter, which López de Cogolludo describes as "a throne of hammered silver, very costly and eye-catching" (*Historia de Yucathán*, 720). This is likely the same litter imaged in both of her paintings.

74. Ibid., 317.

75. Sabás Camacho, *Concilio provincial mexicano IV*, 22.

76. This cartouche has been generously translated by Laurent Cases. Apparently, the canvas was damaged at some point, and a hasty restoration was attempted over a tear that went right through the top right corner of the paragraph. As such, the entirety of the text cannot be translated perfectly. In its current state, it reads, "In the year of the Lord 1648, on the 23rd of August, while the greatest plague was advancing in this city in such a way that very many houses were once again deserted, because none of the . . . owners were spared with life/from life. And this Illmum and also the venerable Caetus celebrated on the behalf of that one a gathering of the few remaining *capitulares* [chapter members], and devotedly for the solstice of the faithful and the people, and also cared for the elucidating the Catholic faith that the most Blessed always Virgin Mary be chosen against the contagious plague in her miraculous image as the greatest of miracles, and she was venerated with great devotion of the people in the place commonly known as Ytzmal and he vowed a vow to God to celebrate through the other chapter members with ministers and the clerics from the clergy of his diocese the vespers Mass and he celebrated in the church the procession for the miraculous Assumption into heaven of the most blessed virgin Mary and he similarly decreed that the charges necessary for this were to be deducted from the estimated tax. He renewed the vow again through the illustrious and venerable chapter in the year of the Lord 1769 on the fifth of December and he ratified with all his heart his own private piety for the most blessed virgin in order that he might

be seen in agreement in the mentioned year and he dedicated this true image of the most blessed Virgin Mary, decorated with the greatest skills and depicted at his own expense with the same Illmum (?) and also the venerable chapter and our Lord Agustín Francisco de Echano consecrated it himself, the Vicarius Deacon of the holy church."

77. For a lucid discussion of the iconographic complexities of the virgin's multiple advocations, see Peterson, *Visualizing Guadalupe*, 119–29.

78. Francisco Pacheco's treatise served to standardize representations of the virgin, according to the published decrees of the Tridentine Council. It was originally published in 1649, but the ideas were quickly disseminated throughout the Iberian Peninsula and beyond to dictate proper modes of Catholic representation. For Pacheco's textual descriptions of the proper modes of representing the various advocations and life events of the Virgin Mary, see *Arte de la pintura*, 481–507.

79. López de Cogolludo, *Historia de Yucathán*, 317.

CHAPTER 4

1. For an overview of Diego Valadés's early biography and a possible explanation for his early dismissal by King Philip II, see Leone, *Saints and Signs*, 237–38.

2. The author included five engravings to illustrate the finer points of the art of rhetoric, but scholars have paid more attention to his seventeen images illustrating themes of the conversion effort, such as his now infamous engraving of an idealized American atrium. Although the work is composed in Latin, a partial Spanish translation exists in Palomera, *Fray Diego Valadés, O.F.M.*

3. For a detailed discussion of the relationship between Valadés's rhetorical practices and those of his contemporaries, see Abbott, *Rhetoric in the New World*; and Venier, "*Rhetorica Christiana* de Diego Valadés."

4. Valadés, *Rhetorica christiana*, 218.

5. Valadés's contemporaries, such as Theodor de Bry, would have likely pictorialized the more expected tropes of cannibalism or idol worshipping. See Gaudio, *Engraving the Savage*.

6. Valadés, *Rhetorica christiana*, 218. Providentially, the two conversational pairs at the far right are shown receiving divine intervention. Behind them two small angels hover, luring one repentant to physically remove the "snake-speech" from his fellow conversant. In another an angel's heavenly influence causes an additional participant to cover his ears against the serpentine words of his conversational partner. The fourth register displays further divine intervention; two Mexica men are reunited in the name of God, as Christ is presented as an "immovable column." The fifth register is kind of cautionary tale, illustrating in five pictorial moments the movement of a young man back into the stronghold of sin. Finally, the sixth register visualizes the three steps that lead one to sin, the suggestion, the consent, and finally one's delight in the unholy act.

7. A version of this chapter has been published as Solari, "'Contagious Stench' of Idolatry."

8. For an overview of the religious landscape of first-century North Africa, see Dunn, *Tertullian*, 13–18; for a revisionist account of Tertullian's life, see Barnes, *Tertullian*; and, more recently, Dunn, *Tertullian*.

9. While the comparison between the sin of idolatry and the other mortal sins has been apparent since this early moment, scholars have analyzed its cultural weight, specifically using the metaphor of marriage. In particular, see Halbertal and Margalit, *Idolatry*, 11.

10. Tertullian, "De Idololatria."

11. Sánchez de Aguilar, *Informe contra idolorum cultores*, 1r.

12. Ruth Gubler has relayed that Aguilar directly related the continued outbreak of idolatry to "the discord and disputes of governors and justices with the prelates and the resulting obstacles" ("Informe contra idolorum cultores," 126).

13. Gubler has similarly recognized the paucity of Yucatecan documentation in this regard. She provides two possible explanations. The first is that the religious of the province were directly following the cédula dictated by Philip II in 1557, forbidding writing that touched on traditional Amerindian beliefs or practices. Second, Gubler points to the fact that so many colonial Yucatecan texts have been lost to modern generations; the sheer destruction of colonial sources may in fact artificially create a body of scholarly materials that appears disinterested in the topic of idolatry (111–12).

14. Sánchez de Aguilar, *Informe contra idolorum cultores*, 65v–66r.

15. Perhaps even more nauseating is the formalized decree from the 1585 *Concilio II provincial Mexicano* that argued for the removal of all remembrances of precontact traditions, lest indigenous neophytes be "deceived by the devil's cunning, and return again like dogs to the vomit of idolatry" (Arrillaga y Barcárcel and Galván Rivera, 23). The theme of "returning to the vomit" of idolatry was also echoed

twice by Friar Diego de Aduarte in reference to the missionary efforts in the Philippines (*De la historia de la provincia*, 62, 230).

16. Nesvig, *Ideology and Inquisition*, 31–32.

17. The other usage of the term occurs in the context of Aguilar's discussion of Philip II's royal cédula that informed his New Spanish colonists of certain "heretics" trying to come to these parts. The king urged his American religious to enact the "necessary remedy" (*el remedio que es necesario*), prompting Aguilar to state that the king should know that the "Indians of this Province would return to the vomit of adoring idols" (Sánchez de Aguilar, *Informe contra idolorum cultores*, 37v). While not as visceral, but certainly pertinent to the discussion here, in the last section of the text Aguilar repeatedly uses the term *enfermedad* (illness) to refer to the ongoing idolatries and *enfermos* (ill people) in reference to its practitioners. In a similar vein the Franciscan friar Alfonso de Castro penned "dung of idolatry" in his 1543 treatise. For an English translation of Castro's entire text, see Nesvig, *Forgotten Franciscans*, 26–50.

18. The population estimates for the late classic period vary drastically, making a clear assessment of population loss postcontact impossible to ascertain. It is undeniable that the peninsula experienced a devastating demographic collapse, resulting in dire social, cultural, political, and economic consequences for the surviving population. Sherburne Friend Cook and Woodrow Wilson Borah, analyzing more than thirty colonial sources, have provided a detailed overview of population fluctuations during the course of the colonial period (*Essays in Population History*, 177). It is now apparent that severe drought, both precontact and postcontact, also dramatically affected the region's population (Hoggarth et al., "Drought and Its Demographic Effects").

19. Numerous scholars, both inside and outside the field of Latin American colonial history, have attempted to formulate a period understanding of colonial Christianity and ritualized vestiges of precontact religion, what early modern Spaniards would have termed *idolatría*. In this regard, the work of Martin Nesvig, John Chuchiak, and David Tavárez, working in New Spain, and Kenneth Mills and Sabine MacCormack for the Andean region have been paramount. See Nesvig, *Ideology and Inquisition*; Chuchiak, "Toward a Regional Definition of Idolatry"; Tavárez, *Invisible War*; Mills, *Idolatry and Its Enemies*; and MacCormack, *Religion in the Andes*. The list of relevant and noteworthy scholarship on this topic is of course much longer.

20. For an overview of the history of disease during this period, see Lindemann, *Medicine and Society*.

21. Ibid., 51.

22. Intriguingly, even after the discovery of the smallpox vaccination, which was coeval with nascent germ theory, this environmental approach was still en vogue. For example, in 1797, a small booklet that discussed the proper methods of smallpox inoculation was published in Puebla, Mexico. Directly following a succinct but graphic description of how to inoculate small children, the author goes on to discuss the curing of diseases specific to hot and cold environments. It is also recommended that when the pox began to dry out, a bloodletting should be administered. See *Instrucción para inocular las viruelas*, 15–17, 34–35.

23. Hippocrates, "On Air, Water, and Places," in Jones, *Hippocrates*, 135.

24. Durling, "Innate Heat in Galen," 210.

25. Carl Sterner has argued that the term "miasma" was not used to described this phenomenon until the seventeenth or eighteenth centuries ("Brief History of Miasmic Theory," 1).

26. It has been noted by historians of science that even in the medieval period, disease outbreaks were recognized as being different in terms of scale and severity, prompting a distinct discourse that has allowed scholars to reconstruct the particulars of these epidemiological disasters (Carmichael, "Universal and Particular").

27. D'Agramont, "Jacme d'Agramont," 61. D'Agramont's analytical link between putrid air and humors is best summarized by the following quote: "Putrefaction of the air can lead sometimes to the generation of living things . . . and sometimes, on the other hand, its putrefaction does not lead to the generation of any living things. . . . Such air must be most unfavorable to our life. And, for that reason, in our body which is called the microcosm, from decay and phlegm may arise worms and vermin with the spirit of life, while from decay of bile or of black bile nothing can generate, because of the essential antagonism between decayed bile and our body. . . . Therefore . . . no man should wonder if the air is sometimes the cause of sudden death of the people; and of diverse pestilential fevers or sores or of abscesses in the axilla or in the inguinal region or in other parts of the body or that the small-pox or worms or other maladies, most perilous and mortal should prevail. And such times can be called times of epidemic or of pestilence" (60–61).

28. Nutton, "Reception of Fracastoro's Theory of Contagion," 198.

29. Fracastoro, *De contagione*. Today Girolamo Fracastoro is perhaps better known for his epic poem on the origins of syphilis, published as *Syphilis sive morbus gallicus*. Interestingly, this poem dramatizes an allegorical encounter of Columbus's men and the

indigenous populations of the Caribbean islands, but to my knowledge no scholar of colonial Latin America has taken it up as an object of analysis.

30. Vivian Nutton has identified three distinct instances where Galen utilized the "seed analogy"; all three usages occurred in within the span of two to four years, suggesting a development of his theory of seeds ("Seeds of Disease," 3–9).

31. Nutton, "Reception of Fracastoro's Theory of Contagion," 234.

32. Cline, "Relaciones Geográficas of the Spanish Indies," 347. López de Velasco's questionnaire was heavily influenced and perhaps even directly assisted by Juan de Ovando y Godoy, who had spent the past decade drafting similar questionnaires for Spain's Iberian holdings. For an overview of the responses from New Spain, particularly in regard to cartographic practices, see Mundy, *Mapping of New Spain*.

33. The fifty-two Yucatecan responses can be found in AGI, Indiferente General 1530, núm. 5.

34. For a copy of the "Instrucción" (sent to Michoacán), see AGI, Patronato 18/2, núm. 16, fols. 1r–2r.

35. Gerardo Bustos has compiled the Yucatec responses to create a kind of generalized Spanish view of the peninsula's environment (*Libro de las descripciones*).

36. *Colección de documentos inéditos*, 11:164, 11:84, 11:164, 13:205.

37. Coxe, *Writings of Hippocrates and Galen*, 247.

38. *Colección de documentos inéditos*, 11:260. Interestingly, the curatives described by the peninsula's Spanish population perfectly resonate with known Maya healing practices, such as the curing of physical symptoms with objects and herbs that replicate those bodily responses. See Kashanipour, "World of Cures," 258–59.

39. Redfield and Villa Rojas, *Chan Kom*, 130, 165. One is tempted to suggest that this bloodletting that seemed so happenstance to the Spanish audience was actually performed as a form of autosacrifice intended for supernatural intervention, not to physically ease corporeal suffering per se.

40. Ibid., 106. As William Hanks has noted, this sentiment also perfectly plays into the coeval Franciscan and secular Spanish rivalry that was currently being played out in the peninsula, whereby each party actively accused the other of abuses enacted toward the Maya population (*Converting Words*, 33).

41. *Colección de documentos inéditos*, 11:106.

42. In fact, these emerging theories were hotly debated even among medical professionals (Nutton, "Reception of Fracastoro's Theory of Contagion").

43. Sahagún, "Historia general de las cosas," 1r. In most English translations, *espiritía* is usually translated as "experience," but I think it is more likely that Bernardino de Sahagún Hispanicized the plural of the Latin noun *espitirus*, "spirit."

44. To this end, Sahagún and countless friars stationed in Yucatán continually mentioned the need for *lenguas*, friars fluent in the native languages of New Spain. Without friars capable of speaking to their indigenous neophytes, curing them of their malicious ailments was understood as impossible. In this, Sahagún falls in line with contemporaneous theology, which conceptualized refined rhetoric as a kind of social remedy. For an insightful discussion of Plato's conceptual conflation of medicine and morality, see Moes, "Plato's Conception of the Relations."

45. Baird, *Drawings of Sahagún's Primeros Memoriales*, 16.

46. The manuscript is currently housed in Real Biblioteca del Palacio Real de Madrid, MS 3280; the Atamalqualiztli image is on folio 254r. The textual description of this rite can be found in Sullivan, *Primeros memoriales*, 67–69.

47. Translated in Sullivan, *Primeros memoriales*, 68–69.

48. Jeanette Peterson has argued that this image is also casually related to a confessional scene from book 6 of the Florentine Codex ("Rhetoric as Acculturation," 23).

49. In this way Valadés differentiates himself from the opinion of Sahagún, who saw within the precontact rhetorical traditions a mode of easing the evangelical burden, since the indigenous population was already familiar with the convincing function of oration (Abbott, *Rhetoric in the New World*, 32).

50. Valadés, *Rhetorica christiana*, 218.

51. Interestingly, precontact societies do not appear to have the same negative connotations of these kinds of animals. For example, in book 11 of the Florentine Codex, nonvenomous snakes are repeatedly described as "harmless," and there isn't a single description of their inherent evilness, as is found in contemporaneous European encyclopedias. Cecilia Klein similarly argues that amphibian and reptilian animals reference the supernatural powers of Mexica deities ("Wild Woman in Colonial Mexico," in Farago, *Reframing the Renaissance*, 257–59). Pete Sigal has shown that, among the Nahuas of central Mexico, animals, in his example scorpions, were much more evocative in their cultural connotations than is suggested by their mere biology (*Flower and the Scorpion*).

52. Of course, agents deemed hazardous to the human population, either physically or spiritually, had long been visualized as repugnant creatures. Marcia Stephenson has shown that early modern representations of poison were pictorially rendered as reptilian, demon-like beings, best immortalized in Francisco de Zurbarán's image of San Luis Beltrán,

who was, not coincidentally, a seventeenth-century Dominican friar who evangelized in Colombia ("From Marvelous Antidote," 24). Representations of Satan himself had long been animalistic, stemming from his conceptual mixing with classical deities such as the hooved pan in the early Christian period.

53. As stated earlier, the link between behaviors deemed morally reprehensible and environmentally contingent physical disease was not a novel concept even in the early modern world. Scholars of ancient Greek philosophy have long noted the coeval relationship between the development of classical ethics and rhetorical practices along with medical knowledge. While there has been debate regarding the directional influence, it seems clear that these two fields of human inquiry, which now reside at opposite poles (and sometimes site plans) of our modern venue for knowledge production, the university, were once engaged in a kind of dialectical and mutually informing relationship. A revealing overview of this parallel intellectual development is provided in Lidz, "Medicine as Metaphor in Plato."

54. Dr. Don Sancho Sánchez Muñón to the Crown, AGI, Indiferente General 739, núm. 94. I am deeply indebted to Robert Schwaller for bringing this incredibly evocative letter to my attention. Schwaller has discussed Muñón's account in much greater detail, specifically in reference to the formation of racial categories in early colonial New Spain ("Defining Difference in Early New Spain," 225).

55. For a scholarly interpretation of this particular epidemic, see Prem, "Disease Outbreaks in Central Mexico," in Cook and Lovell, *Secret Judgments of God,* 24–27; and Cook, *Born to Die,* 63–70. For additional sources of American epidemics in general, see Alchon, *Pest in the Land*; and Fields, *Pestilence and Headcolds.*

56. Of course, this wouldn't be the first time in history that persons of African descent would be targeted as "patient zero" in a mass epidemic. As early as the sixth century BCE this was a trope, as Thucydides hypothesized that the Attic plague of 432 BCE originally spread from "Ethiopia in upper Egypt" (qtd. in Garza, *Understanding Plague,* 16).

57. Mendieta, *Historia eclesiástica indiana,* 514.

58. Ibid., 18.

59. Philip II removed American Indians from the Inquisition's jurisdiction in a royal cédula of 1571 (Klor de Alva, "Colonizing Souls," in Perry and Cruz, *Cultural Encounters,* 4). For an overview of the colonial Inquisition, see Greenleaf, "Inquisition and the Indians"; Moreno de los Arcos, "New Spain's Inquisition for Indians," in Perry and Cruz, *Cultural Encounters,* 23–32; and Chuchiak, *Inquisition in New Spain.*

60. Francisco de Velásquez Gijón to the Crown, AGI, México 359, ramo 4, núm. 15.

61. Bishop Diego Vázquez de Mercado was particularly outspoken about this aspect of the continued idolatries, penning numerous letters to both the Spanish court and the Mexican Audiencia on the topic. See, in particular, Bishop Diego Vázquez de Mercado to the Crown, AGI, Mexico 359, ramo 9, núm. 50.

62. For a discussion of seventeenth-century medicinal texts imported into the colony that either derived from or directly reference Hipporatic-Galenic theories of disease, see Rueda Ramírez, *Negocio e intercambio cultural,* 429–41.

63. Carlos de Luna y Arellano to the Crown, AGI, México 359, ramo 9, núm. 50, fols. 4r, 13r.

64. In one of the earliest letters written by Franciscans in the province, Comisario Juan de la Puerta similarly referenced the ecological nature of this social ill when he utilized the phrase "desert of idolatry" to describe the Yucatán's pre-Christian religious landscape. Franciscan friars of Yucatán to the Crown, AHN, Diversos-Colecciones 23, n. 7, fol. 1v.

65. Andrés Fernández de Castro to the Crown, 1604, AGI, México 294 (unpaginated ramo), emphasis added.

66. "Méritos de Antonio de Arroyo," AGI, México 294 (unpaginated ramo).

67. Vázquez de Mercado to the Crown, AGI, fol. 1v.

68. The actions taken to avoid the spread of idolatry were hotly debated and stemmed from "kill it with kindness" approaches to the advice of some, such as Pedro Sánchez de Aguilar, who argued for severe physical consequences. Priests such as Aguilar admitted the substantive differences between kinds of idolatry and between different kinds of neophytes. To accommodate these differences Aguilar advocated to adjust the recommended punishments accordingly.

69. Most of the "plague studies" have focused their attention on the medieval outbreaks of the disease in England, France, and Italy, likely owing to the relative dearth of documentary evidence from the Iberian Peninsula. But in recent years some attention has been paid to the Spanish and Portuguese experience. See Moreda, "Plague in Castile," in Thompson, *Castilian Crisis of the Seventeenth Century,* 32–59; Carrascal Muñoz, *Guerra de Dios*; Garza. *Understanding Plague*; Stearns, *Infectious Ideas,* 37–65; and Bowers, *Plague and Public Health.*

70. Chirino, *Menor daño de medicina,* 71.

71. The reality of crisis management was much more lenient. Kristy Wilson Bowers has convincingly argued that civic powers continued to make exceptions to their public decrees based on the economic communal good ("Balancing Individual and Communal Needs").

72. This was certainly the case during Seville's plague threat of 1579, when two vessels (one a cargo ship and the other a slave ship) believed to have originated from Portugal were forced to remain boarded until the threat of contamination had passed (Parma Cook and Cook, *Plague Files Crisis Management*, 16–17). Being a port city, Campeche undoubtedly utilized the same tactic on occasion. For an overview of "port society" in early colonial Campeche, see García Bernal, *Campeche y el comercio atlántico yucateco*.

73. Of course, Tomás López Medel's ordinances stemmed way beyond the reach of space alone and, for example, included edicts aimed toward the proper extraction of tribute payment. As Hanks has pointed out, these decrees must be understood within the context of the failed implementation of the 1542 and 1549 New Laws in Yucatán, and in some cases López Medel's laws directly contradicted the earlier edicts (*Converting Words*, 33–34).

74. López de Cogolludo, *Historia de Yucathán*, 293–302. López de Cogolludo states that he transcribed these edicts *à la letra* (to the letter) from the *libro antiguo* (antique book) held by the *cabildo* (town council) of Valladolid (293). For an overview of López Medel's decrees in reference to Indian advocates, see Cunill, "Tomás López Medel y sus instrucciones."

75. López de Cogolludo, *Historia de Yucathán*, 292.

76. Ibid., 294.

77. Diego de Velasco to the Crown, AGI, México 359, ramo 8, núm. 42, fol. 1.

78. For a discussion of this particular visitation, see Ortiz Yam and Quezada, *Visita de Diego García de Palacio*.

79. "Ordinances of Diego García de Palacio," AGI, Indiferente General 2987, fols. 20r, 22r.

80. So dangerous was the monte that friars sent into it never seemed to return, causing one bishop to refer to it as a "death sentence." Fray Antonio de Ciudad Real, Fray Francisco de Bustamante, Fray Francisco Cardete, Fray Antonio Villalon to the Crown, AGI, Audiencia de México 294 (unpaginated ramo).

81. The Inquisition continually tried Spaniards for engaging in Maya rituals. Although this topic has yet to receive full treatment in the academic record, Matthew Restall and Ryan Kashanipour discuss this phenomenon directly in reference to love magic (Restall, *Black Middle*, 265–77; Kashanipour, "World of Cures," 100–101).

82. "Contra Juan Vela de Aguirre," AGN, Inquisición 455, fols. 303r–307v.

83. Ibid., fol. 303r.

84. "Ordinances of Diego García de Palacio," AGI, Indiferente General 2987, fol. 23v.

85. Of course, there was a pragmatic reason for this particular decree as well. It was believed that without "ready for habitation" domestic architecture, the Mayas would be less likely to run away to the monte.

86. "Méritos de Rodrigo Tinoco," AGI, México 3167 (unpaginated ramo).

87. Tavárez has noted a similar instance of spiritual quarantine in Oaxaca, where Bishop Sariñana utilized the social infrastructure of "perpetual prisons" in a mode identical to that of Maria Dzul's case, "treating idolatry defendants like infectious cases . . . quarantined from their social networks" (*Invisible War*, 272).

88. López de Cogolludo, *Historia de Yucathán*, 295.

89. "Ordinances of Diego García de Palacio," AGI, Indiferente General 2987, fol. 24r.

90. López de Cogolludo, *Historia de Yucathán*, 295.

CHAPTER 5

1. Marta Mis's will was housed in Archivo Notarial del Estado de Yucatán, vol. 4, 1819, fol. 37r, but is now located in the Archivo General del Estado de Yucatán. A transcription and English translation can be found in Restall, *Life and Death*, 176–77.

2. Marta also had an additional daughter, named Augustina, who was intentionally cut out of her mother's will "because she and her husband do nothing on my account" (ibid.).

3. Marta gave this religious icon to the son she had named for her father, so one could perhaps conclude that he was her favorite child, and thus she entrusted him with her most valuable possession.

4. To date, Pete Sigal has provided scholars with the most thorough scholarly treatment of Yucatec Maya understandings of the Virgin Mary. Rather than merely understand the Mother of God as a syncretic result of the conversion effort, Sigal recognizes the processual nature of her indigenous identity, arguing that through the middle years of the colonial period she slowly appropriated aspects of the Ix Chel, whose own cultural import was waning. Sigal posits that a kind of hybridized female deity was created to overcome the seeming contradictions between the virginal Mary and the highly sexualized Ix Chel, a sacred being he refers to as "The

Virgin Mary Moon Goddess." The Yucatec Maya directly associated the Virgin Mary with the act of colonization itself; the virgin was the "colonizing goddess, the Spanish parallel of the Moon Goddess" (*From Moon Goddesses to Virgins*, 242).

5. For this discussion I rely primarily on Ciudad Real's early seventeenth-century "Motul Dictionary," supplemented with entries taken from Bastarrachea Manzano and Brito Sansores's modern *Diccionario Maya cordemex*.

6. Archaeological evidence suggests this even to have occurred at the beginning of the fourteenth century. Yet the Chumayel author maintains that the Itza left the Yucatán because they did not want to be Christian or to pay tribute, circumstances dating to European colonization that didn't begin until the 1540s. This is a perfect example of the conflation of certain events in Yucatecan history from the indigenous conception of time as a cyclical entity.

7. In fact, there are many instances in "The Book of Chilam Balam of Chumayel" when the author seemingly inserts lengthy anecdotes into the wrong narrative locations (Solari, *Maya Ideologies of the Sacred*, 83). While this could simply be scribal error, it is also likely that we are viewing evidence of the book's production. Some scholars have argued that these texts were written using hieroglyphic codices as sources (Bricker, "Last Gasp of Maya Hieroglyphic Writing," in Hanks and Rice, *Word and Image*, 39–50). If this is in fact the case (and I believe that it is), it is possible that a Maya literate in the hieroglyphic tradition read from the ancient codex, while another person, who had been taught to read and write using the Latin alphabet (likely in a monastic school), recorded what was being recited. In the course of this event, the narrator ad-libbed sections of narrative, which were then directly transliterated, resulting in the seemingly incongruous nature of certain sections of these esoteric manuscripts.

8. The Mayan word *emi* is used here, a conjugation of *emel*. Most commonly, *emel* translates into "to descend" or "to drop" (Bastarrachea Manzano and Brito Sansores, *Diccionario Maya cordemex*, 153), but it also can have corporeal connotations such as when blood or another bodily fluid leave the body. So here there is perhaps a triple meaning. Christ is "descending" from the sky as a metaphor for the introduction of Christianity, but he also genetically descending from the familial line of his mother, Mary, and, last, he physically is emitted from her body during his birth.

9. *Chim* directly translates as "bag" or "netted bag," but it is used in Mayan clichés that can be translated as one's "bag of compassion" (ibid., 100). Perhaps it is this connotation that is intended here.

10. *Pati* (past tense of *pat*) translates into "declare," "invent," or, most enticingly, "to give form to something" (ibid., 632). I believe we are dealing with the latter of these possibilities. Ciudad Real provides an insightful reading of the word's root noun, *pat*; he defines this as "something made of clay, wax, or dough" ("Motul Dictionary," 367r).

11. The text uses *cicun*, which is likely a variant of *k'ik*, "blood."

12. *Tabí* is the past tense of tabal, "to tie one thing to another," such as horses being tied together. A metaphorical reading could interpret the toponym as tethering the human world to that of the deities.

13. "Book of Chilam Balam of Chumayel," 10v. The original text is "Paxi cah emal chac: etzmal. = ti emi yix mehen: hahal Kui u yumil caan. Yx ahau: yx suhuy. Yx mactzil = ca yalah ahau = emom chim: Kinich Kakmo:. Ma paat ti ahau. Lil uaye : Uay ti pati: yxmactzil: yx ɔayatzil—emom sum = emom tab tal ti caan : emom u than tal ti caan = lay cicun tabí. Y ahaulili tumen u chucan cahob: cayalahob: ma patí y ahau lilob: emmal."

14. Ciudad Real, "Motul Dictionary," 164v.

15. For an overview of the pictorial use of cords in the classic and postclassic Maya world and beyond, see Looper and Kappleman, "Cosmic Umbilicus in Mesoamerica." To date the best translation and analysis of colonial-period creation stories can be found in Knowlton, *Maya Creation Myths*.

16. Vail and Hernández, "Cords and Crocodilians," in Le Fort et al., *Maya and Their Sacred Narratives*, 97, 95.

17. Looper and Kappleman, "Cosmic Umbilicus in Mesoamerica," 4.

18. At other locations in the text, the Chumayel author also describes Jesus Christ as "descending"; clearly, all the newly introduced Catholic personages were being placed within the Mayas' centuries-old theological frame.

19. This moment of "The Book of Chilam Balam of Chumayel" has been translated and analyzed in Knowlton, *Maya Creation Myths*, 54–67; and Solari, *Maya Ideologies of the Sacred*, 61–63. In the *Popol vuh*, a catastrophic flood occurs after the deities' third attempt to make human beings, thus ushering in the era in which contemporary humans are created (Tedlock, 71).

20. In the seminal translation of the Chumayel text, completed by Ralph Roys in 1933, *pat* is glossed as "declared" to reflect that Kinich Kakmo was not "declared ruler" at Itzmal, and instead the virgin was "so declared here" (*Book of Chilam Balam of Chumayel*, 82).

21. In actuality, there is no evidence internal to the manuscript that Ciudad Real was the dictionary's

sole or even primary author. It is just as likely that it was compiled by a now anonymous Maya scribe.

22. Ciudad Real, "Motul Dictionary," 367r. Interestingly, David Stuart has identified the hieroglyph for *pat* in reference to the physical construction of buildings ("Fire Enters His House," in Houston, *Function and Meaning*, 381–82), prompting Stephen Houston to maintain that the term has "cross-craft inspiration," since *pat* also refers to the "plastic manipulation of moist clay" (*Life Within*, 19).

23. Ciudad Real, "Motul Dictionary," 368r.

24. Of course, the Maya had understood these phenomena for millennia, as is evidenced in the precise alignment of architectural complexes to various astronomical events.

25. The manuscript is replete with generic human faces topped with crowns, all of which reference lords of various *k'atun* (twenty-year calendrical cycle) periods. None of these other images include bodies, but an additional "Chilam Balam," that of Teabo, includes an astronomical section nearly identical to that in the Chumayel. Interestingly, in the Teabo manuscript, the human figure that perches on the *tierra* is clearly male.

26. Although the rest of the glosses that surround the image are in Mayan, the artist labeled the earth with the Spanish appellation, suggesting that he was copying this section from a Spanish-language printed book.

27. "Book of Chilam Balam of Chumayel," 48r. The original text is "Bolon ahua katun : u caɔit katun: cuxocol yeh caan çihoo= uheɔ katun; tiix tu kamah u patanobi = uɔullilob cabi = tiix u liob u yumil ca pixan ni = ti yx hun mol hi cahi = ti tzucen tzucil : tu hol poopobi = ti yx ti hopi u canal santo okolal tix hopi yocol haa tacpol ut tiix = es lahi u chun santo yglesia mayori = u kakal na Dios = uxiuil xitelna = Diod cit bil = tix eɔleheuch [water stain] uucppel sacramentoy = çateba [water stain] tix hopi ban meyah chumuc cah [water stain] numya bal cahi = tix u uatal caui [water stain] lic u than kui = xanomi tali tuchi Dios [water stain] bil = ti yulel çatun lanpal = tal ti caan = çuhuy chuplal u kaba : u na u uc pel chacac ek."

28. Ibid. "Çuhuy chuplal u kaba : un na Uuc pel cha chac ek."

29. "The Book of Chilam of Chumayel," fols. 34v–35r. The original text is "Occi christianoil toon §.1519 años. Eɔlahci kuna Tihoo §.1540 años. Ca ɔoci kuna Tihoo §.1599 años. Uchci xe kik, hoppci cimil toon §.1648 años. U uiihi cimil hoppel hab §.1650, §.1651 años, §.1652 años, §.1653 años, §.1654 años. Ca dzoci uiih lae."

30. The manuscript is held in Museum of Indian Arts and Culture in Santa Fe, New Mexico, and the seminal translation can be found in Whalen, "Annotated Translation." The current transcribed copy was written on paper that dates from 1760 to 1780, but it includes the glossed date of 1576 on page 234 (2, 7).

31. Whalen, "Annotated Translation," 44, 119, 143.

32. Documentos de Tekanto, Archivo Notarial del Estado de Yucatán, i. 27.

33. Ciudad Real, "Motul Dictionary," 110v.

34. There is ample evidence of mendicant orders utilizing this same tactic in the Nahuatl evangelical theater of central Mexico. For a specific example of the translation of "sin" into Nahuatl, see Burkhart, *Slippery Earth*, 28–34. Also, Mark Christensen's *Nahua and Maya Catholicisms* is particularly insightful with this line of analysis.

35. Not a single reference to the concept of sexual virginity has been located in the Mayan textual or visual record. As such, the concept is clearly a product of the Christian evangelization mission. In the era the term *suhuy* was explicitly *not* associated feminine abilities such as childbearing. For an insightful analysis of the role of sexuality during the Yucatecan evangelical campaign, see Sigal, *From Moon Goddesses to Virgins*. In fact, Diego de Landa himself might be responsible for the initial sixteenth-century Spanish association of suhuy and female sexuality. In his description of rites performed during the month of Uo, he maintains that "virgin water" (what he calls *agua virgen*) must be procured from a forest where "no women have been" ("Relación de las cosas de Yucatán," fol. 40r).

36. Coronel, *Arte de la lengua Maya*, 151, 155, 157, 163, 169, 191. For a historical contextualization of Coronel's work, with later examples of the genre in Yucatán, see Hanks, *Converting Words*, 242–76.

37. This collection of wills has been analyzed in Restall, *Maya World*, 124–35, 180–84, 247–50; and Christensen, *Nahua and Maya Catholicisms*, 228–29. Cacalchén was a dependent village of the Itzmal parish, and its inhabitants would have been part of Itzmal's regional religious life.

38. Like the term *suhuy*, the term *pixan* has a complex history in the development of colonial Mayan. In the earliest two wills, the scribe references Mary as "nine-souled" (*bolon pixan*), a descriptor that also appears in "The Books of Chilam Balam" to refer to deities and Catholic personages. By using the phrase "the nine-souled, our holy lady, the ritually pure Saint Mary," these Maya testators have effectively hybridized their colonial deity. Nancy Farriss has argued that this reference to the number nine speaks to the notion that a body endured "nine states of transformation through which souls passed to achieve their immortality" (*Maya Society Under Colonial Rule*, 311). Alternatively, Christensen understands *bolon*

pixan not as an adjective but as a noun, signifying "the title of 'Blessed'" (*Nahua and Maya Catholicisms*, 46). He points out that "nine-souled" isn't used exclusively in reference to Mary, as the phrase had also been used in Ebtun as an appellation for the village's patron saint, Saint Bartholomew, and in Tekanto in reference to Saint Augustine (*Nahua and Maya Catholicisms*, 232, 247). I have also found this term in a land title of 1768, drawn up near the villages of Tahcabo and Kaua: "Ca yumilan ah bolon pixan San bartolome tah cabo y cah cili[c] h Colebil Santa maria layx Canoh cintic uayix" ("Ceme Family Deed of Sale," 1r).

39. The use of *suhuy* is ubiquitous in a variety of Maya-authored colonial-period ritual texts, such as the "Ritual of the Bacabs," "El libro de las cantares de Dzitbalché," and many of the "Books of Chilam Balam."

40. Redfield and Villa Rojas, *Chan Kom*, 103–31. For example, Redfield's and Villa Rojas's informants maintained that the linens used to cover altars should not have previously been used (202).

41. Many thanks to Catherine Popovici and David Stuart for their translation of this passage.

42. Córdoba, *Dotrina christiana*, 13v. Although Pedro de Córdoba's text wasn't published until 1544, it was written while he served as America's first royally appointed Inquisitor, sometime before 1520. As it was published under the direction of New Spain's first bishop, the Franciscan Juan de Zumárraga, it is clear that Córdoba's concerns from the previous two decades continued to plague the mainland's first generation of missionaries.

43. Roys posits that this term represents a scribal error and that he intended to write "Ix Kulem," which could be glossed as the "female holy one" (*Book of Chilam Balam of Chumayel*, 126). As

discussed earlier, I believe the Maya author intended to use "Ix Kalem."

44. Matthew Restall maintains that the Maya stopped using Spanish loanwords, such as "santa maria," sometime in the seventeenth century (*Maya World*, 400n13).

45. Restall, *Maya World*; Bernardino Cot, April 29, 1766, Ixil, doc. 24, fol. 12r; and Juan de la Cruz Coba, November 12, 1766, Ixil, doc. 36, fol. 17r. As Christensen has observed, despite the assurances of friars like Porras and Bernardo de Lizana, the native neophytes of Yucatán displayed a much more restrained relationship to home altars when compared to their central Mexican compatriots (*Nahua and Maya Catholicisms*, 250–51). This observation may be a direct function of archival survivability in the peninsula: not as many wills survive, which seems to skew the number of images bequeathed.

46. British Library, Ms Add 42568.

47. For a more exhaustive overview of this manuscript's history, see Cárdenas Valencia and Gómez de Orozco, *Relación historico eclesiastica*, v–vi.

48. Miguel Bretos has argued that the murals' monochromatic pallet suggests their derivation from period print sources (*Iglesias de Yucatán*, 113).

49. For an overview of the Protogospel's and *Golden Legend's* influence, see Rubin, *Mother of God*, 9–11, 203–4.

50. Ibid., 410. Rubin provides an insightful overview of this advocation's role during these tumultuous years (408–12).

51. Williams, "*Birth of the Virgin*," 724.

52. James, "Book of James."

53. Villaseñor Black, "Inquisitorial Practices Past and Present," in Raguin, *Art, Piety, and Destruction*, 188–92, 191–92.

EPILOGUE

1. Sitilpech had been a dependent visita village of the larger Itzmal since the province's territories were carved up by the Franciscans in the middle of the sixteenth century. These jurisdictional patterns actually reflect much older, precontact traditions of political organization. That is, it is likely that the Mayas who inhabited Sitilpech in the centuries prior to Spanish contact paid tribute and were dependent on the royal lineage, the Ah Chel, who controlled Itzmal.

2. This ritual is reminiscent of the Roman Virgin of Santa Maria Antigua, who similarly receives her son annually.

3. The entirety of this tale can be found in Briceño López, *Leyendas Izamaleñas*, 81–85; quote on 83.

4. This part of the Black Christ legend immediately reminds one of the role Provincial Sosa served during the 1648 yellow fever epidemic. Like the Black Christ, Sosa was required to physically take the place of the virgin until she returned from Mérida following her novenario. I am tempted to propose that this historical event influenced or was folklorically morphed into the Sitilpech legend that circulates today.

5. Much has been written on this period of Maya history, but for an overview, see Wells, *Yucatan's*

Gilded Age; Wells and Joseph, *Summer of Discontent*; and Levy, *Making of a Market*.

6. For a theoretical consideration of an empathetic response, see Freedberg, *Power of Images*, 162–75.

7. Medina Un and Quiñones Vega, "Peregrinando por los santuarios," 177. The use of the term "temporary" belies the underlying belief that this local icon's numinous ability will inevitably need to be recharged with future contact with the more powerful icon.

8. Estrella Santana, "Incidentes en la fiesta de Sitilpech."

Bibliography

PRIMARY SOURCES

Aduarte, Diego. *De la historia de la provincia del Sto: Rosario de Filipinas, Japón, y China de la sagrada orden de predicadores.* Zaragoça, Nueva Segovia: Santo Hospital Real y General de Nuestra Señora de Gracia, 1693.

Anghiera, Pietro Martire d'. *De Orbe Novo.* Alcalá de Henares, Spain: Apum Michaelem de Eguia, 1530.

Arrillaga y Barcárcel, Basilio Manuel, and Mariano Galván Rivera. *Concilio II provincial Mexicano: Celebrado en México en el año de 1585, confirmado en Roma* [. . .]. Mexico: Maillefert, 1859.

Baeza, D. Bartolomé José del Granado. *Informe del cura de Yaxcabá.* Translated by Erik Boot. 2008. https://www.wayeb.org/download/resources/baeza.pdf.

"The Book of Chilam Balam of Chumayel." Garret-Gates Mesoamerican Manuscript. Department of Rare Books and Special Collections, Princeton University Library.

Bracamonte y Sosa, Pedro. *La conquista inconclusa de Yucatán: Los Mayas de las montañas, 1560–1680.* Mexico City: Centro de Investigaciones y Estudios Superiores en Antropología Social, 2001.

Brasseur de Bourbourg, Charles Étienne. *Relation des choses de Yucatán de Diego de Landa.* Paris: Bertrand, 1864.

Calderón, Santiago. *Novena de la santísima Virgen de Izamal.* Mérida: Espinosa, 1854.

Cárdenas Valencia, Francisco de. "Relación historical eclesiástica de la provincia de Yucatán de la Nueva España." Manuscript copy of 1643. Egerton Manuscript 1791. British Library, London.

Cárdenas Valencia, Francisco de, and Federico Gómez de Orozco. *Relación historico eclesiástica de la provincia de Yucatán de la Nueva España, escrita el año de 1639.* Mexico City: Antigua Libería Robredo, de Porrúa e Hijos, 1937.

"Ceme Family Deed of Sale." Tahcabo, Kaua, January 23, 1789. Garret-Gates Mesoamerican Manuscript. Department of Rare Books and Special Collections, Princeton University Library.

Charnay, Désiré, and Par M. Viollet-Le-Duc. *Cités et ruines américaines, Mitla, Palenqué, Izamal, Chichen-Itza, Uxmal.* Paris: Gide, 1863.

Chirino, Alfonso. *Menor daño de medicina.* Madrid: Sucesor de Hagenbach, 1504.

Christoval, D., and D. Felipe de Zúñiga y Ontiveros. *Novena de la santissima Virgen de Ytzmal.* Mexico City: Zuñiga y Ontiveros, 1764.

Ciudad Real, Antonio de. "Motul Dictionary." Motul, Yucatán, 1577. John Carter Brown Library, Providence, Rhode Island.

———. *Tratado curioso y docto de las grandezas de la Nueva España: Relación breve y verdadera de algunas cosas de las muchas que sucedieron al padre Fray Alonso Ponce en las provincias de la Nueva España, siendo comisario general de aquellas partes*. Mexico City: Universidad Nacional Autónoma de México, 1993.

Colección de documentos inéditos relativos al descubrimiento, conquista, y orginación de las antiguas posesiones españolas de ultramar. Vols. 11, 13. Madrid: Real Academia de Historia, 1898, 1900.

Colón, Fernando. *Historie del S. D. Fernando Colombo: Nelle quali s'ha paticolare, & vera relatione della vita, & de' fatti dell' ammiragio D. Christoforo Colombo, suo padre*. Venice: Sanese, 1571.

Córdoba, Pedro de. *Dotrina christiana para instrucción y información de los indios: Por manera de hystoria*. Mexico: Casa de Cromberger, 1544.

Coronel, Juan. *Arte de la lengua Maya*. Edited by René Acuña. Mexico City: Universidad Nacional Autónoma de México, 1998.

Coxe, John Redman, trans. *The Writings of Hippocrates and Galen*. Philadelphia: Lindsay and Blakiston, 1846.

D'Agramont, Jacme. "Jacme d'Agramont: 'Regiment de preservacio a epidimia o pestilencia e mortaldats.'" Translated by M. L. Duran-Reynals and C.-E. A. Winslow. *Bulletin of the History of Medicine* 23 (1949): 57–89.

Díaz del Castillo, Bernal. *Historia verdadera de la conquista de la Nueva España*. Madrid: Olmedo, 1632.

Dunn, Geoffrey D. *Tertullian*. London: Routledge, 2004.

Edmonson, Munro E., trans. *The Ancient Future of the Itza: The Book of Chilam Balam of Tizimin*. Austin: University of Texas Press, 1982.

Estatutos de la venerable cofradía del santísimo sacramento de la ciudad de Izamal. Mérida: Imprenta Literaria de Molina Solis, 1875.

Florencia, Francisco de. *La estrella del norte de México aparecida al rayar el dia de la luz evangelica en este Nuevo Mundo* [...]. Mexico City: Viuda de Ribera, 1688.

Florencia, Francisco de, and Juan Antonio de Oviedo. *Zodiaco mariano*. Mexico City: Colegio de San Idelfonso, 1755.

Fracastoro, Girolamo. *De contagione, et contagiosis morbis, et eorum curatione*. Lugduni: Apud Ioan. Tornaesium, & Guil. Gazeium, 1554.

———. *Syphilis sive morbus gallicus*. Veronae: Sabbio & Bros., 1530.

Gerson, Peter. *Tripartito de christianissimo*. Mexico City: Casa de Cromberger, 1544.

Herrera y Tordesillas, Antonio de. *Historia general de los hechos de los castellanos en las islas i tierra firme del mar oceano*. Madrid: Emplenta Real, 1601.

Hippocrates. "On Air, Water, and Places." In *Hippocrates*, translated by W. H. S. Jones. Vol. 1. Loeb Classical Library. London: Heinemann, 1923.

Instrucción para inocular las viruelas, y método de curarlas con facilidad, y acierto. Puebla de Los Angeles: De la Rosa, 1797.

James, M. R., trans. "The Book of James: Protevangelium." *Gnostic Society Library: Christian Apocrypha and Early Christian Literature*. 1924. http://gnosis.org/library/gosjames.htm.

Landa, Diego de. "Relación de las cosas de Yucatán." Circa 1566. M-RAH. 9/5153. Real Academia de la Historia, Madrid.

———. *Yucatán Before and After the Conquest*. Edited and translated by William Gates. New York: Dover, 1978.

"El Libro de las cantares de Dzitbalché." Eighteenth century. Biblioteca Nacional de Antropología e Historia, Mexico City.

Lizana, Bernardo de. *Historia de Yucatán: Devocionario de Nuestra Señora de Izmal y conquista espiritual*. Valladolid: Morillo, 1633.

López de Cogolludo, Diego. *Historia de Yucathán*. Madrid: García Infanzon, 1688.

Marín, Andres Martín. *Novena de la sacratísima Virgen de Itzmal*. Mérida: Marín, 1824.

Mendieta, Gerónimo de. *Historia eclesiástica Indiana*. Edited by Joaquín García Icazbalceta. Mexico City: Antigua Librería, 1870."

Morley Manuscript." Sylvanus Griswold Morley Collection. Museum of Indian Arts and Culture, Santa Fe, New Mexico.

Novena en honor de la inmaculada concepción en su avocación de nuestra sra. de Izamal reina de Yucatán. Mérida: Díaz Massa, 1948.

Oviedo y Valdés, Gonzalo Fernández de. *La historia general de las Indias*. Seville: Emprenta de Iuam Cromberger, 1535.

Pacheco, Francisco. *Arte de la pintura*. Sevilla: Faxardo, 1649.

Pope Paul III, "Cupientes Judaeos." Bull of March 21, 1542.

Remesal, Antonio de. *Historia de la provincia de San Vicente de Chiapas y Guatemala, o Historia general de las indias occidentales y particular de la gobernación de Chiapa y Guatemala*. Madrid: Angulo, 1619.

Roys, Ralph L. *The Book of Chilam Balam of Chumayel*. Norman: University of Oklahoma Press, 1967.

———. *Ritual of the Bacabs*. Norman: University of Oklahoma Press, 1965.

Sabás Camacho, D. Rafael. *Concilio provincial mexicano IV*. Queretaro: Escuela de Artes, 1898.

Sahagún, Bernardino de. "Historia general de las cosas de Nueva España." Circa 1577. Mediceo Palantino 218, 219, 220. Medicea Laurenziana Library, Florence.

———. "Primeros memoriales." 1558–61. MS 3280. Real Biblioteca del Palacio Real, Madrid.

Sánchez de Aguilar, Pedro. *Informe contra idolorum cultores del obispado de Yucatán*. Madrid: Viuda de Gonçalez, 1639.

Scholes, France V., and Eleanor B. Adams. *Documents Relating to the Mirones Expedition to the Interior of Yucatan, 1621–1624*. Culver City, Calif.: Labyrinthos, 1991.

Seguí, Lorenzo. *Novena de la sacratísima Virgen de Itzmal*. Mérida: Oficina del Sol, 1824.

Stephens, John Lloyd. *Incidents of Travel in Yucatan*. 2 vols. New York: Harper and Bros., 1843.

Sullivan, Thelma D., trans. *Primeros memoriales*. Norman: University of Oklahoma Press, 1997.

Talavera, Gabriel de. *Historia de Nuestra Señora de Guadalupe*. Toledo: Guzmán, 1597.

Tedlock, Dennis, trans. *Popol Vuh: The Definitive Edition of the Mayan Book of the Dawn of Life and the Glories of Gods and Kings*. New York: Touchstone, 1996.

Tertullian. "De Idololatria." Edited by Roger Pearse. Accessed November 13, 2018. http://www.tertullian.org/latin/de_idololatria.htm.

Torquemada, Juan de. *Monarquía indiana*. Seville: Mathias Clavijo, 1615.

Tozzer, Alfred M., trans. *Landa's Relación de Las Cosas de Yucatán: A Translation*. Vol. 18. Papers of the Peabody Museum of Archaeology and Ethnology, Harvard University. Cambridge, 1941.

Valadés, Diego. *Rhetorica christiana*. Perugia: Petrumiacobum Petrutium, 1579.

Whalen, Gretchen, trans. "An Annotated Translation of a Colonial Yucatec Manuscript: On Religious and Cosmological Topics by a Native Author." 2003. Foundation for the Advancement of Mesoamerican Studies. http://www.famsi.org/reports/01017/index .html.

"Will and Testament of Thomas William Francis Gann." *Archives and Collections Online*. Jersey Heritage. Accessed September 22, 2018. http://catalogue.jerseyheritage.org /collection/Details/archive/110081233?rank=.

SECONDARY SOURCES

Abbott, Don Paul. *Rhetoric in the New World: Rhetorical Theory and Practice in Colonial Spanish America*. Columbia: University of South Carolina Press, 1996.

Adorno, Rolena. *The Polemics of Possession in Spanish American Narrative*. New Haven: Yale University Press, 2014.

Alchon, Suzanne Austin. *A Pest in the Land: New World Epidemics in a Global Perspective*. Albuquerque: University of New Mexico Press, 2003.

Appadurai, Arjun, ed. *The Social Life of Things: Commodities in Cultural Perspective*. Cambridge: Cambridge University Press, 1986.

Baird, Ellen T. *The Drawings of Sahagún's Primeros Memoriales: Structure and Style*. Norman: University of Oklahoma Press, 1993.

Barnes, Timothy David. *Tertullian: A Historical and Literary Study*. Oxford: Oxford University Press, 1985.

Bassett, Molly H. *The Fate of Earthly Things: Aztec Gods and God-Bodies*. Austin: University of Texas Press, 2015.

Bastarrachea Manzano, Juan Ramón, and William Brito Sansores, eds. *Diccionario Maya cordemex*. Mérida: Ediciones Cordemex, 1980.

Blom, Frans Ferdinand. *The Conquest of Yucatan*. New York: Cooper Square, 1971.

Bowers, Kristy Wilson. "Balancing Individual and Communal Needs: Plague and Public Health in Early Modern Seville." *Bulletin of the History of Medicine* 81, no. 2 (2007): 335–58.

———. *Plague and Public Health in Early Modern Seville*. Rochester: University of Rochester Press, 2013.

Brading, D. A. *Mexican Phoenix: Our Lady of Guadalupe; Image and Tradition Across Five Centuries*. New York: Cambridge University Press, 2001.

Brenner, Anita. *Idols Behind Altars: Modern Mexican Art and Its Cultural Roots*. New York: Biblo and Tannen, 1929.

Bretos, Miguel A. *Arquitectura y arte sacro en Yucatán*. Mérida: Editorial Dante, 1987.

———. *Iglesias de Yucatán*. Mérida: Editorial Dante, 1992.

Briceño López, Ramiro. *Leyendas Izamaleñas*. Mérida: Universidad Autónoma de Yucatán, 1996.

Bricker, Victoria R. "The Last Gasp of Maya Hieroglyphic Writing in the Books of the Chilam Balam of Chumayel and Chan Kan." In *Word and Image in Maya Culture: Explorations in Language, Writing, and Representation*, edited by William F. Hanks and Don Stephen Rice, 39–50. Salt Lake City: University of Utah Press, 1989.

Bricker, Victoria R., and Rebecca E. Hill. "Climatic Signatures in Yucatecan Wills and Death Records." *Ethnohistory* 56 (2009): 227–68.

Bricker, Victoria R., and Helga-Maria Miram. *An Encounter of Two Worlds: The Book of Chilam Balam of Kaua*. New Orleans, La.: Middle American Research Institute, 2002.

Burkhart, Louise M. *Before Guadalupe: The Virgin Mary in Early Colonial Nahuatl Literature*. IMS Monograph 13. Albany: Institute for Mesoamerican Studies, 2001.

———. *The Slippery Earth: Nahua-Christian Moral Dialogue in Sixteenth-Century Mexico*. Tucson: University of Arizona Press, 1989.

Bustos, Gerardo. *Libro de las descripciones: Sobre la visión geográfica de la península de Yucatán en textos españoles del siglo xvi*. Mexico City: Universidad Nacional Autónoma de México, 1988.

Bynum, Caroline Walker. *Christian Materiality: An Essay on Religion in Late Medieval Europe*. New York: Zone Books, 2011.

Canedo, Lino G. "Fray Lorenzo de Bienvenida, O.F.M., and the Origins of the Franciscan Order in Yucatan: A Reconsideration of the Problem on the Basis of Unpublished Documents." *Americas* 8, no. 4 (1952): 493–510.

Carmichael, Ann G. "Universal and Particular: The Language of Plague, 1348–1500." *Medical History Supplement* 27 (2008): 17–52.

Carrascal Muñoz, José María. *La guerra de Dios: Peste y milagro en la Bahía de Cádiz (1680–1681)*. Sevilla: Universidad de Sevilla, 2006.

Carrillo y Ancona, Crescencio, and Don José D. Espinosa Rendón, eds. *El repertorio pintoresco*. Mérida: Espinosa, 1863.

Chamberlain, Robert S. *The Conquest and Colonization of Yucatan, 1517–1550*. Washington, D.C.: Carnegie Institution of Washington, 1948.

Christensen, Mark Z. *Nahua and Maya Catholicisms: Texts and Religion in Colonial Central Mexico and Yucatan*. Stanford: Stanford University Press; Berkeley: Academy of American Franciscan History, 2013.

———. *The Teabo Manuscript: Maya Christian Copybooks, Chilam Balams, and Native Text Production in Yucatan*. Austin: University of Texas Press, 2016.

Christensen, Mark, and Matthew Restall. *Return to Ixil: Maya Society in an Eighteenth-Century Yucatec Town*. Boulder: University Press of Colorado, 2019.

Chuchiak, John F. "The Indian Inquisition and the Extirpation of Idolatry: The Process of Punishment in the Provisorato de Indios of the Diocese of Yucatán, 1563–1812." Ph.D. diss., Tulane University, 2000.

———. *The Inquisition in New Spain, 1536–1820: A Documentary History*. Baltimore: Johns Hopkins University Press, 2012.

———. "Pre-Conquest Ah Kinob in a Colonial World: The Extirpation of Idolatry and the Survival of the Maya Priesthood in Colonial Yucatán, 1563–1697." *Acta Mesoamericana* 12 (2001): 135–60.

———. "Toward a Regional Definition of Idolatry: Reexamining Idolatry Trials in the 'Relaciónes de Méritos' and Their Role in Defining the Concept of 'Idolatria' in Colonial Yucatán, 1570–1780." *Journal of Early Modern History* 6, no. 2 (2002): 140–67.

Ciaramella, Mary A. *The Idol-Makers in the Madrid Codex.* Austin, Tex.: Center for Maya Research, 2004.

Clendinnen, Inga. *Ambivalent Conquests: Maya and Spaniard in Yucatan, 1517–1570.* New York: Cambridge University Press, 2003.

———. "Disciplining the Indians: Franciscan Ideology and Missionary Violence in Sixteenth-Century Yucatán." *Past and Present* 94 (February 1982): 27–48.

Cline, Howard F. "The *Relaciones Geográficas* of the Spanish Indies, 1577–1586." *Hispanic American Historical Review* 44, no. 3 (1964): 341–74.

Coggins, Clemency. *Artifacts from the Cenote of Sacrifice, Chichen Itza, Yucatan: Textiles, Basketry, Stone, Bone, Shell, Ceramics, Wood, Copal, Rubber, Other Organic Materials, and Mammalian Remains.* Cambridge, Mass.: Peabody Museum of Archaeology and Ethnology, 1992.

Cook, Noble David. *Born to Die: Disease and New World Conquest, 1492–1650.* Cambridge: Cambridge University Press, 1998.

Cook, Sherburne Friend, and Woodrow Wilson Borah. *Essays in Population History: Mexico and the Caribbean.* Berkeley: University of California Press, 1974.

Crosby, Alfred W. *The Columbian Exchange: Biological and Cultural Consequences of 1492.* Westport, Conn.: Greenwood, 1972.

Cunill, Caroline. "Tomás López Medel y sus instrucciones para defensores de indios: Una propuesta innovadora." *Anuario de Estudios Americanos* 68, no. 2 (2011): 539–63.

Curcio-Nagy, Linda A. *The Great Festivals of Colonial Mexico City: Performing Power and Identity.* Albuquerque: University of New Mexico Press, 2004.

Curtin, Philip. "Disease Exchange Across the Tropical Atlantic." *History and Philosophy of the Life Sciences* 15, no. 3 (1993): 329–56.

Damian, Carol. *The Virgin of the Andes: Art and Ritual in Colonial Cuzco.* Miami: Grassfield Press, 1995.

"Descubren universitarios un cenote debajo de la pirámide de Kukulkán, en Chichén Itzá." Dirección General de Comunicación Social. August 13, 2015. http://www.dgcs.unam .mx/boletin/bdboletin/2015_466.html.

Doremus, Anne. "Indigenism, Mestizaje, and National Identity in Mexico During the 1940s and the 1950s." *Mexican Studies/Estudios Mexicanos* 17, no. 2 (2001): 375–402.

Dundes, Alan. "Folk Ideas as Units of Worldview." *Journal of American Folklore* 84, no. 331 (1971): 93–103.

———. *Interpreting Folklore.* Bloomington: Indiana University Press, 1980.

Durling, Richard J. "The Innate Heat in Galen." *Medizinhistorisches Journal* 23, nos. 3–4 (1988): 210–12.

Dyck, Jason. "The Sacred Historian's Craft: Francisco de Florencia and Creole Identity in Seventeenth-Century New Spain." Ph.D., University of Toronto, 2012.

Early, John D. *The Maya and Catholicism: An Encounter of Worldviews.* Gainesville: University Press of Florida, 2006.

Elkins, James. "On Some Limits of Materiality in Art History." *31: Das Magazin des Instituts für Theorie der Gestaltung und Kunst, Zürich* 12 (2008): 25–30.

Engel, Emily A. "Visualizing a Colonial Peruvian Community in the Eighteenth-Century Paintings of Our Lady of Cocharcas." *Religion and the Arts* 13, no. 3 (2009): 299–339.

Estrella Santana, Flor Lourdes de. "Incidentes en la fiesta de Sitilpech." *Diario de Yucatán.* September 5, 2014. http://yucatan.com.mx/yucatan/izamal/incidentes-en-la-fiesta -de-sitilpech.

Farriss, Nancy M. *Maya Society Under Colonial Rule: The Collective Enterprise of Survival.* Princeton: Princeton University Press, 1984.

Fernández Repetto, Francisco J., and Genny M. Negroe Sierra. *Izamal festivo.* Mérida: Instituto de Cultura de Yucatán, 2006.

Fields, Sherry. *Pestilence and Headcolds: Encountering Illness in Colonial Mexico.* New York: Columbia University Press, 2008.

Freedberg, David. *The Power of Images: Studies in the History and Theory of Response.* Chicago: University of Chicago Press, 1991.

Gann, Thomas William Francis. *Maya Cities: A Record of Exploration and Adventure in Middle America.* London: Duckworth, 1927.

García Bernal, Manuela Cristina. *Campeche y el comercio atlántico yucateco (1561–1625).* Campeche: Universidad Autónoma de Campeche, 2006.

Garza, Randal Paul. *Understanding Plague: The Medical and Imaginative Texts of Medieval Spain.* New York: Lang, 2008.

Gaudio, Michael. *Engraving the Savage: The New World and Techniques of Civilization.* Minneapolis: University of Minnesota Press, 2008.

Gibson, Charles. *The Aztecs Under Spanish Rule: A History of the Indians of the Valley of Mexico, 1519–1810.* Stanford: Stanford University Press, 1964.

Giffords, Gloria Fraser. *Mexican Folk Retablos.* 1974. Reprint, Albuquerque: University of New Mexico Press, 1992.

Graham, Elizabeth. *Maya Christians and Their Churches in Sixteenth-Century Belize.* Gainesville: University Press of Florida, 2011.

Greenleaf, Richard E. "The Inquisition and the Indians of New Spain: A Study in Jurisdictional Confusion." *Americas* 22, no. 2 (1965): 138–66.

Gruzinski, Serge. *Images at War: Mexico from Columbus to Blade Runner (1492–2019).* Translated by Heather MacLean. Durham: Duke University Press, 2001.

Gubler, Ruth. "El informe contra idolorum cultores del obispado de Yucatán." *Estudios de Cultura Maya* 30 (2007): 107–38.

Guillén, Bertha Pascacio. "Tras las huellas de una tradición: La Virgen de Izamal en Yucatán; Historia, cambios, permanencias, y adapaciones de una imagen de devoción." *Entre Diversidades* 4 (2015): 117–45.

Hahn, Hans Peter, and Hadas Weiss, eds. *Mobility, Meaning, and Transformations of Things: Shifting Contexts of Material Culture Through Time and Space.* Oxford: Oxbow Books, 2013.

Halbertal, Moshe, and Avishai Margalit. *Idolatry.* Translated by Naomi Goldblum. Cambridge: Harvard University Press, 1994.

Hanks, William F. *Converting Words: Maya in the Age of the Cross*. Berkeley: University of California Press, 2010.

Headrick, Annabeth. "'The Street of the Dead . . . It Really Was': Mortuary Bundles at Teotihuacan." *Ancient Mesoamerica* 10, no. 1 (1999): 69–85.

Hoggarth, Julie A., Matthew Restall, James W. Wood, and Douglas J. Kennett. "Drought and Its Demographic Effects in the Maya Lowlands." *Current Anthropology* 58, no. 1 (2017): 82–113.

Houston, Stephen. *The Life Within: Classic Maya and the Matter of Permanence*. New Haven: Yale University Press, 2014.

Jones, Grant D. *Maya Resistance to Spanish Rule: Time and History on a Colonial Frontier*. Albuquerque: University of New Mexico Press, 1989.

Joyce, Rosemary A., and Susan D. Gillespie. "Making Things Out of Objects That Move." In *Things in Motion: Object Itineraries in Anthropological Practice*, edited by Rosemary A. Joyce and Susan D. Gillespie, 3–19. Santa Fe: School for Advanced Research Press, 2015.

Kashanipour, Ryan Amir. "A World of Cures: Magic and Medicine in Colonial Yucatán." Ph.D. diss., University of Arizona, 2012.

Klein, Cecilia F. "Wild Woman in Colonial Mexico: An Encounter of European and Aztec Concept of the Other." In *Reframing the Renaissance: Visual Culture in Europe and Latin America, 1450–1650*, edited by Claire Farago, 245–63. New Haven: Yale University Press, 1995.

Klor de Alva, J. Jorge. "Colonizing Souls: The Failure of the Indian Inquisition and the Rise of Penitential Discipline." In Perry and Cruz, *Cultural Encounters*, 3–22.

———. "Spiritual Conflict and Accommodation in New Spain: Toward a Typology of Aztec Responses to Christianity." In *The Inca and Aztec States, 1400–1800: Anthropology and History*, edited by George A. Collier, Renato Rosaldo, and John D. Wirth, 345–66. New York: Academic Press, 1982.

Knaut, Andrew L. "Yellow Fever and the Late Colonial Public Health Response in the Port of Veracruz." *Hispanic American Historical Review* 77, no. 4 (1997): 619–44.

Knowlton, Timothy W. *Maya Creation Myths: Words and Worlds of the Chilam Balam*. Boulder: University Press of Colorado, 2010.

Kopytoff, Igor. "The Cultural Biography of Things: Commoditization as Process." In Appadurai, *Social Life of Things*, 64–91.

Lara, Jaime. *City, Temple, Stage: Eschatological Architecture and Liturgical Theatrics in New Spain*. Notre Dame: University of Notre Dame Press, 2004.

Leone, Massimo. *Saints and Signs: A Semiotic Reading of Conversion in Early Modern Catholicism*. Religion and Society 48. Berlin: De Gruyter, 2010.

Levy, Juliette. *The Making of a Market: Credit, Henequen, and Notaries in Yucatán, 1850–1900*. University Park: Pennsylvania State University Press, 2012.

Lidz, Joel Warren. "Medicine as Metaphor in Plato." *Journal of Medicine and Philosophy* 20, no. 5 (1995): 527–41.

Lindemann, Mary. *Medicine and Society in Early Modern Europe*. Cambridge: Cambridge University Press, 2010.

Lindsay, Mark Childress. "Spanish Merida Overlaying the Maya City." Ph.D. diss., University of Florida, 1999.

Looper, Matthew G., and Julia Guernsey Kappleman. "The Cosmic Umbilicus in Mesoamerica: A Floral Metaphor for the Source of Life." *Journal of Latin American Lore* 21, no. 1 (2001): 3–54.

MacCormack, Sabine. *Religion in the Andes: Vision and Imagination in Early Colonial Peru.* Princeton: Princeton University Press, 1991.

McGee, R. Jon. *Life, Ritual, and Religion Among the Lacandon Maya.* Belmont: Wadsworth, 1990.

McNeill, J. R. *Mosquito Empires: Ecology and War in the Greater Caribbean, 1620–1914.* New York: Cambridge University Press, 2010.

Medina Un, Martha, and Teresa Quiñones Vega. "Peregrinando por los santuarios de la península de Yucatán." *Estudios de Cultura Maya* 27 (2006): 165–80.

Milbrath, Susan, and Carlos Peraza Lope. "Mayapán's Chen Mul Modeled Effigy Censers: Iconography and Archaeological Context." In *Ancient Maya Pottery: Classification, Analysis, and Interpretation*, edited by James John Aimers, 203–28. Gainesville: University Press of Florida, 2013.

Mills, Kenneth. *Idolatry and Its Enemies: Colonial Andean Religion and Extirpation, 1640–1750.* Princeton: Princeton University Press, 1997.

Moes, Mark. "Plato's Conception of the Relations Between Moral Philosophy and Medicine." *Perspectives in Biology and Medicine* 44, no. 3 (2001): 353–67.

Montgomery, John. *Dictionary of Maya Hieroglyphs.* New York: Hippocrene, 2002.

Moreda, Vicente Pérez. "The Plague in Castile at the End of the Sixteenth Century and Its Consequences." In *The Castilian Crisis of the Seventeenth Century: New Perspectives on the Economic and Social History of Seventeenth-Century Spain*, edited by I. A. A. Thompson and Bartolomé Yun Casalilla, 32–59. Cambridge: Cambridge University Press, 1994.

Moreno de los Arcos, Roberto. "New Spain's Inquisition for Indians from the Sixteenth to the Nineteenth Century." In Perry and Cruz, *Cultural Encounters*, 23–32.

Mundy, Barbara E. *The Death of Aztec Tenochtitlan, the Life of Mexico City.* Austin: University of Texas Press, 2015.

———. *The Mapping of New Spain: Indigenous Cartography and the Maps of the Relaciones Geográficas.* Chicago: University of Chicago Press, 1996.

Nesvig, Martin Austin. *Forgotten Franciscans: Works from an Inquisitional Theorist, a Heretic, and an Inquisitional Deputy.* University Park: Pennsylvania State University Press, 2011.

———. *Ideology and Inquisition: The World of the Censors in Early Mexico.* New Haven: Yale University Press, 2009.

Nutton, Vivian. "The Reception of Fracastoro's Theory of Contagion: The Seed That Fell Among Thorns?" *Osiris* 6 (1990): 196–234.

———. "The Seeds of Disease: An Explanation of Contagion and Infection from the Greeks to the Renaissance." *Medical History* 27, no. 1 (1983): 1–34.

Oliver, José R. "Tiempos difíciles: Fray Ramón Pané en la Española, 1494–1498." In *El caribe precolumbino: Fray Ramón Pané y el universo Taíno*, compiled by Museo Barbier Mueller de Arte Precolombino, 75–95. Madrid: Comgrafic, 2008.

Olson, Glending, D. S. *Literature as Recreation in the Later Middle Ages*. Ithaca: Cornell University Press, 1986.

Ortiz Yam, Inés, and Sergio Quezada. *Visita de Diego García de Palacio a Yucatán, 1583*. Mexico City: Centro de Estudios Mayas, Instituto de Investigaciones Filológicas, Universidad Nacional Autónoma de México, 2009.

Palka, Joel W. *Maya Pilgrimage to Ritual Landscapes: Insights from Archaeology, History, and Ethnography*. Albuquerque: University of New Mexico Press, 2014.

———. *Unconquered Lacandon Maya: Ethnohistory and Archaeology of Indigenous Culture Change*. Gainesville: University Press of Florida, 2005.

Palomera, Esteban J. *Fray Diego Valadés, O.F.M.: Evangelizador humanista de la Nueva España; El hombre, su época, y su obra*. Mexico City: Departamento de Historia, Universidad Iberoamericana, 1988.

Parma Cook, Alexandra, and Noble David Cook. *The Plague Files Crisis Management in Sixteenth-Century Seville*. Baton Rouge: Louisiana State University Press, 2009.

Patch, Robert W. *Maya and Spaniard in Yucatan, 1648–1812*. Stanford: Stanford University Press, 1994.

Perry, Mary Elizabeth, and Anne J. Cruz, eds. *Cultural Encounters: The Impact of the Inquisition in Spain and the New World*. Berkeley: University of California Press, 1991.

Peterson, Jeanette Favrot. "Creating the Virgin of Guadalupe: The Cloth, the Artist, and Sources in Sixteenth-Century New Spain." *Americas* 61, no. 4 (2005): 571–610.

———. "Rhetoric as Acculturation: The Anomalous Book Six." Unpublished manuscript, n.d.

———. *Visualizing Guadalupe: From Black Madonna to Queen of the Americas*. Austin: University of Texas Press, 2014.

Pollock, H. E. D. *The Puuc: An Architectural Survey of the Hill Country of Yucatan and Northern Campeche, Mexico*. Memoirs of the Peabody Museum of Archaeology and Ethnology 19. Cambridge: Harvard University, 1980.

Poole, Stafford. *Our Lady of Guadalupe: The Origins and Sources of a Mexican National Symbol, 1531–1797*. Tucson: University of Arizona Press, 1995.

Prem, Hanns J. "Disease Outbreaks in Central Mexico During the Sixteenth Century." In *"Secret Judgments of God": Old World Disease in Colonial Spanish America*, edited by Noble David Cook and W. George Lovell, 20–48. Norman: University of Oklahoma Press, 1992.

Quezada, Sergio. *Maya Lords and Lordship: The Formation of Colonial Society in Yucatán, 1350–1600*. Translated by Terry Rugeley. Norman: University of Oklahoma Press, 2014.

Quiñones Cetina, Lucía. "Del preclásico medio al clásico temprano: Una propesta de fechamiento para el área nuclear de Izamal, Yucatán." *Estudios de Cultura Maya* 28 (2006): 51–65.

Redfield, Robert. *The Folk Culture of Yucatan*. Chicago: University of Chicago Press, 1941.

Redfield, Robert, and Margaret Park Redfield. *Disease and Its Treatment in Dzitas, Yucatan*. Washington, D.C.: Carnegie Institution of Washington, 1940.

Redfield, Robert, and Alfonso Villa Rojas. *Chan Kom: A Maya Village*. Washington, D.C.: Carnegie Institution of Washington, 1934.

Remensnyder, Amy G. "The Colonization of Sacred Architecture: The Virgin Mary, Mosques, and Temples in Medieval Spain and Early Sixteenth-Century Mexico." In *Monks and Nuns, Saints and Outcasts: Religion in Medieval Society*, edited by Sharon Farmer and Barbara H. Rosenwein, 189–219. Ithaca: Cornell University Press, 2000.

———. *La Conquistadora: The Virgin Mary at War and Peace in the Old and New Worlds*. New York: Oxford University Press, 2014.

Restall, Matthew. *The Black Middle: Africans, Mayas, and Spaniards in Colonial Yucatan*. Stanford: Stanford University Press, 2009.

———. "Gaspar Antonio Chi: Bridging the Conquest of Yucatán." In *The Human Tradition in Colonial Latin America*, edited by Kenneth J. Andrien, 13–31. Lanham, Md.: Rowman and Littlefield, 2013.

———. "A History of the New Philology and the New Philology in History." *Latin American Research Review* 38, no. 1 (2003): 113–34.

———. *Life and Death in a Maya Community: The Ixil Testaments of the 1760s*. Palo Alto: Labyrinthos, 1995.

———. *The Maya World: Yucatec Culture and Society, 1550–1850*. Stanford: Stanford University Press, 1997.

———. *When Montezuma Met Cortés: The True Story of the Meeting That Changed History*. New York: Echo Books, 2018.

Restall, Matthew, and John F. Chuchiak. "A Reevaluation of the Authenticity of Fray Diego de Landa's *Relación de Las Cosas de Yucatán*." *Ethnohistory* 49, no. 3 (2002): 651–69.

Restall, Matthew, John F. Chuchiak IV, Amara Solari, and Traci Ardren. *The Friar and the Maya*. Boulder: University of Colorado Press, forthcoming.

Ricard, Robert. *La "conquête spirituelle" du Mexique: Essai sur l'apostolat et les méthodes missionaires des ordres mendiants en Nouvelle-Espagne de 1523–24 à 1572*. Paris: Institut d'Ethnologie, 1933.

Rice, Prudence M. "Rethinking Classic Lowland Maya Pottery Censers." *Ancient Mesoamerica* 10, no. 1 (1999): 25–50.

Rubin, Miri. *Mother of God: A History of the Virgin Mary*. New Haven: Yale University Press, 2009.

Rueda Ramírez, Pedro J. *Negocio e intercambio cultural: El comercio de libros con América en la carrera de Indias (siglo xvii)*. Sevilla: Escuela de Estudios Hispano-Americanos, Universidad de Sevilla, 2005.

Rugeley, Terry, ed. *Maya Wars: Ethnographic Accounts from Nineteenth-Century Yucatán*. Norman: University of Oklahoma Press, 2001.

Scheper Hughes, Jennifer. *Biography of a Mexican Crucifix: Lived Religion and Local Faith from the Conquest to the Present*. New York: Oxford University Press, 2010.

Schwaller, John F., ed. *Sahagún at 500: Essays on the Quincentary of the Birth of Fr. Bernardino de Sahagún*. Berkeley: Academy of American Franciscan History, 2003.

Schwaller, Robert C. "Defining Difference in Early New Spain." Ph.D. diss., Pennsylvania State University, 2010.

Scott, Mary Katherine, and Jeff Karl Kowalski. "Imaging the Maya: Carvings, Carvers, Contexts, and Messages." In *Crafting Maya Identity: Contemporary Wood Sculptures from the Puuc Region of Yucatán, Mexico*, edited by Jeff Karl Kowalski, 3–82. DeKalb: Northern Illinois University Press, 2009.

Sigal, Pete. *The Flower and the Scorpion: Sexuality and Ritual in Early Nahua Culture.* Durham: Duke University Press, 2011.

———. *From Moon Goddesses to Virgins: The Colonization of Yucatecan Maya Sexual Desire.* Austin: University of Texas Press, 2000.

Solari, Amara. "The 'Contagious Stench' of Idolatry: The Rhetoric of Disease and Sacrilegious Acts in Colonial New Spain." *Hispanic American Historical Review* 96, no. 3 (2016): 481–515.

———. *Maya Ideologies of the Sacred: The Transfiguration of Space in Colonial Yucatan.* Austin: University of Texas Press, 2013.

Solís Acalá, Emilio, trans. *Códice Pérez: Traducción libre del Maya al Castellano*. Mérida: Imprente Oriente, 1949.

Stanfield-Mazzi, Maya. *Object and Apparition: Envisioning the Christian Divine in the Colonial Andes.* Tucson: University of Arizona Press, 2013.

Stearns, Justin K. *Infectious Ideas: Contagion in Premodern Islamic and Christian Thought in the Western Mediterranean.* Baltimore: Johns Hopkins University Press, 2011.

Steiner, Wendy. *The Scandal of Pleasure: Art in an Age of Fundamentalism.* Chicago: University of Chicago Press, 1995.

Stephenson, Marcia. "From Marvelous Antidote to the Poison of Idolatry: The Transatlantic Role of Andean Bezoar Stones During the Late Sixteenth and Early Seventeenth Centuries." *Hispanic American Historical Review* 90, no. 1 (2010): 3–39.

Sterner, Carl S. "A Brief History of Miasmic Theory." Working paper, University of Cincinnati, 2007.

Stuart, David. "'The Fire Enters His House': Architecture and Ritual in Classic Maya Texts." In *Function and Meaning in Classic Maya Architecture*, edited by Stephen D. Houston, 373–425. Washington, D.C.: Dumbarton Oaks Research Library and Collection, 1998.

Taube, Karl Andreas. *The Major Gods of Ancient Yucatan.* Washington, D.C.: Dumbarton Oaks, 1992.

Tavárez, David Eduardo. "Idolatry as an Ontological Question: Native Consciousness and Juridical Proof in Colonial Mexico." *Journal of Early Modern History* 6, no. 2 (2002): 114–39.

———. *The Invisible War: Indigenous Devotions, Discipline, and Dissent in Colonial Mexico.* Stanford: Stanford University Press, 2011.

Taylor, William B. *Theater of a Thousand Wonders: A History of Miraculous Images and Shrines in New Spain.* Cambridge: Cambridge University Press, 2016.

Thompson, J. Eric S. "Deities Portrayed on Censers at Mayapan." *Carnegie Institution of Washington Department of Archaeology* 40 (1957): 599–632.

———. "Thomas Gann in the Maya Ruins." *British Medical Journal* 2 (1975): 741–43.

Thompson, Philip C. *Tekanto, a Maya Town in Colonial Yucatán.* New Orleans: Middle American Research Institute, Tulane University, 1999.

Turner, Victor. *The Ritual Process: Structure and Anti-Structure.* Chicago: Aldine, 1969.

Vail, Gabrielle. "Pre-Hispanic Maya Religion: Conceptions of Divinity in the Postclassic Maya Codices." *Ancient Mesoamerica* 11, no. 1 (2000): 123–47.

Vail, Gabrielle, and Christine Hernández. "Cords and Crocodilians: Creation Mythology in Late Postclassic Maya Iconography and Texts." In *The Maya and Their Sacred Narratives: Text and Context in Maya Mythologies*, edited by Genevieve Le Fort, Raphaël Gardiol, Sebastian Matteo, and Christophe Helmke, 89–108. Munich: Verlag Anton Saurwein, 2009.

Venier, Martha Elena. "La *Rhetorica Christiana* de Diego Valadés." *Caravelle*, nos. 76–77 (2001): 437–42.

Villaseñor Black, Charlene. "Inquisitorial Practices Past and Present: Artistic Censorship, the Virgin Mary, and St. Anne." In *Art, Piety, and Destruction in the Christian West, 1500–1700*, edited by Virginia Chieffo Raguin, 173–200. Surrey: Ashgate, 2010.

Vogt, Evon Z. *Zinacantan: A Maya Community in the Highlands of Chiapas*. Cambridge: Harvard University Press, 1969.

Ward, James S. *Yellow Fever in Latin America: A Geographical Study*. Liverpool: Centre for Latin-American Studies, University of Liverpool, 1972.

Webster, Susan Verdi. "Native Brotherhoods and Visual Culture in Colonial Quito (Ecuador): The Confraternity of the Rosary." In *Faith's Boundaries: Laity and Clergy in Early Modern Confraternities*, edited by Nicholas Terpstra, Adriano Prosperi, and Stefania Pastore, 277–99. Turnhout, Belgium: Brepols, 2012.

Wells, Allen. *Yucatan's Gilded Age: Haciendas, Henequen, and International Harvester, 1860–1915*. Albuquerque: University of New Mexico Press, 1985.

Wells, Allen, and Gilbert M. Joseph. *Summer of Discontent, Seasons of Upheaval: Elite Politics and Rural Insurgency in Yucatán, 1876–1915*. Stanford: Stanford University Press, 1996.

Whitehead, Neil L. *Of Cannibals and Kings: Primal Anthropology in the Americas*. University Park: Pennsylvania State University Press, 2011.

Williams, Linda K. "The *Birth of the Virgin with Saint Michael* Mural at Tabí: The *Inmaculada*, Eschatology, and Christian Orthodoxy in Seventeenth-Century Yucatán." *Ethnohistory* 61, no. 4 (2014): 715–38.

Yonan, Michael. "Toward a Fusion of Art History and Material Culture Studies," *West Eighty-Sixth* 18, no. 2 (2011): 232–48.

Index

Copán, 45
Córdoba, Pedro de, 121, 168 n. 42
Coronel, Juan, 119
Cortés, Hernando, 22, 60, 97
Cot, Bernardino, 122
Council of Trent (Tridentine Council), 10,
    161 n. 78
Counter Reformation, 126
Cozumel, 24, 60, 71, 155 n. 53
Cuyoc, Andres, 54

d'Agramont, Jacme, 90, 162 n. 27
Decalogue (Ten Commandments), 9, 87
Díaz de Alpuche, Giraldo 92
Díaz del Castillo, Bernal, 65, 150 n. 8
disease, 4, 12, 14, 25, 55–57, 86–87, 89–93,
    97–98, 100, 103, 114, 123, 134–35, 150
    n. 10, 151 n. 20, 164 n. 53
Dominican Order, 79, 164 n. 52
Dresden Codex, 47, 111, *111*
Dzitás, 56–59
Dzonot Aké, 92
Dzul, Maria, 102–3

Early, John D., 11
Echano, Agustín Francisco, *5*, 82, 160 n. 76
Esquivel, Amado, 34
estofado, 82–83, 123

Farriss, Nancy, 72, 149 n. 16, 167 n. 38
Florencia, Francisco de, 60–61, 63, 68, 70,
    73–75, 156 n. 1
Fracastoro, Girolamo, 90–91, 99, 162 n. 29
Franciscan order, 4, 13, 15, 16, 17, 21, 121
        in Yucatán, 11, 21, 22–23, 25, 26, 57,
            63, 65, 71, 89, 98, 100, 119, 124, 148
            n. 8, 164 n. 63, 168 n. 1

Galen of Pergamum, 89–91, 92, 93, 94, 97,
    99, 163 n. 30
Gann, Thomas William Francis, 34–38, *35*,
    43, 153 n. 4
Garate, Juan de Ribera y, 30
García, Rodrigo Alonso, 124

Garcia de Palacio, Diego de, 101–3
Giffords, Gloria Frasier, 6–7
Great Famine, 79
Grijalva, Juan de, 21–22
Gruzinski, Serge, 10
Guarionex, 1–3
Guatemala, 41, 60, 62, 67–68, 69, 100, 108,
    111, 123, 146, 157 n. 27

Hanks, William 10
Hecelchakán, 54
Hernández, Christine
Hernández de Córdoba, Francisco, 21
Herrera, Baltasar de, 39–40, 54–55, 153 n. 9,
    155 n. 53
Herrera y Tordesillas, Antonio de, 65
Hippocrates, 89–90, 92, 94, 97, 98
Holy Spirit, 129
Homun, 101, 142
Houston, Stephen, 8–9

idolatria (idolatry), 4, 9, 10, 12, 13, 14, *20*,
    38, 39–40, 49, 54, 60, 71, 72, 84–89, 89,
    93–94, 96–98, 99, 100–103, 127, 134–35,
    145, 162 n. 17, 162 n. 19, 165 n. 87
Isla Mujeres, 21
Itzmal, 3, 13, 15, 19, 23, 26, 27, 29, 31, 32, 59,
    63, 65–67, 68, 70, 71, 72, 79, 108, 110, 118,
    119, 122, 123, 131–33, 136, 137, 140, 141, 142,
    144, 145
        Kinich Kakmo Pyramid, 66, 67, 107,
            159 n. 50
        Monastery of Saint Anthony of
            Padua, 3–4, *4*, 19, *20*, 23, 26, 27, 33,
            62, 67, 68, 71, 75, *76*, *77*, 112, 131,
            132, 133, 138, 140, 141; *camarín*,
            75–77, *76*; confraternity of the
            Immaculate Conception, 27, 31, 72;
            fire in, 13, 76, 77, 160 n. 66
        mission of, 62, 65–67, 70
        Ppop Hol Chak Pyramid, 66, 67
        precontact city, 22, 62, 65–66, 108,
            168 n. 1
        Itzamnaaj, 4, 66–67, 70, 108, 109

Ix Chel, 7, 109, 110, 111, 165 n. 4
Ixil, 105, 106, 122

Jesus Christ, 9, 110, 121, 126, 128, 133–34, 137,
143, 166 n. 18

Kashanipour, Ryan, 31, 70
K'iche', 111
Kinich Ahau, 55, 67
k'atun, 112
k'ex, 56–59, 123–24, 134, 135
k'u (kuh), 9, *46*, 47–48

Lacandon Maya, 47–49, *49*, 153 n. 29
Landa, Diego de, 13–14, 17, 39, 40, 42–43,
49–53, 55, 63, 65–70, 75, 112, 119, 123, 129,
154 n. 32, 154 n. 33, 154 n. 34, 154 n. 37, 157
n. 17, 158 n. 50, 167 n. 35
Las Casas, Bartolomé de, 22
Laso y Castilla, Jerónima de, 74, 76, 146
Lindsay, Mark, 32, 152 n. 35
Lizana, Bernardo de, 1, 3–6, 62–63, *64*, 66,
67–76, 78, 106, 138–45
Lope, Carlos Peraza, 44
López de Cogolludo, Diego, 20–21, 24–26,
29, 30, 31, 62–65, 68, 70, 73–77, 81, 82–83,
100–101, 106, 123, 136, 137, 146–47, 150
n. 2
López de Velasco, Juan, 91, 163 n. 32
López, Medel, Tomás, 100–101, 102, 103, 165
n. 73
Luna y Arellano, Carlos de, 98

Madrid Codex, 47, *48*, 53, *53*, 110, *110*
Mama, 91, 92
Maní, 23, 50, 68, *69*, 159 n. 51
Marian icons, 1–3
Martínez, Francisco, 27
"material turn," 8
materiality, 8–9, 12, 15, 33, 38, 39, 40, 49,
55, 58, 59, 77, 102, 110, 112, 123, 129, 131,
134–35, 149 n. 17
Maya creation narratives, 14
Maya effigies, 13, 15, 33, 38–59

of clay, 42–46, *43, 44, 44, 15, 16*
"eye-opening" ritual of, 53
God M, 42, *43*
of plaster, 34–37
production of, 49–55
of wax, 41–42
of wood, 40–42, *41, 42*, 50–53
Maya theory of disease, 31–32, 55–59
McGee, Jon R., 48
Mendieta, Gerónimo de, 97–98
Mérida, 12–13, 14, 19, 20, 21, 22, 23, 24, 25–33,
66, 68, 69, 75, 79, 82, 86, 119, 124, 132, 137,
140, 142, 143, 146
Casa de Alguacil, 30
Cathedral, 71, 82, 112, 114
Convent of Nuestra Señora de la
Consolación, 30, 79, 102–3, 158
n. 32
Franciscan convent, 20, 25, 26, 30–31,
32, 63–65, 66, 68
processions in, 28–31, 33, 79, 86
Mérida, Juan de, 67
Mexica Empire (Aztecs), 23, 53, 111
Mexico City, 14, 18, 54, 60, 62, 71, 78, 84, 97,
100, 101, 152, n34, 152 n. 38, 160 n. 71
Milbrath, Susan, 44
Mis, Marta, 105–6, 113, 117, 122, 165 n. 2, 165
n. 3
Montejo, Francisco de, 22
Montejo, Juan de Salazar, 30, 31
"Morley Manuscript," 114–18, 122
"Motul Dictionary," 112, 118–19
Moxopipe, 92

Nesvig, Martin, 88
Nicuesa, Diego de, 21
nortes, 91–92
Nuestra Señora de la Navidad (Mérida), 26,
68, 158 n. 32
Nutton, Vivian, 91

Oaxaca, 60, 165 n. 87
Ojeda, Sabas, 34, 152 n. 3